ALTERNATIVE WAR

J.J. PATRICK

First published in the United Kingdom 18th August 2017 by

In association with Byline Media

Alternative War
Copyright© J.J. Patrick (James Patrick) 2017
All Rights Reserved.

Cover Images
Copyright © Cynefin Road 2017
(With gratitude to Paul Kelsey for the background)
All Rights Reserved.

The author has exercised his legal and moral rights.

General Release 2nd Edition
ISBN 978-1-9997854-1-3

WITH SPECIAL THANKS:

I am an independent investigative journalist and was recruited to write for Byline in early 2017. My personal history is not what you would call standard – I was a police officer for a decade and left Scotland Yard in 2014 after sparking the House of Commons inquiry which exposed the manipulation of the crime statistics across the UK. Life afterwards was quite the journey, culminating in my bankruptcy and the grim period during which I simply *existed* below the poverty line.

Losing everything brought out the fight in me and I am now a member of the National Union of Journalists, signed up to the Impress regulations, and have been chasing Russia, the far-right, and their creations: Brexit and Trump. My column at Byline has grown in a short space of time to create a substantial, international following and my work has garnered attention across the established mainstream media too. During the course of my investigations, I uncovered information so bleak I was compelled to submit it in the form of a seventy-page statement to the UK and EU Parliaments, NATO, and the FBI. Independent journalism is now the front line in a war most people don't even know about.

Byline Media provides a vital, independent platform to bring crucial stories and investigations to the public without barriers – no editorial skew and absolutely no advertisers to appease. Nothing between you and the news, just as the tag-line says. Byline provides an essential home for truly unbiased reporting in a world marred by fake news and the billionaires serving their own interests through vast media groups. Most importantly of all, Byline and the journalists who write there are funded directly by you.

Byline Media and I teamed up with independent publisher, Cynefin Road, to produce this book in the public interest. The production was fully funded by public donations in the first few days and I owe a personal debt of gratitude to the supporters, the only people to receive a limited run first edition.

J.J.P.

Because, home.

"I know not with what weapons World War III
will be fought, but World War IV will be
fought with sticks and stones."

Albert Einstein

FOREWORD:

I suppose I should explain how I ended up involved in all this.

My resignation from Scotland Yard came in the wake of the Parliamentary inquiry. The final report was published in April of 2014 and I received not only high praise, but the Metropolitan Police were admonished for their treatment of me. Even the Commissioner, Sir Bernard Hogan-Howe had, by then, admitted not only was there truth in my evidence – not that he faced much of a choice, as it happens – but also that, perhaps, the force would have been better off to look into the matters I raised sooner.

None of it really mattered by the publication date: I'd had gross misconduct charges against me abandoned in favour of a written warning for bringing the service into discredit by telling the truth. But The Job wasn't quite done. I had been interviewed by the BBC about my experience, once for a short film on The One Show and a second time by Victoria Derbyshire, for her Radio 5 talk show. The latter interview took place in a broom cupboard studio of a BBC outpost in Cornwall, where I'd been staying with my sister, and I had to do the recording on my knees as the chair was squeaking so badly it had to be removed from the room. The interviews clearly annoyed Scotland Yard – they reinstated misconduct proceedings on two new charges of speaking to the BBC, thereby bringing the service into disrepute by telling the truth. Again.

I was, however, all out of reasonable responses and the British Broadcasting Corporation were great – if not cynically calculating about the likelihood of making some news themselves for once –so, we arranged for me to go back on both shows as a soon as possible. Hilariously, we did the filming for the second One Show piece directly outside Scotland Yard, right by the spinning sign. I'm one of those people you see: no half-measures.

In any case, I'd already resigned from the office of constable by then. On the 24th of March 2014, in fact.

I remember sitting down to write out a statement on my goodbye to policing – I was pretty much living by press release after two years of restrictions – then publishing it on my blog for all to see. Looking back at it, something I have specifically avoided doing for several years, I'm surprised at how little emotion it generates where once tsunami washed over me.

"With deep regret, I have just resigned from the Metropolitan Police Service ('the MPS'). I am giving several weeks' notice, effectively one week for every complete year of service at this time, plus two to conclude the allegations of misconduct. I had intended to resign after the meeting in any case, but disturbing developments have brought this forward. This has not been an easy decision and has certainly been made with no jerk of the knee.

I am very proud to have served the public, in the Office of Constable, since the 10th of May 2004 – first at Derbyshire Constabulary then transferring to the MPS on the 9th of October 2009 – even though my service could by no means be described as having been an easy ride. My experience led me to see just how flawed the whistleblowing system is, how it fails, but also to firmly believe that no police officer should normally resign or retire while subject to any misconduct investigation; but the circumstances are such that I have no choice.

The decision has not been rushed, and I have given the MPS countless opportunities to set our relationship straight; I have also had to weigh, somewhat extraordinarily, the public interest and the impact such a decision may have on me.

This resignation arises directly from my treatment as a result of making disclosures in good faith and in the public interest. In 2012 I publicly raised concerns over policing, police reform, statistical manipulation, the Olympics and lobbying. I made a permanent record of these concerns in one place, a book, the proceeds of which were destined for and donated to a charity supporting bereaved police families. The result of this was a gross misconduct investigation which had a significant impact upon my work, health and family life. My family and I have had to live under this threat while the MPS pursued it, yet even so I carried on acting in the public interest, resulting in my being effectively bullied at New Scotland Yard and, in the end, with my sparking a parliamentary inquiry into crime statistics which has had a significant national impact. In the wake I had to watch senior officers deny it was happening, but I couldn't reply as I'd been warned that it could result in further discipline. Worse still, Essex Police were sent to my home under the Trojan banner of welfare, concluding themselves that they had been sent to rattle our cages. To add insult to injury, it was then conceded that, in fact, what I had said was a truth that needed to be heard.

Having fought through delays and procedural irregularities in the proceedings before this, and having won the argument of bias, I was then informed that a review had been carried out and the gross misconduct dropped. I had to hear via a reporter, on open social media, that this happened after an external force had reviewed the determination of gross misconduct. I had pleaded for external scrutiny from the outset, had hard won an independent panel against the wishes of the MPS. The situation has had a significant impact on my health, but there has been no real consideration for me. My management has been highlighted as a conflict of interest, driven by questionable motives, and left me subject to open threats of discipline and performance procedures for damage the MPS has caused. Throughout the misconduct process it has been denied that there were any senior level discussions about me, or policy deficiencies relevant to my case. It was discovered on the 19th of March 2014 that significant material does indeed exist. On discovering this, and immediately serving it on the misconduct meeting Chair, the reaction from the MPS has been aggressive; implying that I am the person whose integrity is in question for trying to discover the truth, and threatening me with potential discipline for defending myself.

It is impossible for me to see how I could ever trust the MPS again, that is something which is permanently destroyed. I have held out for as long as I can but enough is enough: the camel's back has been broken with a sledgehammer."

Largely this was a cut and paste from my formal resignation letter – originally drafted as an angry adaptation of the 'Pussies, Dicks and Assholes' speech from Trey Parker's *Team America*. I amended it, somewhat begrudgingly, on the advice of a good friend.

The last few weeks of my service were mainly spent in the Starbucks across the road, or out the back of Scotland Yard smoking, mainly as I couldn't face the drudgery of sitting in the CCTV identification unit – a place where naughty policemen get sent to be babysat. That final period was punctuated by my appeal against the written warning sanction, which was, of course, upheld despite rather some blatant issues forming part of the reviewing officer's final adjudication when it was eventually delivered, in June.

"It's apparent that MPS policies are regarded by some, including it would seem some senior leaders, as difficult to find and interpret, verbose and in need of updating. This applies to the SOP's referred to in this case and the guideline referred to. The Business interest SOP does not explicitly state that prior approval is required prior to taking up a business interest. It is noted that this particular SOP has subsequently been amended. Mr Patrick did submit a business interest [and] was never asked to remove his book from circulation or informed that he was in breach of the SOP's. I accept that Mr Patrick did make some attempts to find guidance on publishing a book [and] it has never been proven by the MPS that Mr Patrick actions have indeed brought discredit upon the MPS in the period since the book was published [and that] many of the views expressed by Mr Patrick in his book are echoed elsewhere by others. Mr Patrick has never tried to conceal his identity [and] appears motivated by a fundamental belief that he has a 'duty' to bring his views to the attention of the public. I also take into account Mr. Patrick's view that the Home Affairs Select Committee has 'thanked' him for bringing his beliefs to their attention. I have not read the transcript of this meeting and I take this observation on face value."

I would have thought, to be honest, the senior officer who wrote this would have had the chance by then to read the Parliamentary report on such a fundamental aspect of policing: the crime figures and how they are recorded. Had he bothered, he would have would have seen a permanent record, generated by the highest democratic institution in Britain, which praised me for *"fulfilment of [his] duty to the highest standards of public service"* and stated that *"[his] actions were both courageous and in the public interest, and that he has done a great service to this country."* But, I suppose, face value is better, depending on which way your bread is being buttered.

The warning they gave me was not even worth the paper it was written on. By the time all this nonsense, for that's really what it all had become, was concluded I'd been out of the police for over a month, having officially ended my service at midnight on the close of the 9th of May 2014. Exactly a decade after I was sworn in.

I forced James Bullock, a Detective Sergeant who'd been ordered to babysit me for the last few months, to travel to Essex to retrieve my warrant card on the last day. It was the last exercise of my sense of humour as a copper, primarily as there had been some ongoing games from HR and Professional Standards, trying to make me "sign the Official Secrets Act." I'd been having a blast with this, sending their form back torn in half or with "refused" scrawled across it in the most generic capital letters I could muster. You see, you don't ever sign the Act. British Citizens themselves never sign any of Parliament's Acts. A simple fact of the matter is an Act of Parliament is a law which applies once passed and commenced. No one has ever signed the Offences Against the Person Act, yet it remains illegal to assault people. It's exactly the same with Official Secrets legislation. The truth of the situation I faced was the Met had created an in-house form with an additional, civil disclaimer – essentially small print underneath the wording of the law itself – and it was that which they wanted me to sign. I owed them no duty to agree to any such thing as avoiding saying nasty things about Scotland Yard, that boat had sailed and sunk, hence my repeated refusal to entertain their requests, which they lumbered James with once more on my last day.

I'd dragged him all the way out to East Anglia for another reason too. Part of his job that day was to take back my warrant card but, in London, your official identification is also your authorisation to travel on the tube and national rail networks. Basically, the Met wanted me to have to pay my own way home but, as it so happened, I couldn't have cared any less what they wanted and was leaving on my own awkward terms. Once poor James arrived, I refused to comply with any of his requests unless he took me to the pub, which he duly did with a roll of the eyes, eventually returning to London with my warrant card and another 'REFUSED' form for HR and Professional Standards to get annoyed with. Sozzled, I was giggling as he left, but that was it. The end of my four times commended career as a police officer. It was a waste really.

Even after leaving, the weight of it stayed chained around my neck as I attempted to take the Met to the Employment Tribunal for automatically unfair constructive dismissal under the provisions of the Public Interest Disclosure Act – the law put in place to protect whistleblowers. Factually speaking, my case was pretty good (I made some disclosures of wrongdoing and got punished for making them) but I'm not a lawyer. I was exhausted and way too close to the thing, so I started to lose on procedural grounds and withdrew. I just couldn't take the kicking anymore. I was a shell of a person after two years of restrictions and discipline, whistleblowing, and media coverage. My marriage had been irrevocably damaged by all of it. Many times since, I've wished I'd had the support of the Federation to provide a lawyer but it wasn't to be and, sometimes, walking away from a scrap is just better. There comes a point where you don't have a jot of fight left and you have to make the tough choice to start all over again. Letting things go does not come naturally to me and, though it was the right thing to do in the circumstances, it haunted me for a long time.

Looking back, I must still have had a little fight left – the tiniest amount – because it was around this time I wrote a series of articles for The Justice Gap, focused on policing. That was the start my journalism, the seed of it, but I was not emotionally ready for the full commitment. I was damaged, still trying to retain a connection to the job, to be part of a world that was no longer mine, and it started to do more harm than good so, I let writing about it tail off. Stopped picking the scab and left it to heal.

After living with the constant ups and downs of adrenaline, brought on by debilitating daily anxiety and stress for the two years of investigation and during the tribunal, I collapsed, spending my days curled in a small ball on the living room carpet, hood pulled up over my face or staring blankly into space. The numb sensation after trauma which left a vacuum in my soul and there was nothing I could do but powerlessly ride the waves as they came and went. All the while, however, I was facing up to the looming consequence of happy endings existing only in films. While my actions had been squarely in the public interest, they rendered me largely unemployable. And by "largely," I mean almost completely. Every large firm has a skeleton in its closet and the last thing anyone wants is an employee likely to start bleaching the damned things with sunlight. This became apparent very quickly as I re-entered the job market. Even with skills like mine, in particular my unique analytical experience, I took a minimum wage job at the local pub, working for someone my now ex-wife knew. It ended in disaster, predictably, but I'm never going to suffer a certain type of person for very long. Sufferance of fools is not in my nature and it is well beyond my capability to restrain certain aspects of my personality.

The new job didn't help with the drink either – a disease of The Job, as they call it. Alcohol had crept up, as it does, ably assisted by someone I once thought of as a friend. During my rollercoaster they would meet me every day, taking me for a pint after work. Then two pints, then three. I was so worn out and ground down it was too late before I even began to grasp what was happening. If I'm brutally honest, the nightly oblivion was a release too. The friend, though, had been a long-term drinker and were using me to enable them, all the while becoming my enabler too, creating this downward spiral into a nightly drunken blur. Giving birth to this unseemly thirst which could only be quenched by repetition. Leaving the police and losing the warrant card went a long way to rectifying this unpalatable situation, mainly by distance alone, a physical separation from the supply. And, even though they had taken to visiting me at home as an excuse for their own indulgence – often with embarrassing consequences – I had it under control until the pub. But, suddenly, I was in a situation where customers were finishing their orders of rounds with the phrase "And one for yourself," and I'd racked up months' worth of drinks in only a few weeks. So, I started joined them once my shifts finished and on at least one occasion fell over on the way home and split my mouth open. I hadn't really begun to understand the depths of the damage done over the course of the whistleblowing but these were the last warning signs as my marriage's fingernails finally started to lose their strained grip on the cliff's edge.

As the pub job came to its rather argumentative – yet oddly satisfying – end, I hit upon the idea of opening my own pub, focusing on a dilapidated old building at the opposite end of town. I felt a kinship with the building, intent on seeing it as something damaged but not broken beyond repair and fixating upon it with the same deadly commitment which had caused all the problems in the police. That inability to let go of the bone. I wasn't looking at the building like that at all, in truth. I was already seeing myself as a failure but, also, as someone who just needed the right amount of TLC and a helping hand to be turned around. I considered myself on a last chance in life and, by a quirk of psychology, used the pub as a physical manifestation of subconscious thoughts. A kind of desperate hope, I suppose. With that, I started to plot how I would take the project on, a scheme which neatly coincided with Mexico's first raps on my door.

Anna Cabrera wasn't someone I knew. I hadn't ever even heard of her, yet there she was, popping up on my Twitter followers list and sending me a message. She worked, she said, for the Assuntos Internos – Internal

Affairs – department of the Federal Police in Mexico City and was interested in speaking to me about my whistleblowing experience. It was not, by any means, the first time I'd ended up speaking to curious sounding people about what I had done – I've been very privileged to chat with other whistleblowers like Adhyl Polanco, a cop in the NYPD who exposed the misuse of quotas in the department and was treated horrendously for the privilege. Dr Eli Silverman too, an academic who'd once praised the use of CompStat but turned coat on discovering the wholesale manipulation of New York's crime figures and published his own book, The Crime Number Game, decrying it. My proudest memory of all of these conversations is now a printed and framed email which I keep on a wall, whenever I have one. I'm most ecstatic to say I have had email conversations with the living legend Frank Serpico – the original police whistleblower turned into an international idol after Al Pacino portrayed him in the 1970s film. Frank was shot in the face after exposing NPYD corruption. Anna, however, was still a serving public official and, up until this point, she was the only one who had shown any interest at all in my experience. The UK police forces had deliberately forgotten about my awkward little existence. They changed the code of ethics, sure, but only the words. British policing is still stuck in its insular dark ages. As it turned out, Anna had been introduced to my story by Silverman and, with some funding made available by the US State Department, she wanted to fly me over to Mexico City to take part in an international symposium on ethics in law enforcement as a specialist, guest speaker. I couldn't quite believe it at first and, until I'd seen the official email addresses, found myself unusually wary. The offer was legitimate though and, in October 2014, I was flown out to Mexico City for a week, staying at a five-star hotel on the Paseo De La Reforma overlooking the iconic Angel of Independence.

Mexico City greets you with warm air, even in mid-October, I discovered. I'd been on a plane for around ten hours and was just glad to be outside, cigarette in hand and utterly bewildered by Spanish – which I don't speak – when Anna came to pick me up with her Inspector, Luis Martinez. I recognised Anna from her profile photographs and both of them were in uniform so, I figured, even though the car was unmarked, my chances of getting kidnapped and decapitated had reduced from a ninety-percent certainty to a solid fifty-fifty.

In the car I stared out of the window, taking in the strange sights and sounds, while Luis and Anna jabbered away to each other in Spanish. Even speaking fluent Italian, less than half of it was decipherable as anything more than a general sense of idle chit-chat. Whenever Anna reverted to English, her accent was heavily Americanised, whereas Luis retained his native pronunciation. They took me to the hotel, a grand old building, where we found a large crowd still dispersing from around the Angel, backlit that night in pink and purple.

"We're lucky we just missed the protest," Anna told me. I immediately felt a pang of guilt because I had no idea what was going on, or if this was just a normal fact of life. Something regular. She must have picked up on my quizzical expression. "A group of students were kidnapped in Iguala. It's a town in Guerrero. They're dead. The local police killed and buried them."

It took me a few moments to digest this news. "The police killed them?"

"Yes, we have a lot of corruption, the police chief was arrested today," she replied.

Just under a month before my arrival, forty-three students from the Ayotzinapa Rural Teachers' College had gone missing in Iguala de la Independencia, a small, historic city about sixty miles away from Chilpancingo, the state capital of Guerrero. It's around eighty miles south-west of Mexico City and has a population of over a hundred thousand people. In 1821 the declaration which ended the war of independence was signed in Iguala, hence it's known as the birthplace of the Flag of Mexico – which was originally called the Flag of Three Guarantees. The state itself takes its name from Vicente Guerrero, a prominent leader in the Mexican War of Independence who went on to become the second President, and is the country's only state to take its name from a public figure. While it has a healthy tourism industry, being home to Acapulco amongst other resorts, Guerrero has the highest level of migrants to the United States due to lack of education and employment. Many of the villages have been left with no men at all, women taking up most of the work. In part, this has allowed over fifty prolific criminal gangs to infest the region which is now regarded as the epicentre of Mexico's opium poppy production, with the Mexican supply of street-sold heroin dominating the United States drugs market.

Guerrero also has healthy marijuana and methamphetamine industries, which combine with the trafficking climate to drive continuously high murder rates as the cartel's fight for the ultimate control of the dark economy.

According to the official reports of the Iguala massacre of students, they had commandeered several buses to travel to Mexico City to commemorate the anniversary of the 1968 Tlatelolco Massacre – an event in Mexico City where police and security forces killed up to three hundred political protestors just days before the Olympics opened. It was during their journey that local police intercepted them and some form of confrontation ensued.

Details of what happened may never be known, and it has been alleged the mayor and his wife were directly involved, but an official investigation concluded the students were already in custody when they were handed over to the Guerreros Unidos ("United Warriors") cartel and killed. There were, however, also reports linking Federal units to the incident, with some evidence suggesting military personnel in the area were either directly engaged in the kidnapping, or were present and failed to respond and assist the students. The mayor and his wife fled after the incident, only to be arrested in Mexico City in October, and Iguala's police chief, Felipe Flores Velásquez, was arrested in Iguala on the day of my arrival, October the 21st.

The events caused social unrest in Guerrero itself, with attacks on government buildings taking place. The state Governor, Ángel Aguirre Rivero, resigned in the face of state and nationwide protests – such as the one which was dispersing in front of the Angel after my flight landed. Up until that point in time, it was the biggest scandal Mexican President Enrique Peña Nieto had faced and resulted in broad and scathing, international condemnation of his government.

It was only after I had left, on the 7th of November, that the Attorney General, Jesús Murillo Karam, announced plastic bags containing human remains, possibly those of the missing students, had been found at a riverside in Cocula. It remains the case in 2017 that only two of the students have been officially confirmed dead after their remains were identified by the forensic team at the Austrian University of Innsbruck.

Of the eighty or so suspects arrested in relation to the massacre, forty-four were police officers.

The reality of it hit me like a breezeblock around the back of the head when Anna told me the story and I made my way up to the hotel room in a dazed state. I was halfway around the world, in a place where the police kidnap and kill protestors and I was giving them an anti-corruption speech. Wriggling my toes on the plush carpet as I mulled this over, I was overwhelmed by a new sensation of missing The Job. I felt out of water and incapacitated, unable to act, and my body clock was up the spout. It should have been morning but it was evening, I'd lost or gained a day and couldn't decipher which and I had a full schedule starting early in the morning, so I tried to sleep, wandered to the restaurant next door and ate when I couldn't, then tried again and succeeded.

Waking up the second morning I had no idea where I was. A brief panic engulfed me in the hotel room as my mind reassembled the time and reminded me, dumping an unwelcome burst of adrenaline. A lingering remnant of the damage done by my escapades at Scotland Yard which brought on a full panic attack. Anna picked me up from the bay in front of the lobby a short while later. She was in her own car and took us on a journey much shorter than I had anticipated in the dawn sun – five minutes later we arrived at the Federal Police building on the opposite side of the Paseo.

"I could have walked you know?" I laughed, eyeing her curiously.

"And if something had happened to you, I'd be in a whole world of trouble," she replied. The reality of the security climate hit me once again. For all intents and purposes, I was a foreign dignitary working with the police, which made me, as strange as it sounded even as a thought, a target.

The agenda for the day was a tour of facilities, so we exchanged the car for a seat on a coach and were joined by other Federal agents and a number of staff from the CNS, the Comisión Nacional de Seguridad. The security services people were quite pleasant and thoroughly curious as to who the British guy in jeans and an open-collared shirt was. I raised a few eyebrows, shall we say, as we waited to depart. I didn't understand the delay until I saw the trucks, and again reality bit. At the front and back of the coach were our motorcade escorts, two pick-up trucks with lights and sirens blaring, and two officers armed with assault rifles riding in the back of each, watching traffic and ready to fire. I have never been on a coach journey quite like it, travelling code blue across a city of millions to a Federal Police base where the first part of our facilities tour began.

We arrived in time for an official flag raising ceremony as part of a national celebration, where all of the other guests and a group of children sang the Mexican national anthem. I had no idea what was going on and copied a young girl, placing my hand on my heart which raised a few smiles. Afterwards, Anna quietly whispered to me, "Why did you put your hand on your chest, it's only for women." Normally I'd have been embarrassed but I laughed raucously, shrugged it off and excitedly ran along to the next stop, an armed display by the rapid entry team, followed by a trip to the Blackhawks over at the aerodrome. I was like a school kid through all of this, then we took the two turns I'd been most eagerly waiting for, heading to the Incident Operations Room for the Federal Police and then their Special Operations Incident Command facility.

The Ops Room was much better equipped than I could have imagined and everything was new. Having experienced the crumbling legacy of UK policing's IT infrastructure, my admiration was genuine – the Mexicans weren't playing at it, as we often do. A broad panel of brand new flat screens adorned the far wall and agents busily occupied themselves responding to calls for service while the Duty Superintendent briefed us. The set up was impressive and the cloud-based software was fast and intuitive, with a multiplatform link from vehicle records, driver licence databases, and criminal records, to social security system and employment databases. I excused myself from the overview briefing and spent my time with one of the agents, working on a real-time intelligence package for a live incident, passing the package to the officers on the ground electronically. Somewhere in the city, a fully equipped and robust Dodge Charger kitted out with the latest technology and weaponry, had just received everything they needed to be able to intervene safely in an attempted domestic murder perpetrated by a violent gang member. It was a far cry from an antiquated incident report being delivered to a broken touchscreen in a six-year-old Vauxhall Astra with a solitary traffic cone in the boot if you were lucky.

Special Operations was a treat too. Video link technology had them connected with each officer as they controlled a live anti-cartel operation in the mountains. The deployment was strictly military in style, even utilising mortar weapons on a heavily armed farm complex while the team was under heavy return fire. It wasn't crime-fighting I was watching, it was combat. The Commander was eyeing me intently and asked, via Anna, what my view was. "Where do I sign up?" was my only reply. While I might have left the job, The Job still hadn't left me and had there been a way to make it happen, I'd have started basic training there and then.

After a brief buffet lunch, alongside the weapons of the firearms presentation, it was time to move on to our second port of call: the CNS facility. So, we re-embarked the coach and our escort led us across the city in the same no-nonsense style. I found myself lost in thought, daydreaming really. There had been a point not so long ago when I couldn't think of anything worse than putting on the uniform which I'd once been proud of, but there in Mexico City I would have done it in a heartbeat, volunteering for Special Operations and doing some of the real dirty work. Because, sometimes, that is what needs to be done.

"You miss it?" Anna asked me, catching my private thought with a degree of accuracy I wasn't anticipating as we walked into the President's underground bunker.

"Every single day," I replied, just before I pointed out the military deployments on the huge array of screens were based on flawed crime data.

And that's how I eventually ended up being an investigative journalist – after becoming a bankrupt publican, then heading back to Mexico once again in 2016 and exposing corruption in the murder figures which implicated state governments, including that of Guerrero.

It was gravity, I suppose.

Or, perhaps, just an addiction to kerfuffle.

"1. Russia is deliberately interfering in Western democracy through the use of disinformation, cybercrime, psychological manipulation and the collaboration of well-placed of third parties. This hybrid conflict is live.

2. This interference has decisively impacted upon the democratic process in the United Kingdom and the United States with negative effect, and has attempted to interfere in Swedish and French democratic process. The threat is continuing and extends to additional nations.

3. There is clear evidence of voter manipulation through the use of psychometric techniques, and evidence indicating data-laundering within and outside of the EMEA data protection area by state and non-state actors.

4. The current legal frameworks and responses of the UK and the US are inadequate and have contributed to the continuance the live threat."

J.J. Patrick

Statement to EU and UK parliaments, NATO, and the FBI – 19th May 2017

ONE:

I didn't know any of this in 2016. Like everyone else, I thought the world had simply fallen victim to a deceitful bus and some idiotic, gun-toting rednecks. I was wrong, I'm not ashamed to admit. We all were. But from that mistake arose what I see as a collective duty, to at least try and put things right and make sure it never happens again.

The term 'hybrid warfare' was first mentioned sometime around 2005, so the story goes, and the year after it was used to try and describe the tactics deployed by Hezbollah in Lebanon. Since then, the term "hybrid" went on to occupy most of the discussions around modern and future warfare, while also being broadly adopted by senior officials and military groups.

The concept of a "hybrid threat" was first introduced in the North Atlantic Treaty Organisation's Strategic Concept of 2010 and then incorporated in the NATO Capstone Concept, defining hybrid threats as "those posed by adversaries, with the ability to simultaneously employ conventional and non-conventional means adaptively in pursuit of their objectives." Their 2010 Strategic Concept, entitled *Active Engagement, Modern Defence* (AEMD) was, according to the organisation: "A very clear and resolute statement on NATO's values and strategic objectives for the next decade." They set their stall out decisively, I suppose as an aid to the uninitiated, saying: "Collective defence, crisis management and cooperative security are the Alliance's essential core tasks in today's transformed security environment, an environment the Alliance is equipping itself for both politically and militarily."

I have always thought of myself as relatively aware of the world in which we live, dared to believe I was in the know, even, but the first concession I had to make was that I knew very little – and not least about NATO. It was just something I'd grown up hearing mentioned all the time but my understanding of it, even after policing, was limited. I now understand this was simply because I have been privileged to have lived through a period in history when war was always very far away. When things were comfortable on the doorstep. I've been lucky enough, like many of us, to not need to know.

According to the organisation itself, recapping essential history in the concept's preamble: "The political and military bonds between Europe and North America have been forged in NATO since the Alliance was founded in 1949; the transatlantic link remains as strong, and as important to the preservation of Euro-Atlantic peace and security, as ever. The security of NATO members on both sides of the Atlantic is indivisible. We will continue to defend it together, on the basis of solidarity, shared purpose and fair burden-sharing." Straight away it became obvious why NATO is perceived as a threat to its enemies, and why – very squarely – Russia is placed in the category of a potential threat, with particular focus on its ballistic and nuclear weapons being placed on or located within reach of the European borders. NATO makes clear an active and effective European Union contributes to the overall security of the Euro-Atlantic area, defining the union as a unique and essential partner. "The two organisations share a majority of members, and all members of both organisations share common values. NATO recognizes the importance of a stronger and more capable European defence," the AEMD states, adding: "We welcome the entry into force of the Lisbon Treaty, which provides a framework for strengthening the EU's capacities to address common security challenges." They also clearly refer to the value of the United States, saying non-EU Allies make a "significant contribution" to these efforts. From the beginning, it is easy to see why a country such as Russia may have wished to involve themselves in the affairs of both EU member states and the United States. A response to a response, to a response. Yet, the hand of reciprocal co-operation was firmly on offer.

"Notwithstanding differences on particular issues, we remain convinced that the security of NATO and Russia is intertwined and that a strong and constructive partnership based on mutual confidence, transparency and predictability can best serve our security," the AEMD adds.

Though the idea of a hybrid threat has come a long way since the concept was first introduced, it was drafted to included cyber-threats, political disruption, state-engaged criminality, and extremism, in addition to traditional warfare threats. Reading it in 2017, it feels like they had a good idea something was cranking up but not precisely what. Perhaps it was the deus ex machina moment, a device introduced to solve the unsolvable. The draft Capstone Concept, while it sounds like something straight out of Jason Bourne was a document completed in August 2010. It articulated the "unique challenges posed by current and future hybrid threats" and explained why these developing challenges required an adaptation of strategy by NATO, so it could adjust both its structure and capabilities accordingly. Capstone discussed both a general approach to dealing with the (then) new hybrid threats, as well as laying down a framework for the organisation to deliver an effective response should such threats manifest in reality. The draft was central in informing the development of the new AEMD Strategic Concept and, even in those early days, NATO was sure "analysis and maturation" would support Capstone's implementation. The paper also suggested broader implications for NATO's core military components.

Capstone's Integrated Project Team (IPT) was established in early 2009, indicating how long the threat we face now had been on the horizon. The IPT subsequently developed a detailed campaign to "assess both hybrid threats and the broader challenges facing NATO within the emerging security environment," according to Royal Marine Lieutenant Colonel Richard Hills, the IPT's Lead Concept Developer. "Between 2009 –2010 a number of ACT led international workshops were held to both focus the key analysis and better inform the development of the concept. The workshops included a broad range of participants from NATO and non-NATO organisations," he said.

Capstone, led by the IPT, asserted that hybrid threats involve any adversaries, including "states, rogue states, non-state actors or terrorist organisations," who may employ a combination of actions in an increasingly unconstrained operating environment in order to achieve their aims. Almost ten years later, they were proven right.

While not a new problem, at the time NATO said "the interconnectedness of the globalised environment now makes hybrid threats a far more significant challenge for the Alliance and its interests, whether encountered within national territory, in operational theatres or across non-physical domains." I found the description used chill-inducing: "Hybrid threats will apply pressure across the entire spectrum of conflict, with action that may originate between the boundaries artificially separating its constituents. They may consist of a combination of every aspect of warfare and compound the activities of multiple actors."

On behalf of the IPT, Hills set out NATO's role at an early stage, saying Capstone "also asserts that NATO's role in managing the emerging security environment will invariably be a supporting one. The Alliance needs to develop its understanding of how it can cooperate with other organisations and stakeholders to both deter potential threats and mitigate their impact."

With principal support from Joint Irregular Warfare Centre (JIWC), NATO set out to conduct its first Counter Hybrid Threats Experiment in Tallinn,

Estonia. The primary purpose defined at the time was "to explore and discuss the key implications of the new draft concept and develop with other international stakeholders an understanding of potential approaches in addressing the likely challenge areas." Academic centres, businesses and international bodies attended. Explaining the experiment, Hills said "one of the key outcomes of the event will be clear recommendations to NATOs Political and Military leadership of what the organisation must do to support the international community in tackling the array of potential hybrid challenges. The results will feed directly into the further development and refinement of the CHT Concept Paper with the aim to potentially produce a more informed draft, by late 2011."

The experiment, according to the official report, was conducted to examine the utility and feasibility of the Military Contribution to the Countering Hybrid Threats Concept. The Tallinn activity also centred on NATO's potential support role in the wider context – what they called a "comprehensive approach" in addressing hybrid threats in a "steady state, security environment." The complex environment of hybrid threats was "examined through three different lenses." The first dealt with cyber, technology and economic threats – followed by the second on stabilisation, conflict prevention and partnership. The final aspect of the experiment examined the "Global Commons and Resource security." The global potential for resource-based conflict has been well established in the defence community for many years, but this is the first time it appeared to have been fully considered in the context of a multifaceted conflict.

During the Tallinn test, Supreme Allied Commander Transformation, French Air Force General Stephane Abrial, stated: "Unforeseen NATO Operations in Libya remind us of a historical string of 'strategic surprises'-central in assessing Hybrid Threats." He went on to say that hybrid conflict situations are linked to "the versatility of threats and a lack of strategic predictability."

Hybrid threats gained renewed traction in response to Russian actions in Ukraine and the Da'esh campaign in Iraq. In 2014, Russian military forces made several aggressive incursions into Ukrainian territory. After subsequent protests and the fall of the then Ukrainian President Viktor Yanukovych, Russian soldiers without insignias (often referred to as the Green Men) took control of strategic positions and infrastructure within the Ukrainian territory of Crimea. Russia went on to annexe Crimea after a disputed referendum concluded the electorate wanted to join the Russian Federation. In August 2016 the SBU, the Security Service of Ukraine, published telephone intercepts – dated 2014 – showing details of Sergey Glazyev, a Russian presidential adviser, Konstantin Zatulin, a Russian politician, and others discussing the covert funding of pro-Russian activists in Eastern Ukraine and arranging the occupation of administration buildings, along with other activities, which led to the eventual armed conflict. Glazyev did not deny the authenticity of the intercepted records and Zatulin confirmed they were real but claimed they were "taken out of context." The intercepts showed that, as early as February 2014, Glazyev was giving direct orders to pro-Russian parties in Ukraine, asking them to instigate civil unrest in the key locations of Donetsk, Kharkiv, Zaporizhia, and Odessa.

Meanwhile, Barack Obama declared Da'esh a hybrid threat in 2014, with world security services at the time reporting the sophisticated use of social media for worldwide propaganda in a campaign which attracted thousands of foreign fighters from Europe, the Maghreb and Asia. The combination of conventional and non-conventional warfare, with disinformation and terrorist operations, saw Da'esh placed in the centre ground of the hybrid conflict arena from that point on. The ripples spread rapidly and, by February

2015, EU Defence Ministers meeting in Riga called for more unity and decisive action across the union. By May, the European External Action Service had created a circular entitled *Countering Hybrid Threats*, which encouraged member states to recognise the risks and build individual responses. The report was particularly bleak in its outlook, setting the full potential of hybrid threats against a more developed context than Capstone initially outlined. It stated: "Elements of hybridity can be traced in many other dimensions of the current security environment" with "various governments in the EU's southern neighbourhood (i.e. the Gaddafi regime in Libya or the current government of Turkey)" having "used the complexity of migratory movements as a pretext to demand various concessions from the European Union." It also concluded that ISIL/Da'esh simultaneously sought to instil fear in EU citizens and governments which, in turn, had the effect of "pushing them to take more hostile attitudes towards refugees, ultimately strengthening the image of the EU as an anti-Muslim society, to its discredit." There is no doubt such a response, in fact, fed (and feeds) the continued propaganda necessary to drive the cycle, escalating the conflict steadily.

In addition to intentional actions, the EU report cited increasing concerns about the potential consequences of complex crises resulting directly from, or even combining the different elements, which would require an equally complicated response. The concerns they documented included ideas rarely thought of in connection with war or conflict, including observations that: "Abnormal weather conditions and climate-induced resource scarcity, for instance, increasingly influence relations between states, and might provoke confrontation over access to water or crops production." At the time, researchers on the impact of climate change in the Middle East and North Africa had estimated, by 2050, summer temperatures across the region would reach around 46 degrees Celsius and hot days would occur five times more often than at the beginning of the 2000s. "Such extreme temperatures," the report stated, "in combination with increasing air pollution by windblown desert dust, will render living conditions in parts of the region intolerable, leading to a 'climate exodus' and social unrest, that might be exploited to destabilise the region by state and non-state actors alike."

An unchecked hybrid threat, such as any of these individual examples, ultimately results in the situation we now face: a full-scale, world hybrid conflict. The Alternative War.

Most references to hybrid war are commonly based around the idea of the existence of an "adversary who controls and employs a mix of tools to achieve their objectives," and this brings with it a layering effect, a structure obfuscating the direct responses available in a traditionally declared military conflict. A hybrid conflict has been given the globally accepted definition of "a situation in which parties refrain from the overt use of armed forces against each other, relying instead on a combination of military intimidation falling short of an attack, exploitation of economic and political vulnerabilities, and the deployment of diplomatic or technological means to pursue their objectives." There is no doubt whatsoever we find ourselves in the middle of an Alternative War by this very description.

Despite the relatively early horizon identification, the world's response has not been sufficiently effective – or unified – in updating the international framework to reflect this developing landscape.

As with all conflicts, attributing responsibility and intent is absolutely necessary, not only to ensure state and allied policy responses are proportionate, but they are legitimate and appropriately targeted. However, a cluster of problems is generated in hybrid conflict situations, arising from international law limitations, technological constraints, and the diffusion of actions to non-state actors working together to give an adversary in such a conflict substantial deniability. For instance, the involvement of a third party not immediately identifiable as being state-sponsored (such as Wikileaks) becomes incredibly difficult to set against the legal concept of beyond reasonable doubt when a response is being tabled. Nonetheless, the US have done this with North Korea after the Sony Pictures hack. Additionally, at a NATO Summit in 2014 the organisation set out that the application of Article 5 of the Washington Treaty in the event of a cyber-attack would apply.

The heads of state of NATO's member countries met in Wales at what the organisation called a pivotal moment in Euro-Atlantic security. They released a joint statement which said: "Russia's aggressive actions against Ukraine have fundamentally challenged our vision of a Europe whole, free, and at peace. Growing instability in our southern neighbourhood, from the Middle East to North Africa, as well as transnational and multi-dimensional threats, are also challenging our security. These can all have long-term consequences for peace and security in the Euro-Atlantic region and stability across the globe." Looking to the future of conflict, NATO correctly anticipated cyber threats and attacks would continue to become more common, sophisticated, and potentially damaging, and, in response to the developing challenges, the alliance endorsed an enhanced cyber defence policy. The commitment, they said, reaffirmed the "principles of the indivisibility of Allied security and of prevention, detection, resilience, recovery, and defence," making clear the fundamental cyber defence responsibility of NATO was to protect its own networks. The policy emphasised assistance would always be addressed in accordance with the spirit of solidarity and went to lengths to press the understanding it remained the individual responsibility of allies to develop "relevant capabilities for the protection of national networks."

NATO's cyber defence policy, a key concept developed through Capstone, recognised something crucial: that international law, including international humanitarian law and the UN Charter, applies equally in cyberspace. According to the policy, a decision as to when a cyberattack would lead to the invocation of Article 5 would be taken by the North Atlantic Council on a case-by-case basis. "Cyberattacks can reach a threshold which threatens national and Euro-Atlantic prosperity, security, and stability," the NATO leaders agreed, adding their impact could be as harmful to modern societies as a conventional attack, before confirming the provision of cyber defences as part of NATO's core task. This marked an extraordinary development in respect of the recognition of hybrid conflicts as the future battleground, making the internet inseparable from a traditional, hot war zone. The phrase "without a bullet fired" suddenly looks grim when you realise a legitimate military response could be launched in response to a technology-based campaign. Article 5 of the Washington Treaty sets out the principle of collective defence – the very heart of NATO's founding treaty signed in the ashes of World War 2. It remains, NATO says: "A unique and enduring principle," which "binds its members together, committing them to protect each other." Collective defence as a term means an attack against one NATO member is considered to be an attack against all and the response is subsequently a joint one. They invoked Article 5 for the first time since the treaty was formed after the 9/11 terrorist attacks against the United States.

In Wales, NATO made a clear commitment to developing national cyber defence capabilities, saying they would "enhance the cyber security of national networks upon which NATO depends for its core tasks, in order to help make the Alliance resilient and fully protected." They identified bilateral and multinational cooperation played – and would continue to play – a central role in building the cyber defence capabilities of the organisation and its members. All the members also agreed to integrate cyber defence into NATO active operations and operational contingency planning, with enhanced information sharing and situational awareness as a focus. Other international organisations, including the EU, agreed and NATO also set out to intensify cooperation with private industry through the NATO Industry Cyber Partnership – having identified technological innovations and expertise from the private sector were crucial to achieving their objectives. Currently, however, no specific international legal framework is in place to regulate hybrid warfare, despite the efforts of NATO and others, which creates a conflict between the ability to invoke Article 5 and compliance with the regulations and legalities established and monitored by the UN. Use of force in international relations is still catered for under the United Nations Charter, which states: "In the absence of an armed attack against a country or its allies, a member state can use force legally only if authorised by a United Nations Security Council resolution."

The grey area, of sorts, arises in the definition of using force at Article 2 of the Charter, which reads: "All members shall refrain in their international relations from the threat or use of force against the territorial integrity or political independence of any state." Article 2(4) does not use the term "war", sticking to "the threat or use of force," which creates an ambiguity as to whether the provision refers to pure military force or extends to incorporate "economic, political, ideological or psychological force." The Declaration on Principles of International Law Concerning Friendly Relations, signed in 1970, states: "No State or group of States has the right to intervene, directly or indirectly, for any reason whatever, in the internal or external affairs of any other State. Consequently, armed intervention and all against its political, economic and cultural elements, are in violation of international law." The absence of a specific provision for hybrid use of force clearly arises from the dated nature of the charter itself and, to muddy the waters further, while a number of developing nations continue to argue force includes non-military force, it is the well-established states within the UN who resist adaptation.

The charter also permits self-defence and first strike, but both fall foul of the elderly definition of force, which has doubtlessly caused some hand-wringing among the states wishing to openly respond to live hybrid threats. Of course, the secondary issue with the dated law, is the UN are subsequently hamstrung by the charter in identifying and dealing with those actively engaged in hybrid conflicts. In addition, while the rules regarding traditional armed conflict are firmly laid down in international humanitarian and human rights law, hybrid conflict and threats are only covered by a patchwork of legal instruments covering specific policy areas. These are the seas, counter-terrorism, money laundering, terrorist financing, and human rights.

The impact of this coalition of defects allowed the growth of complex hybrid conflict operations to run almost unchecked, despite the best efforts of parties such as NATO and the EU, leading the world almost inevitably to the precipice it now stands upon. Trump, Brexit, the attacks on the French and Dutch elections, the world cyber-attack on infrastructure and health organisations, even fake news – these are the multiple fronts in a very real conflict from which there may be no return unless a response begins. Yet, any such response is hampered at the outset by the very structure which has permitted the threat to grow – made it necessary, even, by leaving room for tactics to be developed which exploit the inherent weaknesses.

Europe itself, along with much of the West is, in spite of the complex problems, very much aware of the ongoing war. A fact made even clearer by the attendance of a substantial number of delegates at a Summit held in Prague, in May 2017. The specific focus of the partly open, partly restricted meeting was to discuss a coordinated international response to Russian aggression and to collaborate on addressing the fact "a wide gap remains between mere acknowledgement of the threat and the development of concrete and viable counter-measures." Senior NATO figures and high-ranking representatives from a large number of countries were in attendance, including a senior specialist delegate from the United Kingdom. Over one hundred people representing twenty-seven countries attended the restricted part of the summit, apparently a Chatham House Rules type of affair. The obviously controversial and diplomatically delicate meeting was facilitated by the Czech Think-tank European Values, no stranger to pushing boundaries themselves.

In 2016, the Prague-based organisation compared Czech President Miloš Zeman to a "Russian Trojan horse" actively engaged in an information war. A spokesperson at European Values, Jakub Janda, made the statement as part of a presentation setting out the results of a study which identified Czech websites serving disinformation purposes. "In the Czech space, Miloš Zeman plays the role of a Russian Trojan horse, systematically embracing and repeating Kremlin's position on various issues," Janda said. And, while the president's spokesman, Jiří Ovčáček, dismissed the allegations as "nonsensical" saying they were "part of an ongoing campaign against the head of state," there is some fire behind the smoke. In May 2017, during a meeting with Russian President Vladimir Putin in China, Zeman took aim at the media and was caught on a recording. Shortly before a joint press briefing with Putin, he said there were too many journalists present, adding they should be "liquidated." The reaction was, understandably, furious. The Czech Foreign Minister, Lubomír Zaorálek, condemned the President's comment as having been "in extremely bad taste," while Marián Jurečka, deputy chair of the Christian Democrats, declared that such a statement in the presence of the Russian leader, "in whose country journalists die mysterious deaths," was unforgivable. Pavel Telička, a Czech MEP also weighed in, suggesting Zeman was "no longer fit for office and should not be running for a second term."

Zeman's call for the "liquidation" of journalists came in the wake of a Czech scandal surrounding his Finance Minister and Deputy Prime Minister Andrej Babiš, exposed in secret recordings attempting to influence media coverage. The outcry centred around the daily newspaper Mladá fronta Dnes, which Babiš formerly owned and involved requests to print coverage against political rivals. Journalists went on to raise significant concerns about press freedoms and interference in the media, leading to a situation in which the European Parliament was set to intervene, such was the gravity of the situation. "This tendency has been present here for quite some time, as it is in Poland and Hungary, not to speak about Russia. So it is high time the European Parliament started paying attention to it," said Jan Urban, a prominent Czech journalist.

The last European Values summit drew a great deal of attention and significant responses from attendees, including General Petr Pavel, Chairman of the NATO Military Committee, who said afterwards: "The 2016 StratCom Summit in Prague was organised at a crucial time when Russian disinformation [was] increasingly targeting Western audiences, trying to sow confusion, distrust and division. I came away from the Summit encouraged by the level of awareness and expertise across Europe, its governments and organisations, who are all actively engaged in countering Russia's disinformation operations."

A primary activity which builds towards the annual convention comes under the title Kremlin Watch, a strategic program run by European Values which aims, it says: "To expose and confront instruments of Russian influence and linked disinformation operations focused on working to destabilise the Western democratic system." The introduction to their annual report, the premise for the 2017 gathering, made clear the threats faced across the West, in particular in Europe, are only too real. "Demand is growing for a coordinated international response to Russian aggression, with many EU heads of state, other European politicians, and security experts voicing alarm about the threat. As of May 2017, several Western countries have experienced Russian interference in their elections, while the number of cyberattacks across Europe continues to rise," the publication said.

The organisation's comprehensive strategic assessment for 2017 made for a sobering read, covering the twenty-eight EU countries in detail including, for now, the United Kingdom. The report immediately identifies two countries as being collaborators with Russia: Greece and Cyprus, who have shown – across a number of assessed factors – "no resistance to Russian influence." According to the analysis, the Cypriot government considers Russia an ally in supporting the integrity of the country, although there are doubts about Russia's actual interests amongst some journalists. It also states the Cypriot media have been speculating about Russia's hypothetical ulterior motives for "meddling in Cyprus' internal affairs with an agenda different than publicly claimed," though the country's political representation has not acknowledged these speculations in any way, explain the authors.

Cyprus, the assessment concludes, belongs to the group of countries within the EU which do not perceive or recognise any threat coming from Russia, instead maintaining a close relationship with the Federation. Historically, Russia supported the "integrity of the island," a legacy of the Soviet era, which makes "Moscow a key foreign partner of Nicosia." Cyprus is also Russia's primary offshore banking haven – a well-established matter of fact – and provides a home away from home for around forty thousand Russians. It is also a popular destination for tourists from Russia. The Cypriot government additionally stands opposed to sanctions or other similar measures against Russia, apparently on the basis of the two countries' economic ties, even despite the physical evidence of economic impact of the sanctions remaining limited. At the same time, the analysts state there is "considerable Russian intelligence activity in the country and Cyprus fears Moscow is using social and mass media, as well as its ties to fringe nationalist parties and the Greek Orthodox Church, to undermine the settlement talks." Bilateral relations with Russia remain consistent, even despite events in Ukraine, and the report concludes, on the topic of policy to combat Russian influence, that "either no official activities exist or they are not publicly admitted for domestic political reasons."

It is worth observing that Cyprus is not a NATO member and the cooperation between NATO and the EU is not seen as a particularly high political priority. "On the contrary," the report adds, "Cyprus often tries to decrease it. No shift has been noticeable even in the recent years. Cypriot officials are some of the most steadfast supporters of the idea that Russia is Cyprus' true and honest ally and would not partake in any international activities targeted against it, unless absolutely unavoidable."

Several media outlets in Cyprus have begun speculating about their concerns Russia might actually want to block the settlement agreement on the island, a view opposed to official claims of the Federation. These concerns arose following "suspicious activities" of the Ambassador of Moscow in Cyprus, Stanislav Osadchiy, who engaged in talks in a manner considered to have interfered in Turkish and Cypriot negotiations. Makarios Drousiotis, a Greek-Cypriot researcher told the New York Times that events in the United States and Europe were "shaking his compatriots' view Moscow had only their best interests at heart."

"What they have been doing in America and Europe they have been doing for 50 years in Cyprus," Drousiotis added.

In 2014, he published a book entitled *The Cyprus Crisis and the Cold War*, which "demolished the myth" the West was responsible for Turkey's 1974 invasion of the island and the decades of division which ensued. In the book, Drousiotis denounced Russia's diplomatic efforts in Nicosia as politically unacceptable and painted Russia as a "duplicitous partner that had for decades used disinformation, front organisations and other tools of subterfuge to woo support among Greek-Cypriots while working behind the scenes to stoke tensions." He alleged the activity was designed to ensure Cyprus never aligned with the West and chose to steer clear of NATO membership. However, the concerns raised have not been reflected in the actions of Cypriot authorities, with no measures to counter subversive influence having been taken and no known intelligence activities in Cyprus attempting to counter Russian influence operations. The assessment by European Values specifically cites the absence of an identified threat in any strategy documents and highlights the lack of initiatives concerning cybersecurity.

Greece appears slightly more insidious.

According to the Kremlin Watch assessment, Greece has historically been one of Russia's Trojan Horses within the EU, advocating in Brussels on behalf of Kremlin interests. The current Greek government, the report says, maintains "exceptionally close ties" with Putin's Kremlin and other prominent Russian figures and, at the same time, does not acknowledge any threat pertaining to disinformation or subversive influence stemming from Russia.

Greece, surprisingly, is one of the oldest NATO member states and was the first Balkan state to join the EU, though its difficult history with Turkey has "urged it to look to Russia for support." As a consequence, it is believed Greece has purposefully avoided any expressed opposition to EU measures which could act to alienate the Federation. The Greek government, caught in a severe economic and financial crisis, has sought to woo Russia, reportedly in hopes of receiving aid which Brussels is perceived to have failed to provide, thereby also gaining negotiation leverage on the union. In 2016, Greece also signed a military partnership with Russia on the basis it was "necessary to maintain the Greek defence industry during the economic crisis." Subsequently, the report describes Greece as one of the EU's "three Kremlin friendlies, together with Italy and Cyprus." Despite this, Greece remains committed to the EU and NATO, despite apparently extensive efforts to simultaneously maintain warm, bilateral relations with Russia. (According to the latest Eurobarometer, 66% of Greeks had a positive view of the former USSR.)

In Greece, the report says: "There is no political acknowledgement whatsoever of any hostile Russian activity. On the contrary, the government is very sympathetic to Russian interests and worldview, according to which the West is the aggressor and Russia is merely on the defensive." Greek officials do, instead, take the approach of blaming Western propaganda for fuelling the Ukrainian conflict. In 2014, the report highlights, Defence Minister Panos Kammenos stated, "Western NGOs sponsored by Germany or foundations like the Clinton Institute provoked the crisis in Ukraine where a coup d'état overthrew the legal government." This rhetoric has over-spilled and become commonplace in the alt-right narratives deployed in the US, UK, and elsewhere in the EU.

Greece's radical left-wing Syriza party has never supported EU sanctions on Russia and has very close contacts with Vladimir Putin, Russian nationalist Aleksander Dugin, and Russian oligarchs. In May 2016, Putin travelled to Greece hoping to secure agreements on trade, investment, energy and transportation. The Russian President was joined by foreign minister Sergey Lavrov and a number of oil and gas executives, giving some indication of the importance of the visit. Russia went on to express interest in the purchase of Greek railway company Trainose, as well as Greece's second-largest port, Thessaloniki. Further ties are evident in cooperation on weapons projects with Greece and Moscow negotiating purchase and maintenance deals for S-300 air defence systems.

The authors of the Kremlin Watch report continued in their assessment, identifying a group of eight additional EU states who largely continue to ignore or deny the existence of Russian disinformation and hostile influence operations – Hungary, Austria, Croatia, Luxembourg, Malta, Portugal, Slovakia, Slovenia – and three states who only half-acknowledge existence of the threat. They deduce the latter hesitation is attributable either to geographic distance and historical neutrality (in the case of Ireland) or to the presence of pro-Kremlin forces in the political domain which suppress any efforts to place the threat on the agenda (in Italy and Bulgaria). One of the eight, Hungary, has recently been put on notice of proceedings by the European Commission in relation to its asylum laws and is viewed as a major concern to the EU. Hungarian Prime Minister Viktor Orban, in power in the country since 2010, has vocally attacked the EU on a number of occasions and stands accused in Brussels of willingly accepting EU funds while "rejecting EU values or a share of refugees."

A common theme begins to emerge among the other states assessed by European Values.

Belgium "recognises the threat of Russian disinformation abroad, particularly in the Eastern neighbourhood, but does not consider this to be a problem for its internal security, and therefore does not consider it a national priority," the report says, adding: "Its security institutions predominantly focus on the threat of Islamist terrorism." Spain and France, the assessment continues, consider "Islamist propaganda to be the more serious issue and mostly attribute disinformation campaigns to terrorist recruitment. In France, incoming President Macron seems poised to make a shift in this position, but it remains an open question given France's historically sympathetic attitude to Russia." Denmark, the Netherlands, Romania, Finland, Czech Republic, Germany, the United Kingdom, Poland are recognised as cognizant of the risks but their counter-measure strategies are identified as being in infancy and having "weak spots", rendering all of them vulnerable.

The report states, more generally, "for many of the EU28, a wide gap remains between mere acknowledgement of the threat and the development of concrete and viable counter-measures. The implementation of an effective strategy at the state level requires at least partial political consensus, civic support, and strong democratic institutions."

"Strong rhetoric and condemnation of Russian interference comes at virtually no political cost, but developing a pan-government approach necessitates the dedication of all major political parties and government bodies, as well as their active resistance against local obstacles and Kremlin-linked counter-pressures," it adds.

Having investigated the same issues from an independent standpoint, reading the Kremlin Watch report did little more than support the discoveries I'd made and, while it is a deeply disturbing document, there was very little I could do but sigh and agree with it.

The four states showing the highest levels of "activity, resilience, and readiness to respond" to the Russia threat, given their historical experiences, are Sweden, Estonia, Latvia, and Lithuania, according to the report. This assessment in the case of Sweden I know to be accurate following my own investigations in the country – which, in fact, led me to discover the depth of operations deployed by Russia in this Alternative War.

The Baltic States of Latvia, Lithuania, and Estonia, the report says: "Stand at the forefront of the fight against hostile Russian influence, in large part due to their geographic proximity to Russia, historical experience, and sizeable Russian minorities." The report rightly points out these countries have "adopted strong countermeasures against Russian influence, often restricting Russian pseudo-media," adding "they also actively engage their Russian-speaking minorities, to greater or lesser success. The Baltic experience with Kremlin-linked subversion tactics is the most developed within the EU28 and serves for major lessons learnt." Estonia has been at the forefront of hybrid threat countermeasures since the Capstone experiment in Tallinn.

While there is a clear, natural link to journalism and its position in countering disinformation, it's often more of an implied notion, even though there are clear examples of journalists taking a leading role in challenging Russian subversion operations. The Kremlin Watch report, however, was the first time I had seen the importance of the role of the media is set out expressly. The report is explicit on the need for a free and independent press to form part of any successful counter-measures, saying: "There is a strong negative correlation between the degree of Russian subversive influence on the one hand and the state of media literacy and press freedom on the other."

"In countries with deteriorating press freedom, for instance, due to measures that limit serious investigative journalism, submission to Russian influence has increased in recent months (e.g., Hungary and Croatia)," the report adds. But the assessment of the EU nations serves as a stark warning that press freedom alone, while vital in stemming the success of the current hybrid conflict, is not enough. According to the report, the "traditionally powerful European states only begin to display interest in countering Russian disinformation during, immediately before, or even after major domestic elections, when they have experienced or anticipate Russian interference." Sadly, this is true. In particular, in the United Kingdom.

The Kremlin Watch assessment also correctly identifies that France widely ignored the scale of the threat until the recent presidential elections, even though newly elected President Emmanuel Macron experienced flagrant Russian meddling during his campaign against Russian supported, far-right candidate Marine Le Pen of the Front National. Macron's official foreign policy adviser stated: "We will have a doctrine of retaliation when it comes to Russian cyber-attacks or any other kind of attacks." But in France, as yet, no such action has materialised – at least not visibly and this may well be, in part, due to the complicated and outdated rules of warfare. In another example of unpreparedness, the government of the Netherlands barely reacted when Russian disinformation was circulated during the 2016 referendum on the Association Agreement with Ukraine. It must have, however, learned from the jolt because, during the 2017 parliamentary elections, the country decided not to use electronic voting in order to avoid possible Russian interference. Though no hacks of voting machines have yet been confirmed anywhere in the world, interior minister Ronald Plasterk wrote to his Parliament, saying: "I cannot rule out that state actors may try to benefit from influencing political decisions and public opinion in the Netherlands," and confirmed all ballots would be counted by hand. The Dutch intelligence agency AIVD has since concluded that Russia tried to influence the 2017 elections by spreading fake news.

On the publication of their annual report, Rob Bertholee, the head of AIVD, told reporters Russian had no succeeded in "substantially influencing" the election, saying: "I think they have tried to push voters in the wrong direction by spreading news items that are not true, or partially true." According to the report, the agency assessed the threat posed – by Russia to the Netherlands and Europe – as having escalated over the preceding twelve months, adding that Russia had become "extremely active in espionage," not limiting itself just to elections. "In its efforts to position itself as a superpower, Russia is not afraid of using Cold War methods to obtain political influence. Russia is using the freedom of open and democratic societies of the West [to do this]," the agency added.

In Italy, initial concerns about disinformation and hostile influence operations emerged during the constitutional referendum in December 2016, when the rising anti-establishment Five Star Movement proliferated disinformation and pro-Kremlin propaganda. Nonetheless, the report starkly highlighted: "The government is still not taking any action to counter these efforts. Italy is also a Kremlin ally when it comes to halting new EU sanctions related to Kremlin-sponsored atrocities in Ukraine and Syria." From April 2016, then Prime Minister of Italy, Matteo Renzi, complained privately to his counterparts about Russia meddling in his country's politics by supporting anti-establishment parties. He was referring in the main to the Five Star Movement, led by comedian Beppe Grillo (who I've watched on TV and can say, with my hand on my heart, is simply not funny). In November 2016, a month from the vote, Renzi privately discussed the spread of fake news with other European leaders and President Obama at a meeting in Berlin. The Kremlin had previously enjoyed close relations with Italy for a very long period, in particular under the leadership of billionaire Silvio Berlusconi. The former prime minister and media tycoon was a personal friend of Putin.

Converse to Berlusconi's rise with the Mafia-linked Forza Italia, Grillo's party was initially founded as an online movement. Grillo's co-founder was Gianroberto Casaleggio, an entrepreneur who passed away in 2016. Casaleggio's internet and publishing company, Casaleggio Associati, still controls several widely viewed websites which follow the Breitbart mould and the more sensational, alternative reports found on Sputnik Italia, one of the Kremlin-created websites which disseminate Putin's worldview. One of Casaleggio's sites, Tze, ran nonsense articles with titles such as "Is the US trafficking migrants into Italy?" Though Tze makes no mention of its connection to the Five Star Movement, again following the alt-right model and claiming independence from the mainstream media, large portions of content around the referendum were dedicated to damaging Renzi and his reform campaign. Many of the posts appeared to show thousands of people allegedly protesting against the referendum. A newspaper investigation, however, revealed the people had, in fact, gathered to support Renzi and his proposed reform. Grillo himself, producer of the most widely read blog in Italy, went on to post a picture of a Naples piazza, suggesting the crowds had come to protest against Renzi, describing "a sea of humanity in the square, the people can't take it anymore." In fact, the crowd had gathered to hear a speech from Pope Francis.

Recognition of Russian threats, the Kremlin Watch report concludes: "Results in certain efforts to manage the crisis" but, in the fight against fake news, "governments often seek the help of corporations like Google and Facebook in order to protect their elections."

"These companies have very limited assistance options," the authors point out and the conclusion rings true, startlingly so, when set against everything I discovered independently. Particularly in that "most measures undertaken at the last minute turn out to be "too little, too late" and lack necessary coordination. Importantly, policies against hostile foreign influence must be designed and implemented long in advance."

Rightly, the report's authors highlight that Germany's position could be the "game-changer" in the current hybrid conflict. As they surmise: "With federal elections in September 2017, Germany is currently preoccupied with developing resistance against Russian meddling." Over the last few months, Germany has begun taking the threat posed by Russia much more seriously than ever before, "actively boosting its cyber defence and also promoting cyber security internationally, even creating a new Bundeswehr command."

"If the next German government tackles this threat with true German precision and intensity," the Kremlin Watch authors wrote, "it will spill over to EU policy and prompt substantive democratic counter-pressure. Until now, the concerns of mostly smaller EU members on the Eastern flank have been insufficient to instigate a shift in EU policy."

Northern Europe, very often thought of as the exemplar in terms of military, political, and economic standards, is far from exempt from criticism. Disturbingly, the report is clear the United Kingdom had been "supporting many strategic communications projects in the Eastern Partnership region, but the debate on Kremlin subversion in the UK was very limited before the Brexit referendum in 2016."

"The UK's close ties to Kremlin-linked money has also not featured on the agenda until recently" the report added.

It would be easy to assume this obliquely referred to the 2008 story of then Shadow Chancellor George Osborne, who became involved in a conversation with banking heir Nathaniel Rothschild over the possibility Oleg Deripaska, a Russian oligarch, could donate to the Conservative Party. Osborne, of course, insisted he did not seek any money from Mr Deripaska and claimed the Conservative party had simply rejected a donation from a British company owned by the controversial billionaire. "At no point did Mr Osborne solicit or ask for a donation, suggest ways of channelling a donation or express any wish to meet with Mr Deripaska to discuss donations," said a statement released by the party, which detailed five meetings between the men – four of which took place in Corfu. However, as my own investigation went on to find, this wasn't even the tip of a very large iceberg – the ties between British politics and Russia are insidious, often overt, and the money is, somewhat unexpectedly, the wrong trail to follow. The old journalist's adage is as defunct as traditional warfare.

The report correctly states MI5 chief Andrew Parker had warned Russia's threat to the UK was growing and had stated that Russia's spy activity in the UK is extensive, as was its subversion campaign in Europe in general. It also correctly identified that MI6 chief Alex Younger had also highlighted the issue of subversion and the disinformation campaign waged by Russia and that it was the British intelligence services who first alerted the US about the Democratic National Committee hacks and the alleged Trump-Russia connection in 2015. The authors also picked up on the London School of Economics publication of a report raising alarms about "weak British electoral laws" which can "allow foreign interference to undermine British democracy by allowing an influx of funds from unknown or suspicious sources to fund political campaigns."

The conclusion, under the United Kingdom's heading made for grim, but accurate, reading, saying: "The UK government appears to be more concerned with the diplomatic and international aspects of Russian influence rather than malign domestic effects," while "Facebook has warned that the June 2017 British

General Election may become a subject of attack by fake news and other disinformation online."

As things stand, the Information Commissioner's Office launched an investigation into British election interference and voter manipulation, following the submission of detailed evidence I gathered in the course of my investigations, along with submissions by others. But this alone isn't enough – a retrospective action by a statutory body with insufficient firepower to respond to the Alternative War in any effective way.

We really have gotten into a very grave mess and only the benefits of time and distance will, I fear, provide the ultimate resolution.

TWO:

The European Union itself is already fully engaged in dealing with the Russian threat. Though it took me a while to get hold of the right person, mainly due to staff moves, I eventually tracked down Maja Kocijančič, the Spokesperson for EU Foreign Affairs and Security Policy. She was happy to tell me: "The EU coordinates on all substantial threats, such as terrorism, cyber or hybrid attacks, or propaganda, obviously along the competencies it has."

One of the biggest moves the bloc has attempted to make, which Britain – a divisive voice which is soon to step out altogether – has been key in resisting, is the step towards a greater alignment and combined expenditure on defending the member states by creating a combined military force. Brexit has, in a somewhat unexpected benefit to the union, pushed this agenda forwards at pace without dissent. This is unsurprising once you get a handle on precisely how aware of the hybrid threat the EU is.

"Cyber-attacks are a growing concern worldwide – including for the European Union. Recent attacks experienced in different sectors require a coordinated response. While Member States remain in the front line for much of this work, the EU has an important role to play," Kocijančič added. The change in unified position is now moving at some pace. "In this regard, we will update our Cybersecurity Strategy and reinforce the regulatory framework at EU level on cybersecurity," she told me.

When it comes to hybrid threats, insofar as they relate to national security and defence – and the closely interwoven maintenance of law and order – the primary responsibility, according to the centralised parliament, also lies with individual EU member states. The union is very much alive to the fact that many of them face common threats, which can also target cross-border networks or infrastructures, so single country measures alone are unlikely to be effective.

"Such threats can be addressed more effectively with a coordinated response at EU level by using EU policies and instruments," Kocijančič said, highlighting a deep and progressive understanding of the scale and nature of the issues faced and recognising the need for a more cohesive approach in the future. To this end, the Commission and the High Representative have already presented a unified communication entitled *Joint Framework On Countering Hybrid Threats – A European Union Response,* adopted in April 2016 just as Britain's Brexit referendum campaigns officially began. Kocijančič explained the action taken after the framework was launched, telling me: "Finland established the Centre of Excellence for countering hybrid threats in April this year [2017]. While it is a Finnish national initiative, it constitutes a direct response to one of the twenty-two actionable proposals made in the Joint Communication."

On the launch, High Representative of the Union for Foreign Affairs and Security Policy, Federica Mogherini, who is also Vice-President of the European Commission, said: "As the European Union, we will grant our full support to Finland in driving the new Centre of Excellence for countering hybrid threats forward to a full operational capacity and in its future work in delivering expert strategic analysis on countering hybrid threats, which will contribute to security in Europe. The establishment of the Centre in Helsinki will further strengthen EU-NATO cooperation, particularly on one of the greatest challenges in today's world." A coming change in the structure and functions of both the EU and NATO is highly indicated in this statement alone.

In total, nine nations signed the memorandum of understanding which brought the Centre into being. Finland, France, Germany, Latvia, Lithuania, Poland,

Sweden, the United Kingdom and, somewhat surprisingly given the current situation, the United States. Other NATO and EU nations are expected, according to the nine, to join the Centre in the near future. While the European Union will not be a signatory to the memorandum of understanding between the various participating members states and allies, it has been invited to support the steering board with its expertise. As the Centre develops, the EU has openly stated its looks forward to "being able to develop a close working relationship, drawing in particular on the experience gained through the European Union Hybrid Fusion Centre that operates at a technical level in Brussels." The Centre will engage in strategic level dialogue, research, training and consultations. It will also conduct practical training exercises aiming to improve readiness to counter hybrid threats. The purpose of the Centre is to raise awareness of hybrid threats and societies' vulnerabilities which can be exploited in hybrid operations but the aim is also to help foster the resilience of democracies. Based as planned in Helsinki, the Centre brings together a network of experts from the participating countries and the initial annual budget was set low, at around one and a half million Euro. Half of the funding is covered by membership fees and the host country, Finland, provides the other half, covering the premises, telecommunications and, in part, human resources. It opened on the 11th of April 2017.

Things have moved forwards since the EU's initial joint communication, and Finland is not the only concrete action to have been taken. "Cyber and hybrid threats are part of the new, important cooperation between the EU and NATO, agreed through a set of forty-two concrete proposals in seven different areas identified by the Joint Declaration signed in Warsaw," Kocijančič told me. The EU has also put in place its own specialist division aimed at improving the EU's capacity to forecast, address and raise awareness of disinformation activities by external actors. There are no open questions as to who these actors are.

The EU STRATCOM (Strategic Communications) Task Force was set up specifically to address Russia's ongoing disinformation campaigns. From the outset one of the key focus areas was "analysing disinformation trends, explaining disinformation narratives and myth-busting." They publish ongoing fact-checks under the banner of the Disinformation Review Team, which can also be found on Twitter.

Though the following of the scheme is still low – sitting under thirty thousand followers on Twitter versus the millions who follow the false reporting of the alt-right – the content the unit provides is exceptionally good and they don't hold back from calling out Russia as the culprit of ongoing disinformation. In one example, a bulletin from mid-May 2017, STRATCOM, exploded one myth relating to Swedish doctors and the use of chemical weapons in Syria. "As we have previously explained," the bulletin begins, "Russian state-owned media regularly make use of international "experts" to give legitimacy to pro-Kremlin narratives, even if the experts are known as such only by pro-Kremlin media."

During the weeks leading to the bulletin, STRATCOM analysts had identified the strategy in action once again, citing a little-known organisation from Sweden, "Swedish doctors for human rights" (Swedhr). It was virtually unknown in Sweden, or abroad, until the head of the organisation was cited by the Syrian delegation to the UN and by the spokesperson of the Russian Foreign Ministry, Mariya Zakharova. Russian and Syrian representatives used the organisation's analysis of a two-year-old video as "evidence" that the chemical attacks in Syria were fake or false flag operations carried out by the NGO White Helmets. It transpires Amnesty International in Sweden, Human Rights Watch in Sweden, the Swedish

Society of Medicine, and the Swedish Medical Association all say they had never heard of Swedhr, which describes itself as an "alternative NGO," yet the head of the organisation is regularly cited in Russian state outlets such as RT (Russia Today).

In addition to the mystery of the source, nearly all of the outlets and representatives quoting the video as evidence for casting doubt on current chemical attacks in Syria omit the fact the video analysed by Swedhr was already two years old. STRATCOM, citing previous articles on Russian Syria narrative, conclude the bulletin by saying "during several interviews in Russian state media (RT among others), the head of Swedhr, who is a retired doctor of psychiatry and public health, gives supposedly expert opinions on who is behind the chemical attacks in Syria, in line with the pro-Kremlin narrative on Syria."

The role of Swedhr, which was founded in 2015, has also been covered by Swedish newspaper Dagens Nyheter, which concluded Swedhr pursues a clear agenda in its narratives, such as statements the Ukraine is governed by fascists and the Swedish mainstream media (among them Dagens Nyheter) are Russophobes. "These are common pro-Kremlin narratives," STRATCOM confirms.

The diversity of Russian-led strategic disinformation is astonishing and deeply disturbing. I discovered the CIA has provided rather detailed analysis on one Russian outlet, Russia Today. RT's Editor in Chief, Margarita Simonyan, has close ties to top Russian Government officials, according to the Central Intelligence Agency. Especially, they say, to Presidential Administration Deputy Chief of Staff Aleksey Gromov, who reportedly manages political TV coverage in Russia and is one of the founders of RT. She was also on Putin's 2012 presidential election campaign staff. Simonyan has claimed Gromov shielded her from other officials and their requests to air certain reports, and Russian media consider Simonyan to be Gromov's protégé. (She replaced Gromov on state-owned Channel One's Board of Directors.)

Government officials, including Gromov and Putin's Press Secretary Peskov, were involved in creating RT and appointing Simonyan, according to the CIA report. Gromov oversees political coverage on broadcast media on behalf of the Russian state, and has periodic meetings with media managers – where he shares classified information and discusses, or possibly directs, their coverage plans. Some opposition journalists, including Andrey Loshak, claim he has also ordered media attacks on opposition figures. The Kremlin, the CIA states, not only staffs RT but closely supervises the coverage it provides, specifically recruiting people who can convey Russian strategic messaging because of their ideological beliefs. This extends beyond "alternative NGOs" like Swedhr, and includes even British political figures, Nigel Farage being a specific case in point. The structure of RT also confirms additional links between Farage and the upper echelons of the Kremlin, which makes sense of a lot more I uncovered while investigating this rather intricate web. According to Simonyan, the Russian Government sets rating and viewership requirements for RT and, "since RT receives budget from the state, it must complete tasks given by the state." Tasking is a specific indicator of espionage connections and this deepens when you consider additional factors. For example, the head of RT's Arabic-language service, Aydar Aganin, was rotated from the diplomatic service to manage RT's Arabic-language expansion, suggesting a close relationship between RT and Russia's foreign policy apparatus. And, in addition, RT's London Bureau is managed by Darya Pushkova, the daughter of Aleksey Pushkov, the current chair of the Duma Russian Foreign Affairs Committee.

RT has intensified its efforts, dominating social media with an almost viral level of spread – the specific risk STRATCOM is trying to address. Nonetheless, RT has been highly successful at infiltrating and driving its narratives across the Western world. The United States provides one very good example of their achievements and, in her interview with pro-Kremlin journalist Sergey Minaev, Simonyan complimented RT staff in the United States for passionately defending Russian positions on the air and in social media. "I wish you could see...how these guys, not just on air, but on their own social networks, Twitter, and when giving interviews, how they defend the positions that we stand on!" she said.

From the introduction of Capstone to the EU joint initiatives, it is clear the Alternative War had already been a live, covert conflict for at least two years before Trump and Brexit began to be unpicked, despite all the main warning signs being in plain sight. However, what was probably the biggest weapon in the conflict took everyone by surprise. The crucial element of the hybrid assault deployed by Russia – notable by its failure to achieve the desired political manipulation in France due to the government responses and, equally by its success in the UK with Brexit and US with Trump – was the relatively new and still misunderstood technique of psychometrics or psychographics. Now infamously deployed by American company Cambridge Analytica – part of the British SCL Group – in both the Trump campaign and Leave.EU's Brexit campaign, psychometrics (to stick to one term for ease) utilises so-called Big Data, gathered through social media, surveys and other databases, to create a unique personal profile on every voter. A singular assessment of a person and their personality, to which messages can be tailored and targeted. It is a psychological warfare technique and Cambridge Analytica, through ex-board member and special adviser to Trump, Steve Bannon, is believed to be making attempts to woo the Pentagon, with representatives just "dropping by" according to various reports.

Another company in the same market is Palantir Technologies, already linked to the US Department of Defense. One of their systems, Gotham, is used by counter-terrorism analysts at offices in the United States Intelligence Community and United States Department of Defense, fraud investigators at the Recovery Accountability and Transparency Board, and cyber analysts at Information Warfare Monitor. Going back as far as 2013, additional clients of Palantir included Homeland Security, the NSA, the FBI, the Center for Disease Control, the Marine Corps, the Air Force, Special Operations Command, West Point, the Joint IED-defeat organisation and others. According to reporters at Tech Crunch, "The US spy agencies also employed Palantir to connect databases across departments. Before this, most of the databases used by the CIA and FBI were siloed, forcing users to search each database individually. Now everything is linked together using Palantir." US military intelligence also deployed the Palantir product to improve their ability to predict the locations of improvised explosive devices in its war in Afghanistan. The technology was deployed with Marines in 2011 and practitioners reported it to be more useful than the United States Army's in-house Distributed Common Ground System.

By 2015, Palantir's relationships with both the CIA and the NSA had soured to the point where both parted company with the private company, which was founded by billionaire Peter Thiel. One key observation coming out of the resultant spat highlighted the big data method is significantly more successful where it is deployed in a human intelligence environment, rather than signals intelligence – hence only limited success in the NSA integration. Largely, this goes a long way to explaining how the technology has become so instrumental in the hybrid conflict. Until it became widely known in 2017, however, the technique of harnessing enhanced datasets had been identified and perceived as a risk for a number of years.

Back in 2010, cyber security company HB Gary – who also worked on Federal contracts – were in friendly talks about integrating with Palantir on social media based products. Under the subject heading "Social Media, Exploitation, and Persistent Internet Operations," senior employees of both companies were discussing the opportunities and risks by email.

"The rise of the social web has created an entirely new set of useful technologies and security vulnerabilities. It is our experience that most individuals and organisations understand there are risks to using social media but don't understand the full extent, from what types of use, what the real risks are, or how the vulnerabilities can be fully exploited," one exchange said.

The emails were dumped on the internet by Wikileaks after one HB Gary employee exposed alleged members of Anonymous to the authorities in 2011, in an event which ruined his career. Before infamy, however, Arron Barr set out in further emails just how significant the development of big data as a weapon would be. "There is an immense amount of information that can be aggregated from social media services to develop competitive intelligence against any target. Take any US defence contractor. If I could harvest a significant amount of data from sites such as FBO, Monster, LinkedIn, Input, Facebook, Twitter. What type of picture could I put together as far as company capabilities, future plans, contract wins, etc. From a targeting perspective could I identify information exposure points that lead to a defensive weakness...I spoke to INSCOM a few weeks ago about their desire to start to incorporate more social media reconnaissance and exploitation into their red team efforts. Such a capability has a broad applicability that will be more significantly needed in the future," he wrote.

Barr was years ahead of his time in identifying threats which were subsequently exploited to successfully manipulate both British and American electorates. In one briefing email, he expanded, saying: "The explosive growth of social media has created a highly effective channel for the collection and aggregation of personal and organisational information for the purposes of tailoring content for users. To interact in a social media ecosystem requires some release of personally identifiable information (PII), in fact with most services the more information you provide the more tailored and beneficial the experience. In most cases, these are legitimate reasons for providing the information with tangible user benefits, whether it be to more personalise and localise advertising or tailored and real-time information delivery that increases personal productivity. Unfortunately, the same methods are being used to conduct information reconnaissance and exploitation. The most common current examples are spear-phishing attacks."

"Future social media exploitation tactics will likely be applications and service that provide personal benefit or entertainment, but serving a dual purpose to collect information that can be used for more insidious purposes. This marks a new class of exploitation, vehicles directly targeting people rather than the machines they use," he concluded, in an eerie portent.

HB Gary no longer exists as it was and Barr is now a recluse, nonetheless, what they identified many years ago was not only visionary but has become part of the Russian hybrid arsenal, not only by direct use of psychometrics as a weapon but also via one of their third-party hacking and disinformation channels, Wikileaks. I tracked down one former employee of HB Gary and asked them how dangerous social media really was and if it had really had been turned into a weapon. "The Russian stuff kinda proves that out right?" they replied, without prompting.

"There is enough info and interaction purely in the public domain to provide intelligence and to engage in influence. Social media is the perfect mechanism. But we can see that happening right in front of us. Just have to organise and automate," they added.

In the Wikileaks dumps on HB Gary there were a number of mentions about defence from the weaponised use of this data, but nothing concrete. When I asked, the response they gave me was, again, fairly stark. "There isn't really a defence. Not one that can be easily devised. Platforms are of course working to manage fake info but that only will take care of the careless and less sophisticated – if done properly. [It's] taking advantage of people's natural inclinations... but again we can see all this in front of us."

I pressed them on Cambridge Analytica and what they knew through the industry grapevine, but the answer confirmed a lot of the rumours about the company's high commitment to secrecy. "I haven't heard anything...there are people that obviously have the background and talent and are now, and increasingly, going to apply it in the wild. The question is not "is developing the capabilities unethical?" It's what do you do with it."

The arms value of social media-led psychometrics combined with traditional disinformation has changed everything and the damage caused by the hybrid conflict to date, it seems clear, will take years to correct without a more stringent response from unified allies such as NATO and the EU. But, as I found talking to Kocijančič, huge strides are being taken and the pace is accelerating. Feeding into the discussion on the future direction of the European Union, the Commission held an orientation debate on the future of European defence on the 24th of May 2017.

A stronger Europe when it comes to security and defence matters has been a priority for the Juncker Commission since it took office and President Juncker himself announced the creation of a European Defence Fund in his 2016 State of the Union address, saying "Europe can no longer afford to piggy-back on the military might of others...For European defence to be strong, the European defence industry needs to innovate." With a worsening security situation, both traditional and hybrid, in Europe's neighbourhood, and a strong economic case for greater cooperation on defence spending amongst EU countries, the Commission said it believed "now is the time to make strides towards a Security and Defence Union."

The May 2017 orientation debate aimed to help guide the Commission's work in "the weeks to come," rather than months or years, and ahead of the Prague high-level European conference on defence and security, in June 2017, the Commission was already set to launch the European Defence Fund – which was announced in the European Defence Action Plan of November 2016. "In parallel," the Commissions said, "it will present a longer-term reflection paper setting out possible scenarios for the future in the area of European defence." It's clear the EU is trying to balance the introduction of these necessary defence measures with the economics of diverse states.

Vice-President for Jobs, Growth, Investment and Competitiveness Jyrki Katainen made a statement on the announcement, saying: "Strengthening European security and defence requires using the available defence budgets more efficiently. Investment in defence capabilities remains in the hands of the Member States, and the EU budget cannot replace the Member States' on defence. However, there is an overwhelming economic and industrial case for greater cooperation, for example in defence research and procurement. As pressure on national budgets remains high, we need more efficient defence spending and a better use of defence capabilities."

There is clearly a strong case for greater cooperation on security and defence across the union, and it, like

NATO, is cognisant of the fact the threats faced by the EU as a bloc do not respect national borders. "Their scale is increasing. They are best tackled by working together," the Commission said, adding: "A strong European defence requires a strong European defence industry. As Member States begin to increase their defence budgets, the EU can help them to spend these funds more efficiently. The lack of cooperation between the Member States in the field of defence and security is estimated to cost annually between €25 billion and €100 billion. 80% of procurement and more than 90% of Research and Technology are run on a national basis Up to 30% of annual defence expenditures could be saved through pooling of procurement." The argument they make is well-grounded and dispassionate, which strikes me as being a carefully worded approach to drawing the states together on non-controversial grounds of basic finance. This, I believe, makes a more palatable argument for member representatives to take back to their own parliaments and electorates. It's rather shrewd and certainly savvy, in my opinion.

The softly-softly approach has, however, been taken by Juncker from the outset. In his political guidelines in June 2014, he stated: "I believe that we need to work on a stronger Europe when it comes to security and defence matters. Yes, Europe is chiefly a 'soft power'. But even the strongest soft powers cannot make do in the long run without at least some integrated defence capacities."

When Juncker announced the creation of a European Defence Fund in 2016, the leaders of all but one member state concluded that "we need the EU not only to guarantee peace and democracy but also the security of our people." In a challenging geopolitical environment, they agreed on the need to strengthen EU cooperation on external security and defence, a move which was opposed and frustrated only by Britain – who had already voted to leave the union in the Brexit referendum. "There are member states who would like to see...a single set of forces. That looks and sounds to me like a European army, and we would oppose that," said Michael Fallon, Britain's defence secretary.

Despite the protestations of the inexplicably obstructive departing nation, on the 30th of November 2016 the Commission presented the European Defence Action Plan which outlined how a European Defence Fund and other actions could support Member States' more efficient spending in joint defence capabilities, strengthen European citizens' security and foster a competitive and innovative industrial base. The initiative was welcomed by EU leaders during the European Council meetings – in both December 2016 and March 2017 – and the Commission was given the mandate to present proposals before the summer of 2017. Britain's principle objection, cited by Fallon, was that a common EU defence programme would detract from NATO. He was wrong and his obstruction unfounded.

The European Defence Action Plan is part of the broader Defence package agreed to by the twenty-seven members in Bratislava. It was, the Commission said: "Complementary to the other two work strands, namely the Global Strategy's Implementation Plan on Security and Defence," which sets out a new level of ambition for the Union and identifies actions to fulfil it, as well as with the implementation of the EU-NATO Joint Declaration signed by the President of the European Council, the President of the Commission and the Secretary-General of NATO. According to the EU and NATO, the joint declaration includes action on "hybrid threats, which is also linked to the April 2016 Joint Framework to counter hybrid threats, which in turn builds on the European Agenda on Security adopted by the Commission in April 2015." Further, the Rome Declaration, adopted by the remaining twenty-seven EU leaders on the 25th of March 2017, pledged to work towards an "EU27 that helps create a more competitive and integrated defence industry, and which strengthens its common security and defence in cooperation and complementarity with NATO."

An additional white paper on the "Future of Europe" was presented on the 1st of March 2017 and set out the main challenges and opportunities for Europe in the coming decade. Its publication marked the beginning of a process for the EU27 to decide on the future of their Union without Britain.

Even when the Rome treaty was being signed I was not aware of any of this. In fact, up until I visited Malmö, I had no idea about Capstone, STRATCOM, or the joint declaration. None of it. This all began for me with a trip to Sweden, to find out the truth about crime and immigration after a ding-dong with the alt-right on Twitter and that initial investigation opened a door which led me to connect the far-right across Europe to both the American alt-right movement and to Russia. From there I discovered all manner of darkness from Trump to Brexit, and beyond.

If you'd asked me even earlier this year if we were at war, I'd have probably told you I thought one was coming; that I could see the troop movements on Europe's Eastern borders escalating into armed skirmishes. But the idea a war had already started? The suggestion of a hybrid conflict? I'd have probably laughed.

I don't find it so funny now. The Alternative War is quite real.

THREE:

On the 18th of February 2016 news reports of a bomb being thrown into the Turkish Cultural Centre in Fittja, a Stockholm district, reached the headlines across the world. This followed Kurdish protests during Turkey's military intervention in Syria. Code-named by the Turkish military as Operation Euphrates Shield, the cross-border operation of Turkish forces was allied with opposition factions in the Syrian Civil War. The offensive ended in a Turkish occupation of northern Syria and the action, which is thought to have been planned for up to a year beforehand, ended up creating conflict with the United States, a NATO ally. The extent of the deployment ran from the east, by the Euphrates river, to western, rebel-held area surrounding Azaz. The Turkish-allied Syrian forces had been fighting against the Islamic State of Iraq and the Levant (ISIL), as well as opposing the Syrian Democratic Forces (SDF). The operation concluded in March 2017 and was hailed as a success by Turkey's government. The building in Fittja was damaged in the protest against Euphrates Shield but nobody was injured.

In October 2016, a Muslim community centre was fire-bombed in Malmö, causing smoke damage to the building and no injuries. Responsibility was claimed by ISIS according to local reports and a Syrian man was put on trial, but the courts found him not guilty in April 2017. The prosecutor submitted arguments the fire was "started in order to spread fear in the name of Isis," and set out the cost to repair the smoke damage of one million Swedish kronor (about £100,000). The prosecutor also asserted the Polisen, on searching the suspect's computer, discovered a description of how to make a detonator along with propaganda films showing ISIS soldiers fighting and killing "infidels." He also reported the incident to the Isis-controlled news agency Aamaq, which is where the responsibility claim originated. However, Malmö District Court dismissed the terror charges, with Judge Lennart Strinäs recording that: "One of the prerequisites to consider the fire in question as a terror offence is that the act could have seriously damaged the state of Sweden. For that, acts of a completely different and much more serious nature are required and according to the district court that has not been the case. The act should instead be classified as arson."

The court went on to rule the prosecution had "failed to prove beyond reasonable doubt that the 30-year-old man was guilty of arson," highlighting the forensic examination of the crime scene and the witnesses had failed to produce sufficient evidence to support a guilty verdict. "It appears to be obvious that [the man] sympathizes with IS [Isis], something which could indicate he had a motive to start the fire but does not prove that he did," the court wrote. The Swedish security service, Säpo, was less than sympathetic to the verdict and opened a case under Sweden's Act on Foreign Immigration Control legislation, arguing the evidence was enough to prove the man had links with Isis and should be deported. The security situation in Sweden, however, is not restricted to the Muslim community.

On the 3rd of February 2017, three suspected Neo-Nazis of the Nordic Resistance Movement were arrested by Swedish anti-terror police for a bomb attack at an immigration centre in Gothenburg, where a staff member was seriously injured. Säpo very quickly linked the attack with two other failed attempts – one on a socialist café and the other on a temporary housing camp for migrants. According to Mats Ljungqvist of the anti-terror prosecutor's office, all three explosive devices were "placed in public areas."

Formed by members of Sweden's White Aryan Resistance in the 1990s, the Nordic Resistance Movement calls for an "immediate stop to mass immigration to the Scandinavian countries," and seeks to implement "the repatriation of the majority of peoples that are not of North European descent" from Nordic countries at the earliest opportunity. Now made up of a larger coalition of Swedish, Danish, Finnish, and Norwegian movements, it aims to bring about the creation of one "self-sufficient state with a common military, common currency and central bank." Following a well-known fascist model, the group desire control of mass media and openly wish to ban any foreign publications which they consider "hostile to the people of the north." According to their plans, the Nordic State ideologues envisage they would introduce national conscription and significantly expand the military, while those who completed service would always retain their primary weapon and kit. Under the principles they set out, European Union membership and "other similar associations" would also be immediately be terminated and a lasting imposition placed on the public to "aid in the defence of the nation towards domestic as well as foreign enemies."

The movement has a long history of extremism and violence. Even potted examples paint a disturbing picture of an organisation which more than echoes the Islamic State, its declared enemy. In January 2006, a day before the International Holocaust Remembrance Day, a handful of activists held a demonstration, burning the flag of Israel and draping a "we love Aryans" banner over a bridge. A few months later, four members were sentenced to prison for inciting hatred. They have been in Söderhamn, handing out leaflets linking homosexuality with paedophilia. In December 2007, courts sentenced Niklas Frost, an activist, to five years in prison for attempted manslaughter – he was arrested for stabbing an anti-fascism protester during clashes between the groups which had taken place in September. A year later, in 2008, Swedish police seized a large number of weapons and explosives found in Värmdö and its western suburbs. Three members were arrested on suspicion of larceny and "preparation to the devastation and endangering of the public." This is terrorism in all but a name in law.

Even at the start of my investigation, in the initial stages of research, it was apparent Sweden does have problems with violent acts, in particular those aimed at causing fear and harm, some of which are ideologically motivated, rather than simply related to criminal networks – Mafia styled organisations and gangs engaged in targeted intimidation and retaliation. But, in the country's recent history, there had only been one officially recorded terror incident: in December 2010, a suicide bomber was the only fatality in an attempted attack on Stockholm.

On the 11th of December 2010, two bombs exploded in central Stockholm, killing the bomber, Taimour Abdulwahab al-Abdaly, an Iraqi-born Swedish citizen. The first explosion occurred when a parked Audi 80 exploded at the intersection of Olof Palmes and Drottninggatan in the city centre. A forensic examination by the fire service concluded the car had contained bottles of liquefied petroleum gas which caused a sequence of explosions after the main detonation. The car bomb had a very limited impact, luckily, with only two people being treated at the hospital having both been admitted with minor injuries. The second explosion was twelve minutes later at the junction of Bryggargatan and Drottninggatan, a short distance away. The attacker's body was discovered at the location and the police quickly made a statement that the suicide bomber was the only fatality.

Reports published after the bombing state al-Abdaly had carried six pipe-bombs with him but only one exploded. A metal pipe and a rucksack filled with metal fasteners – a home-made a nail bomb – and an unknown substance was found. The substance was thought to be an unsophisticated but effective, home-made explosive. According to witnesses in the packed shopping street, the bomber was shouting "something in Arabic" before detonating the bomb within metres of the doorway of a busy shop. I have watched the closed-circuit television footage of the second explosion, which was released the following day by the Aftonbladet newspaper and, though the bomber himself is just off camera, the lack of other fatalities is astonishing.

It emerged during the course of the terrorism investigation that, about ten minutes before the explosions, an email was sent to Säpo and Tidningarnas Telegrambyrå (TT), a Swedish news agency. The message apparently referred to the deployment of Swedish troops in Afghanistan and drawings of Muhammad as a dog by the Swedish artist Lars Vilks. "Now your children, daughters and sisters will die in the same way our brothers and sisters die. Our actions will speak for themselves. As long as you don't end your war against Islam and degradation against the prophet and your foolish support for the pig [Lars] Vilks," the email is reported to have said. Sound files in Swedish and Arabic were also included.

It appears, however, al-Abdaly was radicalised in the UK, where he obtained a degree at the University of Bedfordshire in 2004. During his stay in Britain, he lived in Luton for almost a decade and reports which came out after the bombing say he became more religious and more angry in the late 2000s. At some point, while Ramadan was taking place in 2007, he allegedly stormed out of the Luton mosque when confronted about his beliefs and was forbidden to return. While preaching, Al-Abdaly had, according to witnesses who approached the authorities in the wake of Stockholm, tried to recruit other Muslims who shared or sympathised with his political views.

2017 brought with it new challenges for Sweden but not all of them were based in fact.

On Saturday the 18th of February 2017, a year after the Turkish Cultural Centre bombing in Fittja, the newly elected President of the United States stood on the podium at a rally in Florida, talking about the need to keep US Citizens safe in the light of world events. "You look at what's happening, last night in Sweden. Who would believe this?" Donald Trump told the relatively small crowd of supporters.

The gathering formed part of Trump's 2020 election campaign, it appears – an oddity made possible by his early registration under the permissible PAC rules in January, meaning he can fundraise and campaign for election under the different standards afforded despite being in office under the constitutional rules of the White House. Effectively, he can legally separate his electioneering behaviour from his official position, even where this creates a reality chasm. There is also a more disturbing element to this early registration. Filed on January 20th, 2017, the paperwork confirms that Trump submitted an "FEC Form 2" in order to "ensure compliance with the Federal Election Campaign Act." For the record, it is worth noting former President Barack Obama did not file for his 2012 re-election bid until April 2011 but the form being filed with the Federal Elections Commission simply meant Trump could engage with and gain support from financial donors and other groups throughout his presidency. But, more importantly, not for profit organisations would no longer be able to engage in political speech under the 501(c)(3) rule of the FEC without running the risk of losing their non-profit status. In practical terms, it prevents activists from forming not for profit groups which they could funnel money into for the purposes of opposing Trump's initiatives for the duration of his term. Seemingly, Trump worked out a simple way to tip the scales in his own favour, which doesn't look much like draining the swamp. It appears to be, to me at least, a calculated act of political eugenics.

Twenty-four hours before Trump spoke in Florida, on Friday the 17th of February 2017, there were no terror attacks in Sweden. Pretty much nothing happened, as a matter of fact. A man was killed in an industrial accident, a drunk driver got chased through Stockholm in a police pursuit, and some roads were closed due to bad weather, but there were no incidents of terrorism. Outside of Sweden but related to it, the only noteworthy and relevant occurrence was the broadcast of a Fox News documentary in the US which claimed a surge in violent crime and rape was taking place since the country adopted an 'open door' immigration policy in 2013.

Trump's remark caused bemusement across the globe, with Sweden officially rebutting the suggestion anything had happened. Some media outlets speculated Trump may have been directly influenced by watching the Fox documentary and attributed the comment to a misunderstanding of this.

The police officers featured in the film, made by YouTuber Ami Horowitz, called the director a "madman" who misrepresented their views. "It was supposed to be about crime in high-risk areas. Areas with high crime rates. There wasn't any focus on migration or immigration," said one of the officers, Anders Göranzon. Discussing the issue with Swedish paper Dagens Nyheter, Göranzon said Horowitz edited their answers to fit segments of film which were to completely different questions in the interview. Horowitz responded, standing by his work, telling the same newspaper: "They are completely wrong about them answering questions I didn't ask. They are one hundred percent wrong. And that is all on the videotape." However, Swedish freelance cameramen Emil Marczak, who filmed the segment with the police officers for Horowitz, has confirmed the footage was edited. He told reporters: "I would never have participated if I had known how unethically and frivolously the material would be edited. To double check that my memory is correct I have gone through the raw material and it confirms the policemen's view of the course of events."

The BBC responded to Trump's comment with incredulity, as many other mainstream outlets did, while Carl Bildt, the former Swedish Prime Minister, simply tweeted: "What has Trump been smoking?" Conversely, right-wing figures including Nigel Farage took to the media to back Trump's claims of immigrant-driven crime afflicting Sweden. Farage himself insisted on his London-based LBC radio show that Malmö was the "rape capital of Europe." Many 'alternative' news outlets, including the ultra-right website Breitbart – once headed by Trump's Special Advisor Steve Bannon – also backed the assertions and Sweden very quickly found itself being portrayed as a violent haven for immigrant criminality on the brink of social collapse. The White House press office, then led by Sean Spicer, backed this further, releasing a list of what they called "un-reported" terror attacks across the world – including reference to the Malmö fire-bomb of October 2016.

As a result, alternative narratives were driven very swiftly into overdrive, gaining traction across the full spectrum of social media and web-based publications used as platforms by alt-right figures and organisations. This included Alex Jones' Info Wars, and it was at this point the self-declared "editor at large," Paul Joseph Watson, stepped in. Tweeting to 503,200 followers, the British video-blogger – who also runs websites Prison Planet and Propaganda Matrix – declared: "Any journalist claiming Sweden is safe; I will pay for travel costs & accommodation for you to stay in crime-ridden migrant suburbs of Malmo." Only a few hours later, Watson had confirmed his offer as genuine, personally donating $2,000 dollars to one journalist, Tim Pool. He then continued posting inflammatory images and messages about Sweden while refusing to engage with any other people who'd accepted his unilateral contract offer, despite media coverage on both sides of the Atlantic. In response, I launched a successful Crowdfunder to take Watson to Small Claims over breach of contract and to raise funds to travel to Malmö and ensure balanced coverage was produced. At this time, the court aspect is still ongoing.

Up until I got involved, my understanding of crime – in particular, rape and sexual offences – in Sweden had been accrued through my reading of Stieg Larsson's Millennium Trilogy. According to interviews with the late writer's family, he'd taken up a narrative against violence towards women having witnessed a gang rape as a young man and carried a form of guilt or horror with him until his unexpected death. Throughout the first book in the series, The Girl With The Dragon Tattoo, Larsson used statistics to punctuate the primary partitions between the chapters, "13% of all women in Sweden have been subjected to aggravated sexual assault outside of a sexual relationship," for example. Whether or not the figures were based in fact has long since become irrelevant, however. The book was first published in 2005, the year sexual assault law was changed in Sweden, with a further overhaul of the legislation taking place in 2013. This made substantial changes to crime recording practice by the police. I am though, still, an international expert in crime data so it didn't take long to make an initial assessment of the likely landscape.

In general, Swedish crime figures show upwards movement in fraud and violence against the person, marginally increasing in 2016, while drug and theft offences decreased over the same year. Although the number of rapes did increase by 13% in the same period, the overall total was still lower than in 2014. It is worth comparing the total number of reported rapes nationally – six and a half thousand in a population of nearly ten million – with the United States, where crime recording varies state to state. In the US there were nearly one hundred and seventy-five thousand victims of rape recorded in the last national count of

2013, though the under-reporting estimates from the Department of Justice indicate only 55% of rape is notified to the American authorities. Set against the much larger population of almost three hundred and nineteen million, the risk of rape – though the figures don't have direct parity, not least due to the higher rate of under-reporting in the US – is almost the same (within 0.01%). However, with the figures adjusted to account for estimated under-reporting, the per capita rate in the US almost doubles. In relative terms, I can say it is clear in the figures that Sweden is a safe country when compared to the rest of the world, and also has a high rating in terms of public trust of the police – a view which foreign visitors to Sweden often confirm too.

While this initial assessment was done remotely, while I was still planning the trip, Watson's funded video-maker, Tim Pool, agreed. He concluded his trip by telling the Swedish media it was a "paradise compared to Chicago," even though he had given an account of being escorted from the Stockholm district of Rinkeby by police over safety fears when youths began to pull hoods up around him. The Swedish police service vehemently denied Pool's account, officially stating that local youths were upset at being filmed without permission, while the police themselves were only in the same area due to a community poetry evening.

With Horowitz already having damaged media relations with the police, tensions in the Rinkeby area were undoubtedly also high in respect of foreign film crews and, only days before Pool arrived, a Russian television unit had been in the same district reportedly offering youths four hundred Kronor (around forty pounds) to "create some action on camera."

"They came up to us and said they wanted to see some action. They wanted to bribe us 400 [Kronor] each," one Rinkeby resident, told the Danish radio station Radio24syv.

Interestingly, in terms of population growth, which captures immigration, there is still little difference between the US and Sweden in the official figures, barring scale. Sweden ranks, for what such tables are worth, at 139th in the world with a population growth rate of 0.79% per year, whereas the United States comes in lower, at 142nd, with a growth rate of 0.77%. In real terms, by which I mean converting this to a basic head count, Sweden grew by seventy-nine thousand people at the last count while the US population increased by around two and half million, over thirty-one times the Nordic figures. Sweden has taken in somewhere in the region of two hundred thousand asylum seekers and refugees since 2013, which is a higher per capita rate than any other European country by some margin. After a spike in 2015, with a huge surge of nearly one hundred and sixty-five thousand people coming into the country in the twelve months, extra border checks were introduced and financial incentives began to be offered to those migrants willing to return to their homes. The statistics are comprehensively reported – with rolling monthly data – by the Migrationsverket and their clear information bulletins show migration plummeted in 2016. The largest incoming ethnic group was then Syrian, which was unsurprising given the current war and chemical weapons deployments in the country. The displacement of the population caused by what was fundamentally a civil war, now muddied by Turkish, Russian, and IS insurgency has been a significant driver for migration to Europe. There is a rational argument that this has also benefitted Russia, at least in terms of the negative impact on European unity over recent years, and the situation has certainly driven the rise of far-right, anti-immigration politics into the mainstream.

Säpo, who currently deploy active monitoring measures on any immigrants travelling away from Sweden to participate in ongoing wars, have also noted a significant and rapid decline in those leaving over the same period. This made a significant change from 2015 when the security service came under fire from the EU for not doing enough to prevent fighters joining conflicts. At the time, their response was: "There is only very little we can do to stop people from travelling from Sweden to join al-Qaeda inspired groups."

"About 50 of those known to have travelled to Syria have returned to Sweden. They travel to Syria, return to Sweden and tend to go back again," said Fredrik Milder, Säpo press officer. The agency confirmed that at least one hundred and fifty Swedish residents were known to have been to Syria or Iraq to fight for Isis or other extremist groups, with intelligence suggesting that at least thirty-five had died in the process.

Of course, statistics the world over are only as good as the method by which they are collected. Because of me, the United Kingdom's crime figures were stripped of their official status in 2013, having been found to have been broadly manipulated for decades and almost every major police force in the United States faced the same level of scandal in recent years. The UK's employment figures are under almost constant fire, largely due to the three-year push of self-employment roles on job-seekers, which potentially distorts the number of unemployed people recorded, along with sanctions recording. My second trip to Mexico is another case in point. In November 2016, I concluded an analysis of data collected by the Mexican federal government since 1997 and found malpractice in collecting and reporting crime in every single one of Mexico's thirty-two states. The main method through which the authorities misrepresented the crime rates was by inflating the number of lower-level crimes in order to make it appear like there had been fewer high-impact crimes, like kidnapping and intentional homicide. I also found the case of one state that criminal threats, accidental homicides, and intentional homicides varied in the same way over the years analysed – an unlikely trend as there is no inherent correlation between those crimes. Without going into distracting detail here, there were clear links between the changes in state administrations and murder, rape, and extortion rates. Basically, corruption in public institutions working in cahoots with cartels.

"There is manipulation clearly visible in the data, in every state in Mexico, across all crime types," I told a packed press conference, wondering all the while if my head was going to end up in a bin truck.

I'm trying to explain that understanding what's behind the figures is crucial whatever situation you are looking at, as the full story is rarely contained accurately in data alone.

Immigration to Sweden itself, I found, is tightly linked to what has been termed the 'Swedish Model' of social structure. The model has, for many years, been widely regarded as a near-perfect blend of the welfare state and capitalist policy, in which citizens are happy to pay up to sixty percent taxes to level the field for everyone across the country – it's currently rated as the tenth happiest country in the world. Immigrants themselves are extended the same hand and may apply on arrival for "introduction benefit" – which is assessed individually, on a case-by-case basis, and is paid out only once there has been a plan agreed with the Public Employment Service. This is administrated by the Försäkringskassan, along with "introduction benefit for housing" (of up to almost four thousand Kronor per month) and "supplementary introduction benefit for children." Under Elevens attract eight hundred Kronor per month and older youths one thousand five hundred up to a maximum of three children, with the total benefit capped at four and a half thousand Kronor per month. Somewhat generously, in the case of more than three children, the benefit is paid on the ages of the oldest children to maximise state support given. Of course, in Sweden's high-value property market, it is a natural consequence that immigrants in receipt of these benefits – and even those without – are driven towards the lower rent, popular schemes, such as those in Eastern Malmö or Rinkeby, the Stockholm district visited by Pool and the Russians.

With my pre-reading done I made the arrangements to get to Sweden and put some real context around what I'd learned. With the world political and media climate as it had become, there was just no way to get to the truth by research alone – something which was once perfectly feasible as a blogger or a "data journalist." I still owe a debt of gratitude to the huge number of people who made it possible by crowdfunding the investigative trip to Malmö, to see what was behind all the information I had gathered. It seemed clear, even sat in a leafy English town, the alt-right were unlikely to be painting a true picture. Then, only three days before I was due to travel, the unthinkable happened.

On the 7th of April 2017, Stockholm was struck by the horror of a vehicle enabled terror attack, mirroring the method used previously in France and Germany. England went on to suffer a vehicle attack in Westminster a short while afterwards, though the attacker's origin and target were notably different. The Stockholm attack itself was unique in that the suspect was arrested rather than shot dead by police during his arrest. He was subsequently identified as a failed asylum seeker from Uzbekistan, a state which remains closely tied to Russia. The thirty-nine-year-old, Rakhmat Akilov, admitted to committing an act of terrorism in the subsequent court proceedings. It also transpired he had been officially wanted since February 2017, after disappearing once his residency was declined by the Swedish authorities in December 2016. No terrorist group claimed responsibility for the Akilov's actions, which also underlined a significant difference in the Stockholm events, and the suspect's claims in court, that he acted on behalf of the Islamic State, have gained no credibility.

Despite the tragic incident and horrific loss of life, I left home as planned on the 10th of April, determined to uncover the truth about crime and immigration in Sweden, doubly so, in fact, because I wanted to try and make it clear that no act of terror could deter balanced journalism.

I didn't know what to expect, arriving in the immediate wake of the country's only attack since 2010, but what I found was quite extraordinary. I also learned the Swedish word for damage: skada.

FOUR:

Nils Karlsson describes himself on social media as the original vagabond and an "unwashed phenomenon." Though he is larger than life – and somewhat crumpled looking – in truth, he's a fascinating character: an ethics lecturer, a Green Party politician, and the Deputy Mayor of Malmö.

Although we'd missed each other via message and went on to have some inexplicable telephone issues while I sat drinking coffee in the fierce, spring sun on Stortorget square, he made time in an incredibly frantic schedule of public engagements to meet with me in his office at the Stadhuset (City Hall), a municipal building at Augustpalms Plats on the busy Föreningsgatan.

The trip to Malmö was quite the experience – an early flight from Gatwick on Scandinavian, landing at Copenhagen to grab the train across the astounding Øresund bridge, spelt the Danish way, for a short ride to Malmö central station. Visually, it's one of the most splendid short journeys in Europe and brings with it a real sense of adventure. The cold, of course, bites as soon as you get outside but when the sun is up and out it bakes you through any glass you sit by. Too early to check into the hotel, I'd wandered for a while and settled down for early lunch and a huge latte in the Coffee House, an impeccably decked out cafe with huge picture windows looking straight onto Stortorget. The staff spoke amazing English, which makes you feel embarrassed really, ignorant, but they were warm, friendly, and swift with the delivery of a monstrous kyckling sandwich. That's chicken, by the way. Predictably, I was hysterical, courtesy of a soon to be short-lived attempt at not smoking while desperately hoping to do the investigative series of articles justice. The panic set in when I couldn't get hold of Karlsson straight away and I'd convinced myself everything was going to go to rat-shit in double time. Then, ping. His Twitter message came through with a number. I called it, nothing, and the panic set in again. Then he sent another number and this time we spoke. He had managed to clear me a slot in an otherwise packed daily schedule, on the proviso I could be there within thirty minutes. The first ten minutes of walking turned out to be in completely the wrong direction due to the GPS on my iPhone going crazy, but I managed to get there, in the end, walking up to the tall, grey, 1970s building via broad steps adorned with flowers and burned candles – another memorial to the Stockholm victims of only a few days ago. Periodically people would stop, quietly reflecting before moving on about their daily business. Karlsson came and met me in the lobby, cutting an interesting figure in a creased suit, shirt hanging out, hair wild. His keenly intelligent eyes gave him away though – behind the outward image was one of the sharpest minds I had ever come across. And I've crossed paths with quite a few.

A trained philosopher before he became a full-time politician, Karlsson lectured at the internationally respected University of Malmö on ethics and epistemology – the theory of knowledge and the distinction between justified belief and opinion. "It's interesting," he told me, "because suddenly I leave the university and 'what is truth' is suddenly international politics on account of Trump." It is not hard to see why epistemology, though not something you'd often use in a daily conversation, is going to become crucial in the world as it eventually rises from the ashes of the Alternative War.

Epistemology comes from the Greek epistēmē, meaning 'knowledge', and logos, meaning 'logical discourse'. The branch of philosophy concerns itself with studies of the genes of knowledge, justification, and the rationality of belief. Fascinatingly relevant, it concentrates on the philosophical analysis of the nature of knowledge itself and how it relates to such concepts as truth, belief, problems of scepticism, the sources and scope of knowledge and justified belief, and the criteria for each. I had no idea the term was first used by Scottish philosopher James Frederick Ferrier in 1854, but it's Scottish roots are even older – King James VI of Scotland, according to experts, personified the concept as the character Epistemon in 1591. Essentially, it's a really complicated way of debating the difference between truth and belief – the former being fact, and the latter able to exist in an alternative way.

On hiatus from teaching others, Karlsson was elected as a deputy mayor of Sweden's large port city and serves with broad ranging responsibilities for democracy, gender equality and human rights. "Interestingly enough, also IT solutions for the city," he added, not hesitating in explaining this apparent curiosity, "which really is a strange thing as it's not part of the others but nobody wanted that so I took it. One of the things I've been working is getting the citizens of Malmö access to the internet by opening up the closed Wi-Fi across the city." He sees access to the internet for all citizens as an essential part of effective democracy, telling me "by amplifying the signals and letting it leak out you can get quite much Wi-Fi...I think it's a nice thing to do." This is hugely divergent from the current, Conservative narrative in Britain, which aims to restrict and monitor the internet and, via the so-called Snooper's Charter legislation, maintain records on the internet searches of citizens and residents.

Karlsson was voted into to the role at City Hall in 2014 having been a part-time politician since 2006. As a member of the Green Party which rules in the city in coalition with the Social Democrats, he reflects on the previous partnership with the far-left, highlighting they still call themselves Marxist. "I know the Labour Party in England does that too, but just on the 1st of May," he quipped before moving on to his true passion, Malmö itself. Part of the reason I first spoke to Karlsson was his vocal opposition to the viral views sprad by the alt-right and the way he continued to talk the city up in the face of their damaging commentary. It's clear from the way he describes his town that he means every single world. "If I was going to try and sell Malmö to you, I would say it was a beautiful city, aesthetically," he said. "Over the past two hundred years, we have been very conscious in saving old architecture and interspacing it with new, so you can see how the city has changed through the ages just by looking, which I think is a nice feature." It's not hard to agree with him, the city being awash with a blend of styles everywhere you look. Truly historic melds with both the utilitarian post-war and the brand new architecture which is flourishing everywhere. While in some towns this doesn't work, creating an odd and ungainly hodgepodge, here it is a triumph.

"What's also nice is the transition from an industry town to a more creative industry – or knowledge-based town – production wise. There are actually more people working in Malmö now than when we were at the height of the industrial era in the 60s, 70s, and early 1980s." He doesn't believe people miss the leading role of industry over creativity, either, and recommended the Western districts to those wishing to move here. I'm sorely tempted, to be honest.

To me, it was apparent integration is a key part of the culture as well as the architecture, with the old and new mingling happily together, but Karlsson pointed out it is still a modern city, meaning it does see the same problems faced around the world. "In some parts, it is [integrated] but Malmö is like two cities: we have Eastern Malmö and Western Malmö. The Eastern part is where we have state-funded, massive, buildings of housing which were built in the 50s, 60s, and 70s. Huge apartment complexes with a bit of green in between. They were always intended to be cheap housing and have continued to be the cheapest housing in Malmö, so the people who are the poorest continue to live there – which also means you have pushed some of the social problems which go hand-in-hand with poverty to the Eastern parts of Malmö." He highlighted to me that the more focused interspacing of historic and modern architecture is found in the central or Western districts which he described as "quite a bit more affluent."

"The difference between the median income between the Eastern and Western parts of Malmö is more than SEK300,000 a year, thirty thousand pounds roughly. There's a big difference," he added as the friendly conversation continued. I found him refreshingly open and utterly fascinating.

Turning to the more provocative issue of crime and immigration, I was unapologetically blunt in asking if there was a link between the two, acknowledging my grossly basic approach to such a complex topic. (It's near impossible to have this discussion without a much broader one about the influence of social and economic issues). Karlsson surprised me with his candour on the highly emotive subject. "Whatever I say it will be a simplification of how things really are," he said, "but I do think yes, immigrants, in particular second-generation immigrants, are over-represented in violent crime and thefts, and those kinds of crimes. That is a fact. But it is also a fact that they grew up in an area where your mother and father don't go to work and they live in poverty, so there is a strong correlation to the socio-economic level of your area and your family."

"What we see," he continued, "is when families get more income and move out of these areas they leave the city altogether – we have a big problem with housing so they often move out of Malmö and another poor person moves in." He could have been describing any poor area, any council estate, anywhere in the world, even where the population is wholly indigenous, and what Karlsson was getting at appeared to be that environment is responsible for crime, rather than immigration. I've worked these areas as a police officer and this is a simple truth of daily life. Karlsson was quite right.

"You can't really say they are committing crimes because they are immigrants," he told me, and I had to agree from the standpoint of experience, but I wanted to know if – as at home and elsewhere – the occurrence of discriminatory factors in society played to the narrative. Specifically, I was asking about the old demon of skin colour. "There is a theory that there is some structural discrimination against people with darker skin, but I don't really buy that because when you look at the immigrants that come to Malmö, which is quite a lot – about 40% of the population is born outside of Sweden or has parents born outside of Sweden – twenty years ago it was people from the Balkans, then ten years ago South America," he replied. Only in recent years was there a change in Sweden, with people mainly from the Arabic states migrating to Sweden and forming the bulk of arrivals, and this has generated a new problem when set against the huge change in the economic output of Karlsson's city. "This is where it gets to be really complex," he said. "The people coming to Sweden now, most of them, do not have a degree of education that is matched with the labour market here. If you came before 1990 there was always some industry looking for unskilled labour and you trained on the job and could have a good career making things."

"Since the decline of the manufacturing and textile industries, the wharf which was here, it's gone and with that is the need for unskilled labour," he concluded, summing up a clear issue again repeated worldwide. "They're not uneducated, they don't know the language of course but you can learn Swedish, that's no problem," Karlsson told me, adding "but you don't have the education necessary for most of the jobs in Malmö and that is a new situation."

However, the Swedish view appears largely positive and pragmatic when compared to other Western countries.

"It is solved within one generation though because the children growing up go through our school system. Fully qualified to get a degree, they can take the jobs here," Karlsson said, making clear he and the rest of City Hall don't see these problems as either permanent or insurmountable. Surprisingly, Karlsson raised the idea of profit from immigration, seemingly tying the idea of people having monetary value in with the concept of productivity output, rather than being individual cost centres – effectively the benefits argument which is always wheeled out in immigration debates.

"Do we profit from immigration?" he asked me. "I always wonder what the time perspective is. Refugees are not profitable in the national sense, not that I think they should be, people are people and should just do what they do." Karlsson did, however, point out that, in terms of the Swedish economy, immigrant productivity at the fourth generation down the line is regarded as a simple win for the country as a whole. They give back more than is taken.

The conversation followed an easy rhythm and we found ourselves discussing the original reason I made contact with Karlsson: Donald Trump's "Last night in Sweden" comment made in Florida during the February rally. The very thing which was taken up by the Alt-Right, with that huge number of right-wing figures using their media platforms to paint a bleak picture of Malmö as a city where immigrant crime runs out of control and "No Go Zones" exist. Karlsson's feelings on the matter were abundantly clear.

"I don't recognise my city in the way it is described in the foreign media. There is, or should I say 'was' because many people have been arrested recently and the crimes have declined because of that, a murder wave. The murder rate was still much lower than the average American city rate but it was high for Malmö and for Sweden. A spike." In my own research, I'd found a time-established trend of people burning cars late in the summer, which – indicating a less than mysterious origin – stops when school starts. I'd also found public records confirming that some people do feel unsafe because of this. "Yes," Karlsson agreed, "some crime is committed by people of a foreign background. Two summers ago there were some grenade attacks, which is highly unusual for Sweden and not many people were harmed by this but a few cars went up. So there was a surge in criminal activity but it is still much lower than in any random American town."

While the grenade attacks are out of, what I consider, the ordinary – a topic I later pursued with a criminologist from Malmö University – there was absolutely no sense of fear on the streets, even being there only days after the Stockholm terror attack. Karlsson re-enforced this, telling me: "the only people who say they feel unsafe on the streets are the people from the Sweden Democrats right-wing political party. They say they don't feel safe and the people they are talking to don't feel safe, so perhaps it's your point of view in this which affects what you feel." I couldn't help but draw immediate comparisons to Britain's Brexit voters, the UKIP political party, and Marine Le Pen's electioneering in France. The rhetoric also mirrored that churned out by alt-right news outlets – such as Breitbart – in the wake of Trump's comment.

"Just a comment about the Sweden Democrats," Karlsson added. "One of their full-time politicians, because we pay even the opposition to have full-time positions, went on one of the English news channels and said that we need to let the military go into Malmö and let them put things to rest. It was really quite a dramatic statement." The city's administration felt this was "really weird" and Karlsson fluidly addressed a concern impacting the whole of the Western world in the same answer. "The thing about these Alt-Righters is they get a lot of mileage out of their view because it gets spread like wildfire across the internet," he said.

Turning to sexual offences specifically, Karlsson was quick to make sure I knew Malmö had not recorded a recent drop in this type of crime.

"The goal for any politician should be to lower it and it had been the case for a long time in Sweden that it actually had gone down." But, he told me – also confirming my own research – recent changes in the law in 2005 and again in 2013 increased what must be recorded by the police. The truth is, the offending rates have remained largely static over the last few years, with only marginal movements.

"One explanation is that we make more and more actions against the law," Karlsson explained, qualifying the statement with confirmation that Sweden records one offence for every incident. A victim can be a victim multiple times with different crimes recorded and crimes in the country are never 'downgraded' or reclassified afterwards, as they are elsewhere. (This was one of the elements in my own parliamentary evidence which ended Police crime figures being used as a national statistic). Again, however, the issue of over-representation raised its head. "Even in the sexual crimes there is over-representation by immigrants but I can't supply a great criminologist's explanation for that. I've spoken to some police officers who say that there have been groups, men who drugged girls in nightclubs. But the instances of rape are so few that any offence like that would be noticed." I couldn't help but think of Rotherham as a British comparison.

Karlsson's view on sexual offences was, on the whole, incredibly progressive and enlightened. He finished up by telling me "the danger in this is that if you think rape is only committed by immigrants you can't work with the things which prevent rape in the long term, which I think is working with the view of 'what is a man'. You should work with boys early on to prevent rape later on." This approach is one the whole world could stand to learn a lot from, with long-term preventative work focused on gender rather than race. It's utterly pointless for society to continue to deny the existence of male privilege and misogyny inherent in every man, no matter what skin colour they are born with. "I don't think you can say it is foreigners per se," Karlsson added, pointing out something which, perhaps, should be more obvious to all of us. "No country in the world is based on rape and murder because it wouldn't be before long that the society would fall apart."

As we drew close on time, Karlsson checking his watch, I asked what his response would be to the world be in the wake of Trump's comments and the subsequent coverage. He took a deep breath and smiled. "Come and find out for yourself! And, of course, check your sources. Don't take all of your information from Fox News or Alt-Right sites. Check just one other site, or two perhaps if you have enough time."

His background in epistemology shone brightly as I asked Karlsson if he thought this formed part of a broader problem in the world.

"Oh yes. We should be able...we are in a situation where more information than ever is available to more people than ever and yet we choose our information before we read it" he said. "This should like the crowning moment of the human race, where all knowledge is available to everybody. But, instead, we misuse this marvellous opportunity we have to seek out information that just confirms what we already think. And that is a total disaster for our...I think it can lead to the destruction of the human race actually." I was staggered at hearing this but found myself vigorously agreeing, mainly as it was the first time I'd heard the thought put concisely and vocalised outside of my own head. The deputy mayor drove the point home with a pertinent example. "The biggest challenges for us globally are the climate changes and if the ones that actually can do something about it are ignoring the problems because they are not reached by news...we are making decisions based on false facts." There is an intricate link between climate and resources, which is broadly considered to form a staple element in hybrid conflicts, as the NATO documents set out, and Karlsson confirmed this without having the faintest idea how pertinent the observation was.

Karlsson's definition of the state of the world, delivered with his academic credentials, was both fascinating and timely, defining a period in history as eloquently as any of us are likely to hear it said. His words stayed with me as I wandered down the steps of the Stadhuset, looking over that combination of flowers and candles which formed just one of the city's memorials to those killed and injured in Stockholm.

Speaking to people like Karlsson, it was easy to believe Sweden was a progressive and caring society, dedicated to democracy and politically active in improving things for all those who live there. But Karlsson was just one voice of the many I needed to hear and my next appointment had already messaged me, this time without problems, to say they were at the Central Station waiting with a coffee.

FIVE:

Manne Gerell is a father of four, juggling those daily responsibilities with his busy work as a Lecturer at the University of Malmö. He made time to speak with me in between work at the office and running home to take care of his children. As a criminologist, Gerell specialises in research on the geography of crime, social disorganisation, and the principles of near repeats – something close to my heart as I developed the background work on predictive policing in the Met. Gerell isn't just a research academic however, he also works closely with the Polisen across the whole of Sweden, assisting them in addressing issues of crime in the poorer neighbourhoods and districts. We met outside the Espresso House, in the huge and incredibly tidy food court area of Malmö's Central Station, and Gerell was relaxed, sipping coffee while working on his laptop. As I had already found, the Swedish welcome was warm and friendly and the criminologist's English was impeccable when compared to my *Hej* (hello) and *Tack* (thank you). We talked briefly about his background, idle but necessary exchanges to break the ice, and I was immediately reassured I'd come to see the right person.

"I'm now a researcher at Malmö University," he told me, pausing to ask if we needed to move when a spontaneous round of piano playing began – the station's instrument is impeccably maintained and open to use. "I mainly study the geography of crime, why there's more crime in some places than others," he continued after I waved away the soundtrack as being okay. "So, I've been doing shootings and I'm working on a project on crime around local bus stops. How many people are going on the bus rather than how many people live in the local area. It's a mix of where it's really dangerous and," he indicated at the station around us. "The victims don't live here, nor do the offenders. So using crime per resident doesn't work."

The world over, transit crime is a significant issue, from London to Mexico City, and it's only relatively recently police forces have begun to tackle its transient nature in a meaningful way. In London, the Met opened a whole command to manage the issue, with the help of funding from then Mayor, Boris Johnson and, on my second trip to Mexico City, the NGO I worked with on the twenty-year crime analysis where building intricate hotspot maps in conjunction with the local authorities. "Also," Gerell carried on, "I work with the police on a project: what the Swedish police call vulnerable or disadvantaged neighbourhoods. Basically, poorer or immigrant neighbourhoods with more than normal crime and, in particular, some types of crime." Rather than being focused on solely the Eastern districts of Malmö, the areas highlighted to me by Nils Karlsson at the Stadhuset, Gerell's work covers the whole of Sweden. "I work with police nationally," he told me, almost shyly dismissive about the monumental scale of his work, "but those districts in Malmö are mainly in the East, the West of Malmö is a lot richer."

"That work by the police, that's where the whole 'no go zones' thing comes from," he added. The concept of an area where nobody could safely go, including the police, was a central theme in the alt-right coverage I was there to investigate. "The police in Sweden actually issue a report to identify which neighbourhoods have criminal networks and that's been distorted into this kind of 'no go zone' discussion," Gerell told me, adamant the term has resulted from nothing more than over-interpretation of the police reports. "The police don't actually say they are 'no go zones' but the ones they label as problem areas, or vulnerable areas, are the ones the media and international media label," he explained, which spoke volumes.

He had worked in the specialist field for seven years and holds well-developed and grounded views on what sets crime and crime recording in Sweden apart from the rest of the world. "There are tonnes of differences, but obviously the actual laws are different in many cases. When it comes to the actual crime recording I think what's been highlighted is how we tend to record every incident, every instance of crime. Someone could come in and say they had been raped every day by their husband and that's one hundred or two hundred crimes. That's one of the peculiarities of Swedish crime statistics," he told me.

From an expert standpoint of my own, I was curious as to what practical impact this has on the crime figures in respect of peaks and troughs, in particular thinking about other countries such as the UK where increases in reported offences are still, even in my wake, often attributed to mass reporting events – using terms like *The Savile Effect*.

"It depends on what crime. On average it shouldn't have too much impact on the trends, but for a single year, in particular for crimes which are less common like rape, it could have a big impact on a single year if you have hundreds of rapes being reported by one person. But, for most crime types, it doesn't really matter that much and would still be a minority of the crimes reported, like bicycle theft, for example." Gerell highlighted, however, that there have been no hard quantitative studies on the impact of spikes in sexual offences caused by multiple reports with one victim. "There are several which mention that for some years it has had a big impact, with maybe a single victim, or a few victims, making up five percent or even ten percent of the crimes recorded," he said.

This analysis has only been done in certain years and Gerell recognised the true impact was unquantifiable. For me it was an area of personal curiosity and, if I were academically minded (which I'm not), I would be leaning towards the pursuit of this as a thesis.

From my own background work before travelling, I had garnered evidence of a change over the last few years which broadly reflected an increase in the reporting of sexual offences in Sweden, allegedly because of enhanced trust in the response of the authorities. I put it to Gerell.

"There have been some studies over the last few years which indicate people are more willing to report sexual offences than they used to be. So that's been discussed and brought out a lot, but it seems that the willingness hasn't gone down or up," he replied.

There had also been further changes in the Swedish definitions of sexual offences, those legislative changes I discussed with Karlsson, which have also been expanded to include internet-based crimes. Gerell was able to provide me with a great deal more, in terms of specifics. "The figures don't distinguish between what happened online and in the physical world, so we really can't distinguish the increase. But it's also possible that people are less bothered to report offences which happened online. Some laws changed, which had a big impact on the rape statistics in 2005 and 2013. In 2005 many of the crimes which were classified as coercion or forced acts became rape, and in 2013 they amended 'helpless state' to a definition which included other vulnerabilities." In more general terms, in respect of Sweden's world crime ranking, Gerell said: "It's probably pretty average to be a western country in north Europe. On a global scale, it's very low because some countries have many more crimes than we do. But it depends on what crime type you look at."

"For instance," he told me, "in western or north-western Europe crime isn't that much lower than in the US but gun crime is much lower." A quick search on the internet had already shown me there are about thirty-two guns per hundred Swedish citizens compared to the US, where the figure is over one hundred and ten per hundred inhabitants. Coming from the United Kingdom these possession figures both seem high, but Honduras had fewer guns per head than the Britain and still ranked number one for shooting homicides back in 2010, so legal possession and death hold no real bearing. The key factor appears to be societal behaviour, which makes sense. Over the last few years there was indeed an increase in Swedish gun violence and, also, in explosions involving the use of hand-grenades, Gerell added.

"These are the trends where Sweden does stand out and, while there is no hard evidence linking it to immigration, it's something that will come up in a discussion," he said.

I asked him about firearms possession rules and he explained you either have to be a hunter to have rifles, or a competitive sportsman to have pistols or automatic weapons. "Very few of the gun crimes are committed with legal weapons," he told me, confirming my very brief conclusion on the Honduras crimes, adding: "They've been smuggled in from the rest of the world."

I pressed him on exactly where these illegal weapons are coming from.

"There's no solid evidence but it appears to come from the Balkans, from the surplus of the wars down there. But there's also a fair share which comes from Slovakia. These are decommissioned or plugged and anyone can buy them without a licence, bring them to Sweden and reactivate them. They recently arrested a gunsmith here in Malmö who had done this with pistols and machine guns on a fairly large scale." I made notes to pursue Balkan military surplus markets at some point, still entirely unaware of what I'd actually end up occupying myself with.

Gerell compared the gun homicide rate with the UK, correctly identifying the figures used to be comparable but they had plummeted in England over the previous ten years, increasing again only recently, while Sweden saw a steady rise. In April 2017, the Metropolitan police told the media gun and knife crime had risen 42% and 24% respectively, and that recorded crime was otherwise elevated across virtually every category. The figures were released two days after Cressida Dick relieved my old nemesis Hogan-Howe as commissioner. Previous rises in some crime types were explained away by Scotland Yard as "statistical anomalies because of changes in how they are measured," which refers to them having to do it properly because of me. Prior to that, they'd been deceiving the public for around thirty years.

"Gun crime in Sweden, was, by 2015, ten times higher than the UK so it's diverging trends there. You can't not notice it steadily going up year after year," Gerell told me.

The hand-grenades, being such an alien idea to me, were another area to pursue. I've been to a few jobs where people have found old ones in gardens and lofts, but never where the pin has been pulled on active weapons with intent. There was of course the murder of police officers Nicola Hughes and Fiona Bone, though it remains exceptional in terms of British history. The devices also appeared to be coming from the Balkans, but most of the cases the police had investigated weren't clear according to Gerell. "Most of the explosions are related to sending a message to someone, scaring. They haven't been thrown at living people but empty stores or restaurants and cars with no one in. They tend to explode either in the disadvantaged areas or around nightclubs in the city centres, where it could be suspected there is some link to gang criminals acting in revenge, or competing criminal groups in conflict over areas," he said. Having spent a lot of time studying the Mafia and Russian criminal gangs, I can't help but think of this as standard extortion and intimidation. Criminal turf war acts.

"I shouldn't say too much," Gerell added, "but a lot of people think it's criminal gangs from the disadvantaged areas or the motorcycle gangs. But many of these cases aren't solved." While we could have speculated on the basis of broader information, the simple answer was neither of us could safely attribute the explosions to anyone with any degree of accuracy. It was not only Balkan grenades being used, however. Home-made explosives of varying complexities often appeared to be used in offences, again targeting empty premises and vehicles but, in rarer cases, people had also been killed and injured. "Up until three or four years ago we had a few cases a year but not a lot. In the last couple of years, there's been twenty or thirty in a year, which is something different and very media friendly," he said.

The theme kept coming up, this idea the media only grab hold of what is a little controversial, and it took me back to a discussion I once had with a reporter from the Daily Mail. "We only print what's likely to cause rage or fear," they'd told me. "That's where the circulation figures come from."

I carried on with my questions, asking directly what the precise link was between immigration and crime in Sweden. The answer surprised me again.

"Honestly, we don't know," Gerell said, without hesitation. "It's not that easy to disentangle the effect of immigration on crime and nobody's even tried to do it, not even on the macro scale. That's on immigration and crime. The related but different issue of immigrants and crime – how many more crimes does an immigrant commit rather than a native born – we have plenty of data on that." This was the most candid conversation anyone was, or is, likely to have on such a sensitive topic and I was absolutely intrigued as he continued. "Immigrants do tend to commit more crime so, in all likelihood, immigration has increased crime in Sweden," he told me. "But that would be not by a tonne. It would be a fairly small number. A few percent or something, but we don't have an actual number."

There was a definite headline here which could be easily adapted to political agenda or meet the Daily Mail criteria for newspaper sales, but that is not how I operate and there was an obvious complexity which needed exploring in detail.

"There's a hypothesis which has been raised by a criminology professor in Sweden, who's actually in the field of immigration and crime, and he suggests immigrants have become the new underclass," Gerell said. "So, while they commit a lot more crimes, they are replacing native-borns that otherwise would be down a class and committing more crimes. He's arguing that immigration hasn't increased crime, just led to other people committing the crimes."

The theory of a new underclass has been around for a long time, since 1970 in fact, when it was coined by Swedish economist Gunnar Myrdal. He described a worldwide portion of the population cut off from society – lacking the education and skills necessary to function successfully in the modern era – and this echoed with Nils Karlsson's comments on the link between education and the new job market which replaced industry in Malmö. Gerell takes the theory into account but holds his own view.

"To me, that hypothesis is not entirely implausible," he said. "It seems likely that, seeing as immigrants do commit more crime than native-borns, immigration should lead to some more crimes but, of course, we're mixing levels of analysis here. Individuals and countries. But, in my opinion, I wouldn't be surprised if immigration has increased crime but not doubling or anything. Five percent or something, and it's different for different crime types."

I put Karlsson's comments on the table and we discussed the issue of the link between vulnerability, geography, and criminality in the context of immigration and the housing options for immigrants. We also touched on the socio-economic factors of unemployment, non-skilled workers in a competitive job market, and the affordable housing in Malmö's eastern districts. I wanted to know if these factors were reflected in the crime figures to support either the underclass – or, indeed, Gerell's own – hypothesis.

"It kind of depends on how you count," he said. "The highest crime areas in Malmö or anywhere in Sweden is this type of place." He nodded around us at the busy central station again. "Central station, the main square, the nightlife district, that is where most crimes are committed. And that's true for most types of crime: theft, robbery, pickpocketing, assaults. But if you take these places aside and look at residential areas there's a lot more crime in the vulnerable neighbourhoods."

But it isn't all types of crime which are higher in the financially challenged districts.

"It's the kind of crimes which are discussed a lot," Gerell said. "So you have burning cars, arsons, shootings, explosives, hand grenades, open-air drug markets. Those types of crime are very much associated with these vulnerable neighbourhoods where people are a lot poorer, most of them are immigrants. There are a lot more problems."

The socio-economic impact on the environment, Gerell agreed, was inseparable from any discussions about criminality. "It's really difficult to disentangle all that, unemployment, social assistance and welfare, crowding and multi-occupancy. All of these issues crowd together in the same neighbourhoods and it's not surprising we see lots of social problems arise there, including crimes," he told me.

Once again, the wider portrayal of events, both in the traditional and alternative media became a huge influence on the perceived impact of crime.

"You see the burning cars in the media, it gets a lot of attention. Also shootings. You hear it, hear the guns. It's different from most crimes, which you don't see. Unless you're the one burglarized, you're not going to notice, not see it, not going to know it happened. But you can hear gunshots, see a burning car, see the burned out wreck," Gerell said. "It adds to the whole discussion that the types of crime which have the strongest level in these neighbourhoods are much more visible. Much more media friendly. Which drives the whole debate and discussion."

In recent years there had been a reduction in crime on the whole in Sweden, with property offences trending downwards, car theft and bike theft being the high volume. But these decreases are being "eaten up," as Gerell said, by increases in fraud, a trend now a common across the western world.

"There's a similar thing in assaults," Gerell added. "Where they had been decreasing there's now an increase in people reporting less serious offences where there's no mark, nothing visible or anything. And also with bystanders reporting crimes, when it only used to be the victims reporting. When a crime is reported it's still counted in the statistics, even if it's proven nothing happened." This was interesting, something I had noticed elsewhere, and Gerell followed up with the information I wanted without even being asked.

"Despite this, the crime survey, the victimisation survey, shows crime going down and this is also shown in the hospital visits due to violence by another person. It was actually a record low last year for hospital visits from violence since they started summarising the statistics ten years ago. So I think we can say violence is actually going down in Sweden." This underlined the balance needed between the accurate recording of crime by the police and the requirement to verify trends against data beyond one recording authority. Interestingly, Gerell continued by describing the social demographic of assaults – again, an indicator of reducing violent crime. "In the highest group open to violent victimisation, men aged 15-24, the hospital rate is down to half of what it was in 2007. That's quite a dramatic improvement and hospital visits are a good external measurement of serious violence."

In Mexico, I'd set the murder rates against public health data to expose the scale of manipulation in respect of the homicide rates, so Gerell was on the money. There was, however, something we hadn't touched on yet – the status of immigrants as victims of crime rather than offenders – and I wanted to find out what statistics there were on this.

"We have the crime survey," Gerell explained, "and it shows immigrants are a bit more likely to be victimised, but the over-representation isn't as high as in the offending." Having heard the term over-representation with Karlsson too, I was desperate to get to the bottom of its true meaning.

"It has many connotations and is used in many ways," Gerell said. "But, basically, the word was chosen by the National Council of Crime Prevention because they wanted to emphasise that most crimes are committed by native Swedes." It appears, however, that the exercise exposed something entirely different, and gave rise to the expression which was the source of my intrigue. "Not that they commit more crimes, but relative to their share of population, immigrants commit more crime than would be expected. Crude estimates, native born compared to immigrants, show a difference that is quite big," Gerell added.

This was interesting and Gerell got straight to the obvious point before I could ask.

"There are many more males who are immigrants and, also, because more young people are immigrants compared to native-borns, so when you start adjusting for factors like that the representation goes down. Some studies have taken socioeconomic differences into account on top of this more thoroughly, looking at a family situation and the neighbourhood where you grow up. Then you can actually explain away most of the over-representation."

Even taking these factors in and weighing them up, Gerell says there is an over-representation of immigrants in the crime statistics of between 20-70% depending on which crimes you look at. This ended up pointing to the existence of structural discrimination clearly for the first time. "Over-representation is bigger if you look at convictions compared to arrests," he told me. "We're not sure why but maybe, in part, it could be because of some implicit bias." This gets straight to the heart of the issue I had mulled earlier. One which faces most societies now. "They'll be more likely to be charged or spotted to begin with, then convicted. They then have fewer resources to draw on for the defence. There are tonnes of potential biases which could explain how this increases," Gerell explained, then pointed me towards a study in the British Journal of Criminology from 2013, which explored the links to immigration, socio-economic status, and over-representation.

After chatting for longer, both enjoying ourselves, we turned the conversation towards Donald Trump and his "last night in Sweden" comment – which Gerell knew was the reason I had ended up coming to Malmö in the first place.

"I think Carl Bildt, the previous Prime Minister of Sweden, was right when he said 'what has he been smoking?' on Twitter," Gerell said with a smile. "Eventually he [Trump] kind of cleared it up that he meant the whole piece on Fox news about immigration and crime and there is some fire behind the smoke. It's not entirely wrong but, because it's been distorted, it is entirely wrong." I understood the contradiction Gerell was raising, which also went back to Karlsson's epistemology approach.

In respect of whether what Trump said was justified as a throw away comment about terror attacks, Gerell was clear. "No, I don't think it was justified. There are problems but it's not like society is going down or something."

What I really wanted to know after all this was whether or not people feel safe in Sweden, and Gerell was the national expert.

"There was a reduction last year in perceived safety. Fear of crime increased in the survey quite a bit but that's just one year of measurement and it still tells us that seventy-five percent of the population feel safe and are not scared. So it's too early to say that we are doomed," he told me.

The world climate had shifted significantly in the months leading to my trip, with an increase in hard political leanings more commonly being expressed in the media, and I asked Gerell for his view.

"It's complicated and difficult to disentangle all these things but media and media reporting can have an impact on perceptions of safety and fear of crime," he reiterated. "The whole public discourse and media climate changed dramatically a year and a half ago with a big influx of refugees coming. Literally, in one week our prime minister was at a refugee demonstration saying 'in my Europe we don't build any walls' and a couple of months later they put up border controls to stop the refugees coming here."

Gerell described the change in approach as "huge", an almost complete U-turn. "That was the Social Democrats in government with the Greens, who are traditionally pro-immigrant, but they are now supporting these measures where Sweden completely turned its policy around. That influences everything, the discussion, how people see the issues of crime and immigration," he said, which left me wondering how does such a significant change happen. "What happened was, everyone saw our nice policy and when they came here we couldn't handle it so they had to clamp down and now we are at the minimum level of the European Union, having really strict rules on everything."

I had been reading the Sapö intelligence service reports on the huge reductions in people being tracked travelling from Sweden to war zones such as Syria and wanted to cross check my understanding these numbers had also reduced significantly.

"It's not really my area of expertise, but there's lots of discussion on it," Gerell replied. "Similar trends, maybe not as strong and dramatic, but similar trends have been seen elsewhere in Europe. Likely it has things to do with tighter border controls with Turkey and our local controls. Mainly, probably, it's to do with the war in Syria and how the Islamic State is faring in the conflict. It's not going so well anymore, so it's not as attractive to go down there." This was far from difficult to agree with.

Sombrely, before it came time for me to move on, I asked Gerell for his view on the horrifying Stockholm attack which had occurred only days before I travelled to Sweden.

"It's unusual. We've only had one failed Islamic terror attack before so obviously...he only killed himself. On the other hand, I don't think it's extremely surprising in a way. Most people were expecting it to happen eventually. We don't consider ourselves invulnerable so when this stuff happens elsewhere it's not unlikely to come to Sweden as well," he concluded pragmatically.

Wandering out of the station I felt conflicted. There was much hypothesis around crime and immigration but no concrete data and some of the information which did exist was contradictory. All I could say with any degree of certainty was areas with less money and status were more likely to be the places where media friendly, visual crimes happened. That was no different to London, or Derby, or anywhere else.

The only thing to do, I decided, was to get out on the ground and take a look around for myself.

SIX:

Malmö is a port city, the capital of Sweden's Skåne County, and the third largest population centre in the country. The wharf faces the Øresund (which, apparently, is written Öresund in Swedish), where a joint venture between Denmark and Sweden built the tremendous bridge which spans the waters separating them. In many ways, Malmö has the look and feel of Liverpool or Hull, with a population of around three hundred and fifty thousand meaning it sits somewhere in between both.

As Nils Karlsson pointed out to me during our meeting at the Stadhuset, Malmö has undergone a huge transformation in its economy, shifting from traditional industry to biotech, IT, and the creative sectors. A key driver in this change of once declining fortunes appears to have been a combination of the Øresund Bridge itself and the foundation of the University of Malmö in 1998.

The bridge, which is estimated to generate around six and a half billion Kronor a year in terms of economic benefit, runs nearly eight kilometres from the Swedish coast to an artificial island, Peberholm, in the middle of the strait. The connection is completed by the Drogden Tunnel, which runs the four kilometres from Peberholm to the Danish island of Amager. It's the longest combined rail and road bridge in Europe. The massive additional cost and engineering related to digging the tunnel, rather than raising one section of the bridge, was met to avoid interfering with air traffic Copenhagen Airport, to maintain a clear channel for shipping, and to prevent ice from blocking the waters. It was originally proposed in the 1930s but dropped due to World War Two – though the legacy of the conflict did mean they uncovered sixteen unexploded bombs during construction.

Due to the Schengen Agreement and the Nordic Passport Union, which I'd never heard of, there aren't usually passport inspections, just random customs checks when entering Sweden. But, since January 2016, checks have become significantly more frequent due to the tightening of borders in response to the migration issues. As I travelled in the wake of Stockholm, the passport checks of every passenger were somewhat unsurprising but I didn't realise the country had been granted a temporary Schengen exemption.

The University, which was able to expand rapidly in part because of the bridge, provides a campus for more than twenty-four thousand students and employs about sixteen-hundred staff. It's the 9th largest institute of learning in Sweden and has been awarded a number of honours, including that of "Centre for Excellence" in respect of dentistry. It has developed, in a relatively short number of years, exchange agreements with more than two hundred universities around the world and roughly a third of the students have an international background. It seems natural, by extension of this, that the university has a particular focus on migration, international relations, political science, sustainability, urban studies, and new media and technology.

The combination of the enhanced access to Europe provided by the bridge and the swift growth of the university have doubtlessly contributed to the changed landscape of Malmö's economy – causing the knock-on effect on the social demographics of the city.

Sitting in the independent Coffee House, baking in the Nordic sun which shone through the huge windows onto Stortorget, the historic city square, I could imagine Malmö as quite bleak during the winter. Stepping outside, I really felt the last bites of the chill, even despite the low daylight washing the colour out of the spring streets. My imagination was, in this case, supported as I wandered along the bustling Lilla Torg, where the restaurants provide blankets at every outdoor table, along with powerful gas heaters. Having arrived early in the morning by train, that hop which took only twenty minutes from Kastrup, Copenhagen airport, I'd noticed the prominence of darker skin tones on the near empty streets – as Malmö's immigrant communities made their way to work. But, by the time I'd interviewed Karlsson at the Stadhuset and criminologist Manne Gerell back at the Central Station, white Swedish faces dominated everywhere. Two observations leapt out at me immediately.

White, Swedish men appeared to be much more likely to openly ogle women, in particular if they were wearing skirts, and the same group were singularly prone to spitting or blowing their nostrils out, straight onto the pavement. I didn't see anyone else doing the same, even watching keenly as I walked. According to hundreds of online articles claiming it's saliva free, the spitting is not linked to the country's consumption of snus – snuff – but I saw plenty of empty packets, like small tea bags, littering the floor. This is a fairly solid indicator that what the internet says may not be true in this case. The debris, however, was swiftly cleared by the regular passes of street-sweepers.

In terms of misogyny, the Swedish nation is heavily involved in advancing gender equality, with most political parties representing the issue. Women make up almost half of the political representatives in the Swedish Parliament and the country has a permanent role for a Minister for Gender Equality – the government allocates money specifically to advancing this balance in the annual budget and in 2014 they allocated over two hundred and fifty million Kronor. Still, the wandering eyes are bothersome and it seemed obvious to me, even at a glance, there remains a quite blatant societal issue which these political moves have not yet addressed.

Meandering up and down the side streets I was approached by a beggar. The man, a heavyset African, blind in one eye, approached me and I felt a little apprehensive – my experiences policing in England still haunt me in many ways – but he politely switched from Swedish to English and asked for a cigarette. I could not oblige as I had none, but he wished me a friendly good day with a smile. The same polite approach played out several times during the course of the day, with a Middle Eastern woman sat quietly between some bicycles and a few native Swedish men and women huddled in blankets on the bridges which cross the canal surrounding the wharf. Even with the arrival of better weather, I couldn't imagine being homeless on the bitter nights here, so I offloaded what change I had in Kronor.

Aside from the spitting and ogling, everything in Malmö appeared otherwise civilised and clean. Maintenance crews were everywhere tidying and repairing, and the air did not smell of anything – something which hit me harder when I got back to England. The day I returned, the smell of jet fuel persisted for longer than I've ever noticed as I drove back from Gatwick, and the night air beyond, though warmer, was always intrusively scented with rotting litter and pollution. Even visually, the problem of rubbish on the roadside is much more visible by comparison.

After my own observations, a report was released in April 2017 which concluded up to forty million people in the United Kingdom live under the cosh of illegal air pollution. The data showed 59% of the population is living in towns and cities where nitrogen dioxide (NO_2) pollution breaches the lawful level of forty micrograms per cubic metre of air. According to the Guardian, who reported on the findings, about fifty thousand Britons die prematurely each year from respiratory, cardiovascular and other illnesses associated with pollutants such as NO_2 and what's known as particulate matter. In February 2017, the European Union put the British government on a warning of court action if they didn't release their plans to tackle the issue within two months. The Government lodged an appeal with the high court which was rejected and they were ordered to publish their plans before the general election. The strategy itself, which was released after the court loss, was met with dismay and ridicule. Caroline Lucas, the co-leader of the Green party, responded by saying: "The government is standing idly by while Britain chokes. This feeble plan won't go anywhere near far enough in tackling this public health emergency."

The public health costs of Britain's air pollution problem have been estimated at twenty billion pounds a year, with around six million working days, some experts say, lost throughout the course of each as a direct result of polluting emissions. Conversely, the Swedish strategy is world renowned and they now recycle so much they are seeking imports of recyclable materials from other countries to process. Less than one percent of household waste in the country was sent to landfill in 2015 and this has been the case annually since 2011.

Aside from cleanliness, everywhere I looked in Sweden there were signs of settled, balanced immigration and integration. Kensington High Street looks grubby and dangerous by comparison to the centre of Malmö, to give my observations some easy context. There are no Starbucks – barring a few rare exceptions – but Espresso House shops are everywhere, along with many kebab shops – oddly German in their influence. The worst immigration I saw in the central shopping area was a bizarre English outlet selling random tat and I still can't fathom what it was doing there, even after the trip. Certainly not propping the British economy with artisan jam. Nothing was really empty or boarded up, either and the streets were free from what British people now call 'Chavs' – an acronym meaning Council Housed and Violent, which apparently originates from Stab Proof Scarecrows, a book by Lance Manley.

What I saw in Sweden was people living, working and interacting together in peace. At the foot of the monument in Stortorget were more flowers, burned candles, and a stuffed toy. A few metres away was a large but simple sign declaring "Malmö loves Stockholm." These were the very real signs of a crystallised unity in the wake of an horrific terror attack only days earlier and, almost spontaneously, a crowd gathered in a minute of solemn silence for the victims, before moving on with their usual routines. A group of teenage girls wearing hijabs ran to join the assembly at the last minute.

It was unavoidable, the conclusion that commercialisation hasn't had the same effect there as it has in Britain, with our carbon copy high streets all looking much the same now. The obvious marker was Starbuck's absence, but the brightly coloured feathers, pussy willow, and pom-pom's adorning the trees and windows denoted an Easter utterly free from eggs at three for a fiver. I liked it very much, the visual of a tradition untainted by the economy. The colours of hope simply displayed in a juxtaposition to winter's passing bleakness. Even off the main streets very little changed, everything was still clean and I did not, for one second, feel the pressing sense of alertness I've gotten used to living with in most places in Britain. An unpredictability which, the more I think about it, should be seen as a more glaring indicator of the fact trouble isn't coming at home: it has been around for a while, embedded in our daily lives and normalised.

An orderly queue caught my eye at one branch of the Försäkringskassan – for all intents and purposes the benefits office. The line was almost a fifty-fifty split of white Swedish faces and darker Middle Eastern ones. The feeling I got again was overwhelming and wondrously repetitive: I was visiting a balanced, integrated, clean, and civilised city centre. So far, everything was reflecting Karlsson's account of Malmö as a beautiful, welcoming city. After speaking to him and Gerell about crime though, I knew I needed to look East of the centre. To Rosengård. That was where the truth lived, I had no doubt.

The Rosengård district of Eastern Malmö, literally translated as Rose Manor, had a population of around twenty-three thousand people in 2012, making up only 7.6% of the city's total population. With the exception of a couple of specific areas, most of the district was built between 1967 and the early seventies – when the immigrant population was around low, at about 18%. The construction effort was a substantial investment in affordable housing by the government, the largest project of its kind in the world at the time. The aim of the Miljonprogrammet, as it was called, was to build one million homes in a country of eight million people and make sure everyone had access to them. Over the years, the assignment of housing by the state had almost inevitably increased the population of residents with an immigrant background to 86% in the area.

Of course, there have been racial tensions and, in 2008, there was serious rioting – though nothing like on the scale of 2011's London riots, which spread across the UK and lasted five days. The violence in Malmö, which was centred squarely on Rosengård, lasted only two nights and saw extensive fire damage to vehicles and bicycle sheds. It began when a building owner refused to renew the lease on a space which was rented and used by the Islamic Culture Association. Initially, angry youths who used the centre occupied the basement and refused to leave but, after several weeks, an eviction took place and a broader demonstration involving anti-fascism protesters, some of whom travelled in from outside Malmö, turned violent. The riot was quelled when two-hundred Malmö residents, organised and led by the Islamic Culture Association, mediated with the rioters and brought the events to an end.

Three years before the riots, Rosengård was the location for a film, *Without Borders – A Film About Sports and Integration,* which was hailed at the time as a ground-breaking documentary about the successful integration of immigrants into Swedish society. Featured in the film was a young Swedish-Syrian, Osama Krayem, who went on to be one of the perpetrators of the 2016 Brussels Bombings. Aged eleven during the production, it is believed Krayem was radicalised online during his early twenties and left Sweden in 2014 to fight with ISIS in Syria against the Russian-allied Assad regime. By his return to Europe in 2015, Krayem was using a false Syrian passport in the name of Naim Al Hamed and lived in Belgium rather than Sweden until the attack. His DNA was also found in the apartments used by the assailants in the Paris terror attacks of November 2015. During questioning, Krayem told terror police he had refused to detonate his suicide bomb in Brussels and expressed regret.

Osama Krayem is not evidence of a particular problem in Rosengård, nor indeed Sweden, but his story does highlight how extreme a change the radicalisation process can create in young people, wherever they are from and however it is done.

The same year as the Paris attacks another young Swede, Anton Lundin Pettersson, attacked Kronorn School in Trollhättan, armed with a sword. He killed a teaching assistant and a male student, then stabbed another male student and a teacher. The second teacher died in hospital six weeks later. This was the deadliest recorded attack on a school in Swedish history and the police investigation concluded the assailant was motivated by racism. They also confirmed Pettersson had chosen his target due to its location in a neighbourhood with a high immigrant population and the horrifying CCTV footage showed Pettersson sparing the lives of students with white skin.

Pettersson, the investigation found, had visited right-wing extremist groups social media sites supporting Adolf Hitler and had joined a group on Facebook wanting to stop immigrants coming to Sweden. He had also supported a petition by the Sweden Democrats to initiate a referendum on immigration. On the day of his assault on the school, he left a handwritten note at his home, declaring something had to be done about foreigners and stating he did not expect to survive his spree. Pettersson was killed during apprehension.

I look at these two stories of young Swedish men, both radicalised online, and see no difference. Both were extremists. Both were terrorists.

In terms of Rosengård itself, I couldn't help but wonder how much of a negative influence the closure of the cultural centre in 2008 had on community relations, given the circumstances, and to what degree it created an opportunity for radical extremists to exploit the disaffected youths from the area. On top of all of this, the socioeconomic concerns – which both Karlsson and Gerell raised – still had to be considered so, I briefly looked up the figures and found less than 40% of Rosengård's population was employed and only 60% were completing elementary school education. The latter fed the former, of course, given the now skilled nature of Malmö's technical economy. A trap not uncommon across Western societies.

It was only ten minutes from the city centre to Rosengård on the number five bus according to the travel information clerks so, I bought a return ticket and headed there to find out exactly how bad things were.

SEVEN:

The efficient public transport doesn't take long at to arrive in Rosengård, only being a short hop from Malmö's central station, and the bus itself was clean. The passengers carried themselves with the same quiet civility I'd seen everywhere else in the city and video screens displayed the upcoming stops and journey times on the right and live news on the left. The lead story was still a school shooting in the United States, which had occurred the day before.

While Sweden's most recent and deadly school killing was committed by a right-wing extremist armed with a bladed weapon, the incident at North Park Elementary School in San Bernardino involved a fifty-three-year-old Riverside man who went to his estranged wife's special education classroom and opened fire with a gun. In an apparent act of domestic violence, he fatally shot her and struck two students before killing himself. One of the students, an eight-year-old boy named Jonathan Martinez, died after being rushed to the hospital. With a chill, I grimly noted at the time Trump never muttered the phrase "last night in San Bernardino," a pattern he followed again later, in May 2017, when two men were murdered by a white supremacist in Portland, Oregon, for defending Muslims from an attack on public transport.

Having had the fortune to consult with one of the country's leading criminologists, Gerell, I had decided to leave the safety of public transport at Ramels Väg – allegedly the roughest place Rosengård had to offer – and the bus stop was directly outside the entrance to the infamous estate of Herrgården – announced by a valkommen sign which also showed a clear map of the area.

Herrgården's population, according to published figures, is 96% non-native, with well over two-thirds of those immigrant residents being born abroad, while the remaining thirty percent are shown in the statistics as being born to parents of non-Swedish ethnic origins. Of the diverse nationalities, which include Iraqi, Lebanese, Afghan, Yugoslav, and Somalian, it was estimated that only 15% of the estate's residents were in employment. Almost half of the population was eighteen years old or younger, too, setting the estate firmly in a well-established risk zone in terms of the likelihood of serious violent crime occurring. Sadly, this is internationally recognised and quite logical.

The first thing to strike me was the presence of those famous, Swedish recycling bins. They stand everywhere in the public squares, around which people were toing and froing almost constantly. The municipal agencies, the council, were also busy cutting the grass of the extensive green areas and, I noticed, there was next to no litter. Aside from one piece of graffiti which declared 'Fuck SD', the right-wing Sweden Democrats party, the rest of the décor was an elaborate riot of colourful urban art, often declaring love for Herrgården, Rosengård, and Malmö. Swedish flags flew on the balconies of the tower blocks and none of the windows were smashed or boarded up. It was, in short, a far cry from my experience of popular or municipal housing projects in Britain.

While the estate was well kept, it did feel a little sterile compared to the historic centre, but these are utilitarian sprawls, built as part of that ambitious social programme to construct one million affordable homes. They have, however, stood up to time's test well – the buildings aren't dilapidated and the grounds aren't wild or dirty. Children's play areas are every few hundred metres and each of them was full of happy kids and chatting parents, older people walked the streets without any apparent fear, and bicycle traffic was nearly constant as people went about their daily lives on the extensive, designated networks.

The schools fascinated me. There was clearly a very real social difference between Sweden and the UK – a positive one – because the playgrounds aren't surrounded by ten-foot fencing. Even the nursery fences were low enough for an adult to lean over, indicating their purpose was simply to keep toddlers in.

I keenly perused the carparks, too, looking for burned out vehicles. There were none. Not even scorch marks on the tarmac. Idly, I Googled Buckinghamshire Fire Service and found three reports of burned out cars and one arson on a caravan in the space of three days. Even basic details painted a very different picture to the online horror stories.

Making a cheerful effort, I tried to speak to a few of the locals in passing, not far from a plot where the public ground had been dug over by residents to form allotments, but – unsurprisingly – the people I encountered spoke little or no English on top of their own languages and Swedish. Two very young girls, no older than nine, did, however, run up to me, excitedly asking what I was doing and why I was filming. They giggled, exercising their school English in this unexpected way, and then skipped off holding hands. There was no adult with them, yet they were safe to roam the estate freely – something which I would never consider with my own children, even in leafy, semi-rural England.

The one indication of any problems I found in Herrgården was a clearly recent and heavily decorated memorial to a young man, Ahmed, who appeared to have lost his life in 2017. Flowers, letters, trainers, and an almost overwhelming assortment of carefully arranged candles were piled against a fence adorned with photographs of him. I investigated the story behind the memorial, using the dates and words in the notes, which had been left to weather in laminated cases, and discovered the boy in the pictures was Ahmed Abdulaziz, shot dead around the 31st of March 2017 having been witness to an earlier shooting in

January. Seven gang members were arrested for his murder in a very short space of time and this sad incident formed part of the exceptional, organised criminal spree both Gerell, the criminologist and Nils Karlsson, the deputy mayor, had discussed with me. Interestingly, as the arrests of specific gang members in Malmö quelled the relatively limited violence, London's figures showed the significant rise in gun crime and an increase of nearly a quarter in the number of knife crime offences over the same twelve months. The contrast made it really apparent to me that we face much bigger problems back in the UK, from the security of our children in school to their safety out of it and, beyond that, during their young adulthood. Our council estates are, by direct comparison, much more squalid and less well cared for and, on top of the air being cleaner in Sweden – with millions of us being exposed to illegal levels of air pollution – we recycle significantly less, and have a more noticeable litter problem in general than even in one of the 'roughest' estates in Sweden. This drew another deep sigh from me as the realisation of it all solidified.

Undisturbed in my explorations, aside from the welcome encounter with the two little girls, I made my way across one of the bridges and deeper into the estates, turning left and heading past a social welfare centre – something like a SureStart but much larger – passing a busy medical clinic where older Swedish women stood chatting. The bike racks outside were full and only a couple of the cycles were locked in place. A longer bridge led across to a large mall but a police station caught my eye, nestling below the blue-topped towers of the next sprawling garden estate.

Of course, if I just walked into a police station in England and asked for comment on something contentious, I'd be laughed out of the door – or directed to a press officer countless miles away. As it turns out, and in spite of the damage done by the

Russian escapade in Rinkeby, or Horowitz's film, Sweden is inarguably different from the UK in almost every way.

Rosengård police station's reception was clean, white, and the walls were adorned with a combination of public information posters and community art. The receptionist cheerfully greeted my tentative approach with the now familiar "Hej!" Obviously, I didn't have an appointment and felt it was massively unlikely I would manage to speak to anyone at all – especially not to get a comment on Donald Trump's 'last night in Sweden' remark, the controversial topic of crime and immigration, or the Stockholm terror attack only days before. I was also visibly ashamed that I couldn't communicate in Swedish, while the receptionist listened carefully and told me in flawless English she would make some calls and see who was available to see me, if anyone.

Tenacious but feeling a little hopeless, I took a seat, reading the domestic violence posters and information leaflets on Rosengård's community patrol volunteers, and waited five minutes. Unexpectedly, a heavy metal door swung open and grey-haired man in the dark blue Polisen uniform stepped out, greeting me with a curious look, a firm handshake, and "Hi!" in English. He introduced himself simply as Jansåker and said he had five minutes while calling me through to the police station proper and leading me to a conference room. As he offered me a seat around a large table, I noticed the two lines and the crown on his epaulettes. Very shortly I would find out just how lucky I'd been, popping in on the off chance.

Erik Jansåker had been the area Chief Superintendent for five years. Back in the 1980s, he worked with young criminals to address re-offending and, over the years which followed, his work became increasingly important – addressing youth crime is now a central focus of Sweden's policing strategy. Rosengård's policing area is outside of Malmö's central enforcement district and forms one of three areas under Jansåker's command. Of the city's five divisions, Jansåker is in charge of the most deprived. As we began chatting, a second officer was beckoned into the room by the chief.

Zoran Markovic, the head of community policy and officer in charge of South Malmö, joined us at the conference table and we spent half an hour having an incredibly frank and open discussion. As we covered some of the ground I had been over with Karlsson and Gerell, Markovic repeated the point that "We have no 'no go zones'."

"Problems come and go with gangs in different ways but right now it's calm," he told me. "Gun violence is between organised criminal networks. We have a list of two hundred well-known criminals and eighteen-hundred others who are twenty-two or younger. Many are under eighteen, so we're working with social services too, as it isn't always a police issue alone." Markovic, it turned out, was the first person in the country to formally hold the new, community-focused position.

Jansåker clearly was a time-served expert on this, pointing out the complexities of the work to change things extending well beyond policing alone. "It's long term work and each agency has their own legal framework. Prevention is a journey of years and it's only the last year or two it's become a formal role," he said.

"Crime, on the whole, is showing a decline," Jansåker added. "And the figures here are interpreted knowing that our crime recording is different to other places." I knew from my own research, and from speaking to Manne Gerell, that the Swedish crime recording practice was, in many ways, superior to other countries – though it's obvious this can make the figures seem higher in a direct comparison.

Markovic also highlighted one area where they still have a lot of work to do. "In gang violence, there is much less will to report offences, or even act as witnesses in police investigations." But he clarified the diverse range of methods being deployed to capture more reports of crime across the country. "We have our offices like this one open all the time, we have telephone and internet reporting, and you can approach the police openly," he said. The continued presence of an open police station is noteworthy when comparing Sweden to the UK, where austerity has left police forces with little option but to cut back on civilian staff, freeze officer recruitment, and close vast numbers of front counters and offices. Sweden, conversely, appears to recognise the importance of giving the public even more access to the police. At the time, the Manchester terror attack, which would bring the debate around cuts to emergency services to the centre of the general election campaigns in Britain, had not yet happened.

Driving the conversation on, I didn't pull the punch on asking about the link between crime and immigration, even though I realised asking the two senior officers so directly might bring my unannounced visit to an end. They didn't bat an eyelid and there was no hesitation in answering, with Jansåker quipping about difficult questions being his pay grade rather than Markovic's.

"It's a difficult question," Jansåker mused, resting his glasses on the table while he worked the Swedish to English translations through in his head. "Last year we had lots of immigrations, high numbers of immigrants coming to live in different parts of Malmö. Of course, there are some problems which come with this but we cannot say crime has gone up because of it. We simply can't."

Markovic was especially passionate on this topic – he grew up in Rosengård. "It's the area and the system together which create problems, not the people.

Schools, employment, money. You can get stuck. It's the environment which has the greatest effect on people's lives," he told me. The police, the Stadhuset, and the criminology experts were all clearly in agreement: socio-economic factors are the biggest driver of society's problems, including crime. I asked Markovic what could make it better.

"Better homes, better jobs. Education," he said.

"It's the same answer in all of Europe," Jansåker added.

I found their approach and their understanding deeply philosophical, a display of positive policing driven by a genuine passion for reducing problems across society, rather than just reacting and enforcing the law.

Turning less bluntly to the terrorist incident in Stockholm, I wanted to know if this event would drive a change in the police approach to community policing or to their presence. In particular, I was thinking about the Metropolitan Police Service introducing their black-clad, anti-terror teams on the streets of London and the heavily polarised public reaction. Again this was pre-Manchester, which resulted in the even more controversial deployment of troops to the British streets. I was also conscious the Stockholm attack would be raw for both of senior officers but Jansåker surprised me again with his candour.

"It's early but it's been discussed nationally and locally. There are some more officers on high visibility patrols of course, but there's no change in our approach," he told me.

Markovic was also very proud of the way the Polisen responded in the aftermath of the attack, and how the public reacted to the efforts of officers.

"We handled it very well in Stockholm. I'm proud of the positive comments on our handling of such a difficult incident," he added.

We talked for a few more minutes and, as we were exchanging email addresses, it occurred to me they had not asked for my credentials at any point, nor approached any of my questions in a stand-offish or suspicious fashion. It was clear to me that policing in Sweden really was transparent and open to all: Markovic is a Rosengård success story, and Jansåker a talented and progressive commander who saw the potential in tackling issues broader than the law alone a long time before it was a formal part of the job. Leaving, I felt reassured Malmö was in safe hands – but, though I'd seen no overt signs of fear and loathing in Rosengård, I still wanted to double check by speaking to people on the street.

Ann worked on the hotel reception where I was staying in the centre of Malmö. She was what I would think of as typically Swedish: white, blonde and tall. (Oddly, this isn't 'typically' Swedish because, in truth, there is no such thing.)

She greeted me with a friendly "Hej-Hej!" and quickly spotted I was British, seamlessly switching to flawless English with no less sparkle in her tone. I explained to her that I was a journalist, in the city to explore the truth about crime and immigration and, of course, President Donald Trump's comments which caused a tsunami of international coverage.

"It's crazy that he took that and made a big thing out of it," she said, referring to Trump's "last night in Sweden" comment which was based on his watching the falsified Fox News documentary by Horowitz. "But he hasn't said much about what happened on Friday," she added.

Trump had spoken with the Swedish Prime Minister, Stefan Lofven, over the weekend, and, according to a readout of the two leaders' conversation, the US President expressed condolences and "agreed to maintain and strengthen the already close partnership between the United States and Sweden in the global fight against terrorism." However, his public commentary, characteristically via Twitter, said very little which reached Swedish ears in the same way as his Florida statement.

I asked Ann about the reports of riots and the claims by Nigel Farage that Malmö was the rape capital of the world. She waved her hand and laughed, saying: "Of course there is crime, there's crime everywhere, but it's perfectly safe." A criminologist, a deputy mayor, the police chiefs, and my own research all confirmed this so, I briefly asked her about the still raw events in Stockholm and her reply was unhesitant. "Life carries on, we are Sweden!"

Back in Rosengård, I spoke with Deeq, who has owned Safari Fashion – a vibrant and colourful shop in the peaceful but busy mall across the bridge from the police station – since 2006. He spoke three languages and his English was excellent. He arrived in Sweden from Somalia in 2002 and had always lived in Rosengård. "It's always the same here. Always. It's good and, for me, peaceful. I've never had a problem," he told me.

Watching him interact with his customers, from all manner of backgrounds, was a pleasure and he paused between them to continue speaking with me. "There can be problems, nothing unusual though. I see problems in the news but never with my own eyes. Some things are just exaggerated," he said, echoing everything I'd found during the course of my investigations.

I was curious about the significant lifestyle transition from Somalia to Sweden.

"It was a big change," he said sincerely. "The climate, the culture. But they are very kind people in Sweden." I can imagine the shock of the cold was quite something. "I studied in high school when I came, even though I was 26, and went straight to work afterwards." It was obvious Deeq both loved Sweden and feels Swedish, but how did he feel about Rosengård? "There are big cultural differences, lots of different cultures, but we all get on really well."

By this point, I was genuinely struggling to find any trace of the huge problems reported by the international press and Deeq shrugged it off too.

"They never report positives. The journalists never come here to ask me. Swedish people think Rosengård residents are negative people but that's just not reality." It appeared I was a novelty of sorts.

When I asked him about Donald Trump and he sighed loudly.

"I don't know where politics is heading today. The right kind of politics is being lost. I think it's better to focus on positives but it's just every negative thing in Swedish society, not just Malmö. Sweden has always been even and stable but I think it's heading to problems with all of this," he said. I asked Deeq what he thought had changed and he replied with absolute certainty: "It's caused by the media, the politicians. The negative things are everywhere now. Sweden, the EU, the world. We live in a global network and it spreads this way." I couldn't help but think back to Nils Karlsson's comments on us wasting the crowning moment of humanity.

After leaving Rosengård, I headed back to the centre of Malmö and wandered the side streets until my eye caught a solitary broken window. I was hopeful that, perhaps, I would get a different view. A contrast.

The family run cobbler also cut keys and a white Swedish woman in her mid to late sixties was out the back, playing with her grandson, as I pushed the door open and walked inside. She waved, added a cheerful "Hej!" and came to the counter – peering over to look at my shoes and see what was broken. I was sorry to disappoint her by only being there to ask questions.

The owner, Britta, also spoke good English, though she told me she doesn't get to use it much anymore. I asked her about the broken window.

"It was smashed," she shrugged with a smile. "Nobody was trying to get in, you can see that." I was curious as to what the police did when she reported it. It was recorded as an attempted burglary, she said, though she didn't agree, and they did what they could to investigate. "They asked about a camera, but I don't have one. What can they do really, it's just damage?" So, I asked if she had any problems before and she vigorously shook her head. "No, first time."

In terms of general safety, Britta just did not like the big city anymore and told me she was glad to retreat to her village after work, for simple peace and quiet. "I don't know if it changes at night as I don't get out on nights." As Manne Gerell pointed out, most crime is focused on the city centre in the evening – as you would expect anywhere in the world – but it has been falling.

When I asked Britta about Donald Trump, she laughed loudly. "I heard this. It's not true, nonsense! You can come here and look before you say it. Trump is totally wrong." I pressed her a little on immigration too and she surprised me, saying "it's good. They can work and pay taxes! There are always some who come who are criminals but with them, we see. Most are good people."

I suppose the real question then has always been on integration rather than immigration, so I put the question to Britta, asking if new communities do make the effort to integrate. Her response turned the question on its head. "It's up to us! We must take them along and teach them how we live."

Having talked to real Swedes who are warm, articulate, liberal, and welcoming, as well as experts who have the same traits, I was left with some other rocks to kick over. There had to be an explanation for the alt-right focus, so I got back to research and the truth of it all started to tumble out.

Up until that point, I had no idea what a mess I'd stumbled into.

EIGHT:

When Trump said "Last night in Sweden" he had no idea what he was talking about and the right-wing coverage which followed was false. I knew that by the time I had to leave Malmö.

I went there to investigate the reality of crime and immigration but, while there, I had inadvertently discovered a much darker truth. The President of the United States' comment and the alternative narrative which followed was a divisive and deliberate attack on the truth to serve nefarious ends: the creation of fear through propaganda and disinformation.

During the course of my investigation, I learned a lot about Sweden. It's a liberal, open-minded, forward-thinking country which believes open democracy and internet access for all are closely interwoven. People feel safe on the streets and they share values which have no borders or ethnic definition and the country was strong in its unity, even in the immediate aftermath of terror. Yes, Sweden has its fair share of criminality but, at the same time, takes one of the most honest – if not the most honest – approaches to crime recording I've ever encountered. The Polisen works constantly on developing innovative strategies to combat high volume crime and, in conjunction with criminologists and other agencies, they strive to address the socio-economic factors driving serious offending. The country also faces challenges of extremism, both foreign and domestic, but faces up to both without hesitation or self-denial. My digging around for the truth in Sweden uncovered something more, however: the existence of a pattern. Something wrong. There was a thread to untangle and my trip was the key.

Something seedy was visible in the growth of insular, nationalist politics. Right-wing parties of a similar ilk were working together globally, with a vast machinery of alternative media, cyber-attacks, and data-laundering behind them. And, I found, this international network was directly linked to Russia.

People were taken by surprise with Brexit and then Trump but, if they had looked to Sweden, a country where the home-grown nationalists have much clearer Nazi roots – and where the government has acknowledged the political and physical threat posed by Russia – perhaps neither would have even come to pass.

By March 2017, support for the right-wing Sverigedemokraterna (Sweden Democrats) party had almost doubled, with polls showing anticipated votes of between 19% and 23%, putting them in second place, nationally. Contrary to the evidence I'd uncovered through my investigation, the party website claims: "The overall net impact of mass immigration from distant countries [is] strongly negative, both economically and socially."

With roots planted deep in fascism, the party was officially founded in 1988 and rose from the white supremacy movement. The SD logo from the 1990s until 2006 was a variant of the torch used by the United Kingdom's National Front but, after that, was changed to a distinctive blue flower with a yellow centre, the blåsippa (Hepatica). I don't know the significance of it and the internet records on its meaning are not quite simple as they are when it comes to Wales and the Daffodil. Originally at its politically strongest in the South of Sweden, the right-wing party gained 13% of the vote in the 2006 municipal elections in Malmö and, by the 2014 general election, they had gained traction in the North, towards Stockholm – they polled at 12.9%, winning forty-nine seats in the Riksdag (the Swedish Parliament). For now, however, they remain politically isolated due to a policy of the other parties not to enter a coalition with them, which I fully understand having taken a closer look at their affairs.

Gustaf Ekström, a Waffen-SS veteran, was the first auditor of the party and Anders Klarström, once a member of the Nordiska rikspartiet ("Nordic Reich Party"), was an early chair. From the outset, the party sought alliances with the National Democratic Party of Germany and the American National Association for the Advancement of White People – founded by David Duke, Imperial Wizard of the Ku Klux Klan. Duke managed one-term as a Republican Louisiana State Representative, and, bizarrely, went on to be a candidate in the Democratic presidential primaries in 1988. By 1992, he was back to being a Republican and stood in the primaries on that side. Over the years he has conducted unsuccessful campaigns for the Louisiana State Senate, United States Senate, United States House of Representatives, and Governor of Louisiana and, in 2002, pled guilty to defrauding supporters by falsely claiming to be impoverished and in danger of losing his home, in order to solicit emergency donations. It transpired Duke was completely financially secure and had channelled the donations he received towards recreational gambling.

It seems Duke was an early starter in the development of the alt-right, or at least the forerunning attempts to make white supremacy more palatable to the masses. In 1974, he founded the Louisiana-based Knights of the Ku Klux Klan (KKKK), where he became Grand Wizard. One politically astute and forward-thinking follower, Thomas Robb, changed the title of Grand Wizard to National Director and replaced the known white robes with business suits. Duke started in earnest to sell himself – and the Knights – as a new breed of Klansman: well-groomed, engaged, and professional. The self-presentation of alt-right figures in 2017 America was more than inspired by the same approach. Duke's commentary on Trump's rally statement also turned out to be the same fallacy peddled by the modern day versions of him, his Twitter feed being full of such gems as "Sweden had no idea what @realDonaldTrump was talking about. #WhiteGenocide." In a way he was right, of course, Sweden had no idea what Trump was talking about because it wasn't true.

The early leadership of Sweden's own far-right party, the SD, also sought links with publications such as the Nazi Nation Europa and Nouvelle École, the latter being a newspaper which advocates racial biology.

Nation Europa (also referred to as Nation und Europa) was a monthly magazine published in Germany between 1951 and 2009 when it was closed down.

The publication was founded by former SS commanders, Arthur Ehrhardt and Herbert Boehme, and took its title from a quote by Oswald Mosley, which described his "Europe a Nation" ideology. Initially, the largest single shareholder was Swedish neo-Nazi and former Olympic athlete Carl-Ehrenfried Carlberg. In later years, the publication would become more closely associated with Deutsche Liga für Volk und Heimat (The German League for People and Homeland), a far-right political group, and Nation Europa was eventually accused of giving space to Nazism. It was subsequently investigated by the German government. Nouvelle École was equally extreme, being a journal which declared its commitment to "racial purity" in its editorial.

Despite their clear preferences, it wasn't until after photographs surfaced of Swedish Democrat members posing in Nazi regalia that the wearing of any kind of uniform was formally banned in 1996. This was the point when the party began to try and present itself more moderately and the youth branch was eventually expelled due to racism and links to extremist groups in 2015. The youth group has, however, been re-initiated under the name Ungsvenskarna (Young Swedes), though they are far from the only section of the party which hasn't escaped the image it was trying to shake off to make broader progress. In November 2012, Swedish newspaper the Expressen released a series of videos from August 2010 for the second time.

The 'iron pipe scandal', as it subsequently became known, was recorded on film by one member of the Riksdag, Kent Ekeroth, and featured his fellow SD MPs Jansåker Almqvist and Christian Westling. Almqvist was shown arguing with comedian Soran Ismail, while referring to Sweden as "my country, not your country" before the trio went on to argue with another drunken man. Ekeroth was then approached by a woman, who he called her a whore before pushing her. The three then went on to pick up scaffold poles in a continuance of the original argument with Ismail.

As a result, Almqvist left his position as the party's economic policy spokesperson and resigned from his seat on the executive committee after the video's second publication gained more traction. The party itself went on to announce Ekeroth would "take a break" from his position as the SD's justice policy spokesman. Before their own expulsion, the youth movement also argued the Swedish Democrats should not have bowed to the media pressure.

Shortly after the departures, another Swedish Democrat MP, Lars Isovaara, left his seat after reporting to the Polisen that "two unknown men of an immigrant background" had robbed him of his backpack. The party backed the claim until the Expressen revealed Isovaara had simply forgotten his backpack at a restaurant and, it transpired, the two innocent men had only helped him when he fell out of his wheelchair. The same MP was also reported to the police for racial abuse against Riksdag security guards.

After the scandals and dismissals, however, the Sweden Democrats began to rise dramatically in the polls in 2015. This was at the peak of incoming immigration and the party was actively seeking rigid controls of those coming in for "the benefit of indigenous Swedish citizens" while, simultaneously, remaining openly critical of the special rights given to the indigenous Sami people of northern Sweden. In 2008 they had gone as far as adopting a motion against the rights to reindeer husbandry, arguing those "who do not involve themselves with reindeer husbandry are treated as second-class citizens." They had also expressed a desire to abolish funds supporting the Sami and redistribute them "regardless of ethnic identity and business operations" and still appear keen to abolish the Sami Parliament. The position strikes me a deeply hypocritical.

In a mirror of right-wing part policy across Europe, the Sweden Democrats have set out that they reject any notions of joining the Economic and Monetary Union of the EU, stand opposed to the accession of Turkey – an argument also used the Leave campaigns during Brexit – and want to renegotiate Swedish membership in the European Union. Within this political party's background is the key to exposing the global network of purported nationalist parties – a mockery of the 'anti-globalisation' rhetoric they have all now adopted.

The Sweden Democrats not only have long-term links with the extreme right but have also shifted – trying to escape this image and found themselves aligning with the newer, more acceptable face of this politik: what is now known as the alt-right.

During the course of their rise, the party has found itself in regular scandal situations, being accused of antisemitism, having members expelled for extremism, and having its website blocked by the Swedish government for posting anti-Islamic cartoons. They are also still boycotted from advertising space by some Swedish newspapers – something which has helped hinder their traditional reach to the electorate and subsequently goes a long way to explaining the shift to new media. This doesn't always go so well, however. A few weeks prior to the general election of September 2014, the chairman of the Swedish Democrat's

Stockholm branch, Christoffer Dulny, resigned from his position having been found to have been calling immigrants "shameless" and mocking them on alternative media sites. Additionally, in December 2016, Anna Hagwall was thrown out of the party after using arguments associated with antisemitism to argue for a bill she introduced in the Riksdag, intended to "reduce the concentration of media ownership" in Sweden. She was attempting to make way for alternative outlets through legislation. It is somewhat unsurprising, then, that right-wing sites Info Wars and Breitbart have been posting articles with a supporting lean towards the Sweden Democrats since 2015 at least. You can find this out on a cursory search alone, but the meaning is not immediately obvious. The link is easy to miss unless you are looking for it specifically.

Breitbart was founded by a right-wing journalist, Andrew Breitbart who died in 2012 and, though it retains his surname, was headed up by Steve Bannon, chief advisor to President Donald Trump. It is now known Bannon was funded directly by billionaire Republican donor Robert Mercer whose involvement was first mooted while he was still investing in Ted Cruz's candidacy in the eventual Trump/Clinton election race. His involvement, however, was only officially outed well after the election of Trump, in 2017. Breitbart News Network CEO, Larry Solov, publicly acknowledged the family's involvement, though he denied the Mercers held any editorial input.

The idea was first developed by Andrew Breitbart when he visited Israel in 2007 and he then outlined the concept as being a website which "would be unapologetically pro-freedom and pro-Israel." By 2010, Andrew Breitbart had told the Associated Press he was "committed to the destruction of the old media guard," through the site. Later, under Bannon, the site aligned with the European populist right and the American alt-right, at which point the New York Times started to describe Breitbart News as led by "ideologically driven journalists" to churn out controversial "material that has been called misogynist, xenophobic and racist." Bannon himself declared Breitbart as "the platform for the alt-right" in 2016, though he later denied all allegations of racism and even stated he rejected the "ethno-nationalist" tendencies of the movement. The money men behind Breitbart have always refuted any connection with the extreme right though, after the election of Donald Trump, more than two-thousand companies removed Breitbart from their advertising buying lists for this reason. Breitbart has also published a number of false articles and wild conspiracy theories, with inexhaustive examples including Barack Obama supporting ISIS, a number of features about Hilary Clinton's health, and a heavily edited video of Department of Agriculture employee Shirley Sherrod. With the original mission being to "take back the culture", Breitbart launched careers of a host of controversial 'alt-right' figures – none of whom I am giving oxygen to – and the site came to London in 2014, with Bannon saying the coming 2015 election (and subsequent 2016 referendum) were a key focus in their "current cultural and political war."

In November 2015, Breitbart began to post content under the banner "Sweden Yes", though this was limited to five articles, according to reports, until Trump's comment in February 2017. According to the web encyclopaedia Know Your Meme, "Sweden Yes" first appeared on a far-right German message board in 2012, from where it spread to Reddit where it is currently "quarantined" due to "shocking or highly offensive content." Also popular on "4chan", the meme is directly connected to Swedish webcomics which are openly despising of multi-culturalism and show interracial intercourse in a dim light, or feature immigrants engaging in criminality. Breitbart-wise, the content listed under "Sweden Yes" was mostly written by Chris Tomlinson, a London contributor who openly supports Marine Le Pen and Dutch far-right leader

Geert Wilders. Following Trump's Florida speech, Breitbart labelled thirty-two articles of a total of thirty-seven released in the same month, with the "Sweden Yes" tag.

While some of these back links to Sweden are more obvious – for example, Duke and the SD have a long history, and Bannon's appointment in the Trump cabinet was publicly hailed a success by Duke – they are only, in fact, small components which come together and form a broader, more complex picture. And this jigsaw builds to a point where it goes well beyond even the other obvious links between the Sweden Democrats and their EU parliamentary associations with Nigel Farage's UKIP and Marine Le Pen's Front National. Mercer once worked for IBM designing revolutionary technology – which went on to form the basis of today's artificial intelligence – and became CEO of a complex hedge fund which uses algorithms to trade. One of the funds is reported to be the most successful in the world.

Robert Mercer attended a National Youth Science Camp in West Virginia in 1964 where he learned to program and went on to study for a bachelor's degree in physics and mathematics from the University of New Mexico. During his university degree, he also held a job at the Air Force Weapons Laboratory at Kirtland, writing military programs. He's since publicly said the experience left him "with a jaundiced view of government-financed research." In the 1970s he joined IBM, where he developed what's known as "Mercer Clustering" – a standard code now used in speech recognition – and in 2014 received the Association for Computational Linguistics Lifetime Achievement Award for this work. By the end of 1993, Mercer had joined the hedge fund Renaissance Technologies. The founder, James Harris Simons, had a well-known preference for hiring mathematicians, computer scientists, and physicists rather than business school students or traditional financial analysts, and in 2009

Mercer and another colleague from IBM, Peter Brown, became co-CEOs of Renaissance when Simons retired. By 2014, Renaissance was already managing twenty-five billion dollars in assets.

Since the start of the decade, Mercer has also focused millions on right-wing, "ultra-conservative" political donations and the Washington Post called Mercer "one of the ten most influential billionaires in politics" in 2015. According to estimates across the internet, Mercer had already donated about thirty-five million dollars to federal campaigns by 2006. In this, Mercer joined forces with the Koch brothers, a conservative political donor network, but Mercer and his daughter, Rebekah, went on to establish their own political foundation: The Mercer Family Foundation, which is run by Rebekah. Rebekah Mercer later became one of the members of Donald Trump's Presidential Transition Team Executive Committee. Both Robert Mercer and Bannon are also linked to controversial data analytics firm Cambridge Analytica, which uses big data to focus tailored messaging on voters down to an individual level. This company became one the subjects of my investigation beyond Sweden, building a picture of the mass manipulation of the electorate with the aim of controlling not only geopolitics but the financial markets too.

Mercer was a major – if not the major – supporter of Donald Trump's successful 2016 presidential campaign, and Rebekah is broadly accepted to have played the primary role in the ascent of Bannon and controversial peddler of "alternative facts", Kellyanne Conway, into their senior roles in the Trump White House. Rebekah had worked with Conway on the Cruz Super PAC, Keep the Promise, in the Republican primaries, while Mercer also financed another Super PAC, Make America Number One, which supported Trump. According to reports, Nick Patterson, a former colleague of Mercer's, said: "In my view, Trump wouldn't be President if not for Bob." Mercer, I went on to find, also played a part in

Brexit and, by that point, I'd formed a detailed picture of the vital factors in the success of any campaign like Trump or the EU referendum. A combination of the use of psychometrics, big data, propaganda and disinformation, artificial intelligence, and hacking. The unifying feature which the strands hung off was the involvement of Russia – who I found to be involved in state-sanctioned hacking and AI targeting of Western elections.

Once again, Sweden was the key to unlocking everything. You see, the Sweden Democrats do have direct links to Russia and this has raised a significant concern over security within the Riksdag and impacted on foreign and defence policy decisions by the country. This began when a Russian-born political secretary for the SD resigned in September 2016, after making several million kronor in a suspect property deal with a St Petersburg "businessman."

Known by a Swedish name in parliament, having changed it on his arrival in Sweden ten years before, Egor Putilov had wide access to the Riksdag when he entered the deal with the previously imprisoned Russian – a Mafioso type, known to have strong ties to the Russian state. The property deal in question made around six million SKE for Putilov.

Putilov had also become a well-known newspaper columnist, writing with a distinct anti-immigrant tone, who regularly criticised the Swedish government for granting asylum to refugees, in particular those from the Middle East. "If nothing is done, Sweden's lax immigration checks could prove very costly," he wrote in one op-ed for the Aftonbladet, adding comments that Islamic State terrorists were capitalising on Sweden's "porous" borders. In other similar articles, he made claims similar to those of the alt-right which I have since debunked, including allegations that "stone-wielding Muslim youths attacked him in Stockholm's ethnically mixed suburbs." Aftonbladet's editors believed something was wrong when they discovered

Putilov had submitted opinion articles using the false name Tobias Lagerfeldt and found the image he provided belonged to an innocent party. In a subsequent investigation, they exposed what they claimed were Putilov's "connections to Russian state agents and criminals," reporting he had assembled a handful of secret identities to help disseminate pro-Russian and anti-Swedish government views in the media.

Responding to the scandal, Putilov wrote an email to Newsweek, in which he denied everything and claimed "the attack against me has to do with internal political situation in Sweden where the ruling left party and the main left newspaper who reported the story are desperate about growing public support for Sweden Democrats."

Mattias Karlsson, the Sweden Democrats' parliamentary group leader, suggested the accusations against Putilov were only "speculations," saying: "No one has proven so far that he has done anything illegal or that he is a security risk at all."

Center Party group leader, Anders W. Jonsson, was less dismissive, saying "this is about a Russian who came to Sweden and kept applying for jobs at places like the Civil Contingencies Agency, a person who has used five different identities and writes debate articles under false names."

While a property scandal may seem a regular or low-level occurrence in politics, the case was so unusual and disturbing the Riksdag responded without hesitation. Defence Minister, Peter Hultqvist, made a quick public statement that "several people with a high level of competence have declared a potential security risk, therefore, I think that one should take the situation seriously."

Clarifying the threat and indicating Russia had, in fact, acquired a 'hold' over Putilov by way of the property transaction, Lars Nicander, Director for the

Center for Asymmetric Threat Studies at Sweden's National Defence College, said: "You can hear intimate conversations, you can hear the different parties' positions on the Nord Stream [gas pipeline], for example, or on NATO and trade agreements. You can even install listening devices."

The Putilov Affair, as it became known, drew a tight focus on not only Russian business dealings, and infiltration of politics, but the spread of disinformation which had been gaining force. For example, in August 2016, while the debate was underway as to whether Sweden should enter a military partnership with NATO, Swedish social media was flooded with fake news from alternative outlets. The claims included warnings of stockpiling nuclear weapons on Swedish soil, NATO using Sweden to launch attacks on Russia, and sinister claims NATO soldiers would rape Swedish women without fear of prosecution. Hultqvist faced harsh questioning across the country about the false stories, which also started to trickle into the mainstream media. Analysts and experts in American and European intelligence singled Russia out as the prime suspect in the disinformation campaign, as the likely outcome was tightly aligned with their national objectives.

"Moscow views world affairs as a system of special operations, and very sincerely believes that it itself is an object of Western special operations," said Gleb Pavlovsky, who worked with the Kremlin before 2008. "I am sure that there are a lot of centers, some linked to the state, that are involved in inventing these kinds of fake stories."

Some of the pressure which can be exerted, according to Swedish research, is as blatant as Putilov's, while some of it is more nuanced and, often, targeted in places you might not necessarily expect. Russia's Sputnik brand of news stations, for example, use a subtler approach and try to appeal to Western audiences by featuring anti-establishment voices from both the far left and right. Sputnik established a strategically positioned studio in Tallinn, the home of the original Capstone experiment, and another in Edinburgh.

Sputnik is owned by Rossiya Segodny, the Russian state news agency set up by Vladimir Putin in 2013 and, according to David Leask – a journalist with Scotland's Herald newspaper – Sputnik's Edinburgh operation "aims to tap into the growing Scottish independence movement."

"In Scotland, Sputnik is seeking to exploit the deep mistrust felt by many independence supporters in Britain's mainstream media, especially the BBC," he told reporters. "To do so, it has hired some staunch Scottish nationalists to staff its U.K. base in Edinburgh."

Rossiya Sedogny translates as Russia Today and, though the outlet RT denies any link, Margarita Simonyan was also appointed editor-in-chief of the news agency, which was created by an executive order of Putin as a Kremlin operation. There are no degrees of separation between any of these channels, in truth.

By March 2017, in the wake of the discovery of Russian efforts on multiple fronts, the Swedish defence ministry had announced the country was reinstating the military draft and four thousand men and women would be called up for service beginning in January 2018. "The security environment in Europe and in Sweden's vicinity has deteriorated and the all-volunteer recruitment hasn't provided the Armed Forces with enough trained personnel," a spokesperson said at the time, adding "the re-activating of the conscription is needed for military readiness."

Shortly after this reintroduction of military service, Sweden's Prime Minister, Stefan Löfven, set out measures designed to prevent foreign countries interfering in the 2018 Swedish general election. On this news, Anders Norlén, chair of the Riksdag constitutional committee, told Radio Sweden parties should avoid relying on Russian propaganda or other support. "Every party in the Swedish parliament has a responsibility to make sure that the facts they use and the arguments they use are sound and valid and not just a way of repeating propaganda from, for instance, Russia," he said.

Mattias Karlsson, who had played down the Putilov scandal on behalf of the Sweden Democrats gave a statement that Russian interference was "likely" and said the security services should be tasked to investigate, but added "the Social Democratic government are using Russia as a means to try to silence the opposition, and trying to make everybody who doesn't share their political views suspect of being a Russian spy." However, the SD narrative was already ringing hollow and the alarm bells were ringing almost everywhere.

In June 2016, the European Council on Foreign Relations, chaired by former Swedish PM Carl Bildt, had carried out the first comprehensive survey of so-called 'insurgent' parties in Europe and found: "Despite their differences, a majority of them are positively inclined towards Putin's Russia and pursue policies that promote Russia's interests in Europe." The report highlighted this applied left and right, as with Sputnik, but predominantly had become a concern with the right wing. The council went on to say "parties are useful for Moscow in that they help legitimise the Kremlin's policies and amplify Russian disinformation. At times they can also shift Europe's domestic debates in Russia's favour."

"Voting patterns in the European Parliament show that on issues such as Ukraine, the human rights situation in Russia, and association agreements with Ukraine, Georgia, and Moldova, the Dutch PVV leads the pack in pro-Russian votes. UKIP, the Sweden Democrats, Italy's Northern League, and France's Front National come in a shared second place," they clarified.

Crucially, the report did not refrain from adding: "But it is not just in matters of policy that these parties' sympathies with the Kremlin are revealed. In them, Moscow has also found convenient and willing conveyors of its anti-Western, anti-globalisation narratives. Several of the far right leaders, such as Nigel Farage, Geert Wilders and Marine Le Pen, are frequent guests on Russia Today (RT) and Sputnik, with Farage reportedly having been offered his own show on RT."

While the report noted the obvious policy leanings, it was circumspect in saying: "It is less clear to what extent there is collusion." Though it noted pointedly: "The notion that Russia might be funding agents of influence by providing financing to sympathetic parties in Europe has become more salient as relations between Russia and the West have deteriorated." This was published a long time before the extent of the Trump/Russia inquiry began to unravel in the US.

In their conclusion, the council recommended: "European law enforcement agencies should prioritise looking into Russian covert support for populist parties and [take] steps to counter such support. European governments should consider publishing intelligence on this in the public domain. Voters have a right to be informed about whom they are voting for." I've returned to this last sentence often, wondering how much different the world would now be if this had been done by governments and not by me – and others – after the horse had run gleefully from the stable.

What became clear to me, from an investigation which began over something as simple as the fact alt-right narratives didn't fit the publicly available crime figures in Sweden, was the shadow of something much larger loomed over much of the western world. The threat to democracy was credible, substantiated, and it was impossible for me to dismiss the clear and present security risks – for example, no progressive, modern country re-introduces the military draft on a whim. It was also apparent that data, notably 'big data', played some crucial role in what was happening because, without it, the delivery of pro-Russian propaganda would not be able to gain such traction through targeting and tailoring to audiences. In turn, those globally similar messages – too alike to be coincidental – could be traced locally to nationalist parties in individual countries, while the people behind those parties and alternative media sources could be traced back to each other – internationally once again – without much effort.

I didn't even find it hard to briefly study the interactions between shifting geopolitics and the financial markets either – though within this other factors were obviously at play. For example, while I was still in Sweden, Reuters reported that "on eight occasions over the past twelve months, the pound has moved against the dollar in the minutes before the release of the retail sales numbers, correctly anticipating the direction the currency took once the figures were published." Some experts believed the shifts could only have been as a result of leaks – the information only being provided to a short list of forty-one people in the UK, twenty-four hours in advance of publication. Others believed some funds simply became "very good at predicting movements working with technology and broader data sets." AI, such as Mercer's, combined with publicly available 'big data'.

I had thought, starting out, my investigation was only about skada, the damage caused in Sweden by alternative news, but it turned out I was wrong. The truth had become more important in the world than ever and, in Sweden, I saw the shadow of the snowman clearly for the first time.

NINE:

Back in England, I was determined to see what crawled out from the rocks I could see needed kicking over, set out like a trail of breadcrumbs as they were, and the clock was ticking. Because I was working as an independent journalist for Byline, only obtaining funding directly from the public, it was a race against not only time but finances. So, I set to work straight away and started pumping a diverse range of sources.

It didn't take much time at all to break into what turned out to be a very deep rabbit hole. On the 21st of April 2017 the Electoral Commission (EC), the independent body which oversees elections and regulates political finance in the UK, released a statement confirming they had "begun an investigation into Leave.EU's EU Referendum spending return." I had been back from Sweden for ten days, writing up the thousands of words from my trip.

It doesn't take much effort to find out Leave.EU is a limited company created by UKIP donor Arron Banks, who is currently listed as the main shareholder with Companies House – to campaign for Britain's exit from the European Union in the 2016 referendum. While Leave.EU applied to the Electoral Commission to be the designated official campaign this was, in the end, awarded to Vote Leave and an application for judicial review of the decision which Banks threatened was never followed through. The Commission's press release stated their decision to launch an inquiry: "Followed an assessment which concluded there were reasonable grounds to suspect that potential offences under the law may have occurred." The investigation was, they said, focused on whether one or more donations – including of services – accepted by Leave.EU was impermissible and whether Leave.EU's spending return was subsequently "complete."

On clarifying the rather dry release with the press office, a spokesperson told me: "We don't comment on ongoing investigations," but they were happy to explain that "a service would be a donation in kind." They could not give a timeframe for the investigation either, "due to complexities in these cases," and were unable to "speculate on sanctions if a finding was [subsequently] made, as this varies on a case by case basis." The spokesperson simply recommended I refer to the Enforcement Policy on their website, a document giving more detail on offences and sanctions, which I duly did and discovered the EC's powers to investigate offences are granted under the Political Parties, Elections and Referendums Act 2000, known as PPERA, rather than under their statutory supervisory powers. The policy was clear that the EC would only use the PPERA powers as a last resort and that it was a criminal offence to fail to comply with, obstruct, or provide false information to, such an investigation.

On the Commission's publication confirming the commencement of the investigation, Arron Banks made his own rather aggressive statement, saying: "Today's announcement is politically motivated and the timing is intended to cause maximum damage just before the general election. We will not be cooperating any further with the commission and we will see them in court." Banks had been set to stand as the UKIP candidate in Clacton-On-Sea following the resignation of the party's only MP, Douglas Carswell, but withdrew on the 24th of April 2017 in a move which was described in the tabloids as "chickening out."

While I was openly curious as to whether a "see you in court" would class as obstruction, the Electoral Commission spokesperson told me there was no comment to be made on the response of Banks.

Having an initial dig around, it wasn't hard to find some public traces of the concerns which appeared to have sparked the inquiry. Member of Parliament for Aberavon, Stephen Kinnock, openly welcomed the investigation which, in his view, seemed to specifically relate to the donation in kind of services by the psychometric data specialists Cambridge Analytica. According to further reports, Kinnock had also written to the Electoral Commission in March 2017, citing concerns the "market rate for a donation of this kind could amount to hundreds of thousands of pounds" and that "any substantial additional spending between 15 April last year and the referendum on 23 June would have pushed Leave.EU over the spending limit for the regulated period."

"They were allowed by law to spend up to £700,000 but according to the accounts they filed they spent £693,000," he added helpfully.

Cambridge Analytica was, of course, used by the successful Trump campaign in the US Elections and the British-born CEO, Alexander Nix, previously stated this earned the company $15 million dollars from that one campaign alone.

My sources had, by this point, sent me documents confirming Kinnock voiced his concerns in writing to the Special Crime and Counter-Terrorism Division of the Crown Prosecution Service, also in March 2017. I tried to reach him for comment, but even now have received no response. Thankfully, the same source gave me access to documents, which were verified, and which showed a significant level of detail in the allegations made to the Electoral Commission. Specifically, they related to the donation of services by Cambridge Analytica to Leave.EU and the reasons for the EC investigation made for grim reading – not least because they showed signs of a cover-up taking place.

The documents set out that: "In a February [2017] Newspaper interview with The Observer, Andy Wigmore, the director of communications for Leave.EU stated that Cambridge Analytica was 'happy to help' with their EU referendum campaign but that they had not 'employed' them. However, this appears to run contrary to previous claims made by both Leave.EU and Cambridge Analytica." The evidence then started to show a pattern of the retrospective deletion of internet records. For example, it noted: "In a now deleted post on their website titled *The science behind our strategy*, Leave.EU stated that: Cambridge Analytica are world leaders in target voter messaging. They will be helping us map the British electorate and what they believe in, enabling us to better engage with voters. Most elections are fought using demographic and socio-economic data. Cambridge Analytica's psychographic methodology however is on another level of sophistication."

"And in November 2015," the evidence went on, "PR Week reported the following comments from Cambridge Analytica's development programme editor: "Cambridge Analytica director of programme development Brittany Kaiser, who will be spending time split between the UK and US in the coming months, was speaking today (Wednesday) at a press conference hosted by Leave.EU. She later told PR Week that the firm had been approached by the campaign several months ago, but only started working with it more recently. She said the firm's team of data scientists and analysts, some of whom were based full-time in the UK, would be enabling targeted messaging by "understanding why certain things worry people... probing why people care about a certain issue." There's actually a picture of all of them together on the internet and the distancing leaves only suspicion.

The pages of documents also pointed out that "The market rate for a donation of this kind could amount to hundreds of thousands of pounds, based on the previous experience of referendum campaigns and political parties for such analytical tools. Yet Leave.eu have not declared this donation-in-kind at any point in their returns to the Electoral Commission." I'd found that the Commission's guidelines I was directed to specifically defined a donation as "money, goods, or services which is given towards campaign spending "without charge or on non-commercial terms and has a value of over £500." In short, there was definitely a declaration of some kind warranted.

The documents were also explicit in stating:"Neither Cambridge Analytica, as a US company, nor Robert Mercer, as a US citizen, fit the Electoral Commission's list of permissible donors" adding there was "no record that this donation was returned within 30 days as required." Robert Mercer, the American Billionaire and Trump campaign donor, had been funding the use of Cambridge Analytica directly since the time of Ted Cruz's Super PAC and Steve Bannon sat on the board of the company. The rules about foreign donations are very clear, so neither would be acceptable in any case.

In their *Expert Paper On Splitting Campaign Spending*, the Electoral Commission set out the circumstances in which the costs of services might need to be divided – which includes items used before or during the regulated period of a referendum. They highlight that campaign groups must make an honest, factual assessment of the proportion of costs to be attributed to their overall expenditure. What this means, essentially, is you can't just spend a lot of money by getting donations up front for campaign activity and then disregard it if there is an overlap of official and unofficial time periods. My source's documentation specified the identification of this as a serious concern, stating: "In his interview with the Observer, Mr Wigmore states that the service provided by Cambridge Analytica were Leave.eu's most potent weapon...because using artificial intelligence, as we did, tells you all sorts of things about that individual and how to convince them with what sort of advert. And you knew there would also be other people in their network who liked what they liked, so you could spread. And then you follow them. The computer never stops learning and it never stops monitoring."

"Given his stated views on the importance to their campaign of the service which was provided free of charge by Cambridge Analytica it seems inconceivable that the donation was not split and partially included in their returns for expenditure during the regulated period," the evidence continued. The documents also stated that Leave.EU only became a permitted participant in the referendum on the 15th of February 2016, and so would not have legally been allowed to "hold and use the full electoral register for referendum purposes prior to that date." This raised initial questions about the possession of data, which I rather doggedly pursued afterwards.

All of this didn't, however, start and end with Cambridge Analytica. The documents also referred to US-based election consultants Goddard Gunster as being employed by Leave.EU and stated: "This service has not been included in their returns as an item of split spending." Again, Leave.EU's deleted *science behind our strategy* page was cited as saying: "While Cambridge Analytica will be helping with the data, Goddard Gunster, who have fought some of the most contentious referendum campaigns all over the world (with a success rate of over 90%) will be helping us turn that data into a comprehensive strategy. Working alongside them will be Ian Warren, an expert on the issues that matter to people on lower incomes."

I kept searching for information and found the regulated referendum period began on the 15th of April 2016. When the limits on expenditure came into force for the designated official campaigns, the lead campaigns were given higher spending limits of seven million pounds, ten times that of Leave.EU.

The documents I saw also made a number of assessments of potential over-spending by the official Vote Leave campaign but there was no indication of an investigation by the Electoral Commission at the time. However, Guardian journalist Carole Cadwalladr and I had been working almost in tandem, attacking the same issue from two very different angles, and she later managed to assemble evidence of, what she says is: "A close working relationship between the two data analytics firms employed by the campaigns – AggregateIQ, which Vote Leave hired, and Cambridge Analytica, retained by Leave.EU." She states AggregateIQ is, in fact, a Canadian field office of Cambridge Analytica and the two campaigns are linked by a memorandum on joint operations, making both of them illegal. Following her series of articles, the Guardian was confronted with legal action, with the companies using a law firm linked to Russian-owned Rosneft and Donald Trump. Carole told me this while we were sitting on a panel discussing weaponised data at the Byline Festival, at the start of June 2017. Trump himself had also been linked to the Rosneft deal by the now infamous Steele dossier, through his association with Carter Page.

Page was a foreign policy advisor to Trump until September 2016, and British ex-spy Christopher Steele's dossier is – to say the least – disparaging, noting: "The Rosneft president was so keen to lift personal and corporate Western sanctions imposed on the company, that he offered Page and his associates the brokerage of up to a 19 percent (privatised) stake in Rosneft."

"In return, Page had expressed interest and confirmed that were Trump elected US president, then sanctions on Russia would be lifted," Steele added.

At the early stage of the Electoral Commission investigation, when I reported on the documents, I didn't know any of this and there was no reason to believe anyone had been arrested, summonsed, or charged in relation to the Leave.EU investigation. The Commission refused to confirm or deny this too – though they were asked directly, so I could make sure there were no contempt of court issues to consider alongside the distinct matter of public interest in writing the article. It is, however, worth pointing out that, prior to an investigation being launched, an assessment is always made by the EC and – according to their policy – they "robustly dismiss the investigative option without credible evidence." They only open formal investigations themselves where there are reasonable grounds and where the offence is "in the public interest."

Trying to get the other side of the story was a dead end – I found getting hold of Leave.EU nigh on impossible. Andy Wigmore still hasn't replied to a request for the company's official response, even now, and their press inbox is no longer monitored.

In terms of enforcement, the EC can either force compliance of parties with a contempt of court order or prosecute them. They can also issue a Stop Notice, requiring an individual or organisation not to begin, or to cease their activity and, in addition – in the case of impermissible or unidentifiable donations or loans being involved – the Commission may also apply for forfeiture. The formal sanction structure is simplistic and consists of a sliding scale, which runs from a fixed monetary penalty of two hundred pounds, then a variable penalty between two hundred and fifty and twenty thousand pounds, then escalates to Compliance and Restoration notices (which set out what not to do and how conduct must be managed, or force the party to restore 'the position' to what it would have been before the offence). They can also issue an Enforcement Undertaking – a binding agreement to conduct matters in a specified fashion. Taking into account the likely impact of interference in something as serious as a referendum which changes the entire economic model of a country, the options available are clearly woeful. However, the Electoral Commission was instrumental in the electoral fraud investigations arising from the 2015 General Election, despite the fact these cases were left with the Crown Prosecution Service for charging decisions and no further action was taken in around thirty cases – with the exception of South Thanet, where three people were charged with offences.

Looking at other recent cases, reported by the Commission on the 19th of April 2017, it was possible to gain insight into sanctions and financial scales in a more related – though indirectly comparable – case to the non-political party Leave.EU group. Greenpeace and Friends of the Earth worked as campaign groups during the 2015 General Election and, following an EC investigation, Greenpeace was fined thirty thousand pounds for incurring over a hundred and ten thousand pounds in campaign-related expenditure. Friends of The Earth were fined a further grand for a twenty-four-thousand-pound campaigning spend in conjunction with Greenpeace. Despite this, it didn't strike me as something which would be an effective sanction in a case which changed the whole course of a nation.

I'll be the first to admit, while there appeared to be a lot to go at in terms of leads to follow up, there were equally a number of dead ends. I was also conscious, not having the financial backing of a large newspaper group, if I rocked the boat too hard I might face a litigious backlash and have to walk away. After I took a pause for thought, I realised the only way to start to unravel all of this was with cold, hard information. Data. So, I started to treat the investigation like the intelligence-led operations I used to carry out in the old days.

It paid off.

TEN:

Our individual data is electronically stored on thousands of servers across the world. Our employment records, personal lives, medical histories, psychological profiles, political views, and our private communications. When assembled together, this forms what's become known as a Big Data Profile and, in reality, none of us can escape its existence. Though I didn't know this when I first started my investigation, HB Gary had recognised this would become a weapon years ago.

Scientific research, including important work by Michael Kosinski at Cambridge University, has shown that a big data profile can be used to develop targeted marketing or messaging, designed to drive a behavioural response in an individual. The technique is known as either psychographics or psychometrics and became famous, or infamous, following its use by Cambridge Analytica in the Trump and Brexit campaigns. Kosinski's work initially used surveys to develop a profile, then he developed it and, with enough social media likes alone, he got to a point where he could "know" people as well as – if not better than – they knew themselves. There are also rumours his work was less than scrupulously taken elsewhere, though Cambridge Analytica fiercely denied any involvement when this was reported.

Data is, in fact, now the single biggest commodity in the world and can be used to drive electorates in almost every aspect of their decision making – the ownership of this data subsequently controls geopolitics and the world financial markets. But, our data is also unsafe and being deliberately stolen on a regular basis. The largest known hack to date was centred around international technology company Yahoo, with the information of around 1.5 billion users stolen across its platforms. The company believed the attack was "state sponsored" and, in March 2017, the FBI and the United States Department of Justice announced charges against Russian individuals, including Russian Federal Security Service (FSB) agents Dmitry Dokuchaev and Igor Sushchin. The indictment reads: "The FSB officer defendants, Dmitry Dokuchaev and Igor Sushchin, protected, directed, facilitated and paid criminal hackers to collect information through computer intrusions in the US and elsewhere. In the present case, they worked with co-defendants Alexsey Belan and Karim Baratov to obtain access to the email accounts of thousands of individuals." The legal papers also highlight that: "During the conspiracy, the FSB officers facilitated Belan's other criminal activities, by providing him with sensitive FSB law enforcement and intelligence information that would have helped him avoid detection by US and other law enforcement agencies outside Russia, including information regarding FSB investigations of computer hacking and FSB techniques for identifying criminal hackers." This means they actively managed the assets and trained them in counter-espionage.

In commenting beyond the dry indictment wording, the US law enforcement community did not pull any punches. "The criminal conduct at issue, carried out and otherwise facilitated by officers from an FSB unit that serves as the FBI's point of contact in Moscow on cybercrime matters, is beyond the pale," said Acting Assistant Attorney, General McCord, adding: "Once again, the Department and the FBI have demonstrated that hackers around the world can and will be exposed and held accountable. State actors may be using common criminals to access the data they want, but the indictment shows that our companies do not have to stand alone against this threat."

By June 2017, Vladimir Putin had been backed into a corner by the weight of evidence against Russia and started trying to distance himself from any involvement in subverting the 2016 US election. In comments to reporters at the St. Petersburg Economic Forum, Putin glibly described hackers as artists and peddled a line they "may act on behalf of their country." Referring to these "artists", he added: "They wake up in good mood and paint things. Same with hackers, they woke up today, read something about the state-to-state relations. If they are patriotic, they contribute in a way they think is right, to fight against those who say bad things about Russia." By the time these words left his lips, I had accrued more than enough evidence to believe we weren't talking about lone, digital artisans and that the FBI was right: Russia was using outside help in its operations. Deniable assets.

After reading the indictments against the FSB, I carried on researching and found the illegal data trade was well documented across the world – with so-called Data Laundering now clearly defined as: "Obscuring, removing, or fabricating the provenance of illegally obtained data such that it may be used for lawful purposes." Security experts were also well aware of the huge scale of the problem and had been for several years. New Zealand based expert Andy Prow had previously said turning hacked data into a legitimate commercial asset was: "the nature of a maturing industry" and highlighted that hacked data is easily made to look legitimate then sold on to, often unsuspecting, clients. "It doesn't raise too many warnings," he added.

I also found that hackers, traditionally, sell stolen data not for cash currencies, but for Bitcoin payments. In May 2016, one hacker offered the private data of nearly one hundred and twenty million Linked In users, including passwords, in exchange for five Bitcoin and in September 2016, a further sixty-eight million account details, this time from Dropbox, were offered for sale for two Bitcoin. Both offers were made on the Dark Web outlet TheRealDeal.

The Real Deal is a website considered a part of the cyber-arms industry, also reported to be selling code and zero-day software exploits – the latter of which is something I returned to later in my investigation, after a worldwide cyber-attack took out critical infrastructure across several countries and caused major disruption to the National Health Service in the UK. In July 2015 the Real Deal website was down for twenty-four hours at the same time as cybercrime forum Darkode was seized by the FBI and various people were arrested under Operation Shrouded Horizon. The FBI called the raid: "The largest-ever coordinated law enforcement effort directed at an online cyber-criminal forum." However, by December the 1st 2015 The Real Deal announced its reopening for business on DeepDotWeb, a news site dedicated to events in – and surrounding – the Dark Web. (For the uninitiated, the Dark Web is the content which exists on overlay networks that require specific software, configurations or authorization to access them, while the Deep Web is the whole of the internet which isn't covered by mainstream listings and search engines.)

Returning to the financial currency of the shadier side of the internet, Bitcoin are worth around one thousand pounds each, though this varies by the current exchange rates, and their value increased exponentially over the five years leading to 2017. It is worth explaining, though, there have been other electronic global currencies before Bitcoin's creation. Back in 2006, Donald Trump's advisor Steve Bannon was involved in a company called IGE who, via Goldman Sachs investments, spent sixty million dollars on a 'gold farming' enterprise within the online game World of Warcraft. This involved harvesting virtual gold resources and selling it back to players. Eventually, IGE was confronted with a lawsuit, the gold trade came to an end, and Bannon went on to head up the right-wing news site Breitbart, then sat on the board at

Cambridge Analytica before moving to the White House.

In the time after IGE, the online currency market began to change drastically. Bitcoin's cryptographic, decentralised currency first appeared in 2007 and was developed by what is thought to be a collective of people operating under the pseudonym Satoshi Nakamoto. The patents for bitcoin and its encryption first appeared in 2008 and were registered by Neal Kin, Vladimir Oksman, and Charles Bry, though they have always denied being involved with Nakamoto.

The Nakamoto persona itself disappeared from Bitcoin forums – and then altogether – in December 2010 and this came after Wikileaks began to accept the currency for donations, despite pleas from the Bitcoin founder for this not to happen. They wrote at the time, "I make this appeal to Wikileaks not to try to use bitcoin. Bitcoin is a small beta community in its infancy. You would not stand to get more than pocket change, and the heat you would bring would likely destroy us at this stage." WikiLeaks went on to harness the use of Bitcoin regardless and has since reportedly hidden messages in blockchain code associated with the currency transactions. In one such episode after reports of law enforcement raids, they inserted a "we are okay" message into their transaction data. It was this, really, which started to draw my attention to the operation who I had once thought of as transparency champions and I didn't really like what I found.

Following a 'dump' of CIA data on the WikiLeaks site in March 2017, security analysts began to draw conclusions that Assange's site was, in fact, a full-blown Russian interest. Another deniable asset. Dr Andrew Foxall, director of the Russia Centre at the Henry Jackson Institute openly stated: "Wikileaks has secret Russian intelligence but hasn't disclosed anything remotely sensitive about Russia. He [Assange] has taken a consistently pro-Russia stance." Though Assange denied the claims, speaking from the Ecuadorian

Embassy in London, Foxall added: "The documents contained 75,000 redactions. These were codes that would also affect Russia's security, because some of the data was relatively fresh, it is unlikely it had been in the pipeline for a while. And Assange's team is small. The logical conclusion is that the data was given already redacted. This was the work of a sophisticated team, and it fits entirely into a pattern of behaviour demonstrated by Russia in the past."

In fact, in January 2017, the Office of the Director of National Intelligence had already confirmed there was "high confidence that Russian military intelligence relayed material to WikiLeaks."

Interestingly, I found while researching all this, Putin's Russia officially describes Bitcoin as "a virus" but this hasn't deterred legitimate global investments elsewhere, with China investing hundreds of millions of dollars. What was immediately clear, however, is that the market is heavily masked, unregulated by conventional standards, and is used as the currency of data criminality. One particularly relevant example occurred in July 2016, when British citizen George Cottrell was arrested on twenty-one charges including attempted extortion, money laundering and fraud. At the time, he was stepping off a plane at Chicago's O'Hare airport with Nigel Farage.

They were on their way to Heathrow when the arrest took place, after attending the Republican Party's Convention in Cleveland where they both appeared on television, met with US Senators, and engaged in discussions with aides to presidential candidate Donald Trump. Cottrell had been working for Farage during the Brexit referendum and is the nephew of Lord Hesketh, a hereditary peer and former Conservative Party treasurer who defected to UKIP in 2011. It transpired that, in the events leading to his detention, Cottrell had been offering money laundering services on the Dark Web and met with undercover agents in Las Vegas, where he made arrangements for them to send him over fifteen thousand pounds before threatening to expose them to the authorities unless they transferred him over sixty thousand pounds in Bitcoin. A court document filed by the prosecutors in February 2017 advised the judge in the case to offer Cottrell a light prison sentence because he had been willing to "provide federal agents additional information after his arrest," and added that this related to extra details "about his role in the offence and how he became involved." It is not unusual for plea bargains to take place in the US, and the FBI does have a clear interest in criminal operations run on the Dark Web.

Looking into this, however, made me take a closer look at Farage, the former UKIP Leader and instrumental Leave.EU politician. Unsurprisingly, given the general background of the right which I'd uncovered in Sweden, I found he had more documented close ties to the Trump administration than Breitbart alone and, in March 2017, he personally thanked Steve Bannon for his help in making the trigger of Article 50 – the legal start of the UK's departure from the EU – a reality. During the same period, the MEP was also seen visiting Ecuadorian embassy, the "home" address of WikiLeaks's Julian Assange.

Though Farage said at the time of the embassy visit "I never discuss where I go or who I see," and later claimed it was for "journalistic purposes," leaked emails actually show UKIP had been actively supporting Assange since 2011. The Farage-led Europe of Freedom and Democracy group tabled a motion attacking "the possible abuse of the European Arrest Warrant for political purposes," when the law was used to trigger Assange's extradition over Swedish rape allegations and, on RT, a UKIP representative labelled the extradition proceedings against Assange as "legalised kidnap." The Swedish prosecutor eventually withdrew the warrant in 2017 as, after several years of Assange living untouchable under diplomatic immunity in Ecuador's London embassy, it was judged there was a limited likelihood of the extradition ever taking place. This did not, however, change the status of the allegation and Assange's flight was seen widely as a frustration of due process.

Farage had also personally used his LBC radio show to broadcast a repeat Assange's denial of Russian involvement in the hacking of the Democratic National Committee and their presidential nominee Hilary Clinton during the US election. In January 2017, Farage told his listeners "[Julian Assange] is absolutely clear that all the information he has got is not from Russian sources."

In the same month as Farage's Broadcast, senior officials in the CIA completely contradicted both of them, saying the leaked DNC material had been traced to Russian GRU officials and "handed off to Assange via a circuitous route" in an attempt to avoid detection of the original source. That route was a hacker known as Guccifer 2.0 who, between 2016 and January 2017, publicly stated they were not Russian but Romanian. However, despite stating they were unable to read or understand Russian, metadata of their own emails showed a Russian-language-only VPN was used. In addition, when pressed to use the Romanian language in an interview with reporters, Motherboard noted they "used such clunky grammar and terminology that experts believed he was using an online translator." My investigation led me to explore this particular strand in more detail later on, but Wikileaks and the far-right stayed front and centre the whole time.

By spring 2017, with the French presidential elections underway, the right-wing candidate Marine Le Pen – who had travelled to Moscow to visit Vladimir Putin – was given a rather glowing interview by Farage, and Assange had made a statement to Russian newspaper Izvestia that WikiLeaks would: "Throw oil on the fire of the French presidential election." After Le Pen successfully passed through the first round in the presidential race in April 2017, cyber security experts warned that her rival, ultimately victorious centrist Emanuel Macron, had been targeted by the same hacking group involved in the US elections. Trend Micro, a Japanese cyber security company, stated there was evidence APT (Advanced Persistent Threat) 28, a team of hackers linked by US security services to the GRU (Russia's military intelligence agency), was directing its resources to influence the French contest. (I later discovered the group had also, disturbingly, masqueraded as ISIS during previous hacking activities.)

The GRU hackers were said to have been found setting up a number of phishing sites aimed at duping Macron's En Marche! members into attempting to log in, thus giving the group access to their email servers – the technique allegedly deployed against the Clinton campaign which led to the release of the thousands of DNC emails via Wikileaks. The Macron campaign insisted at the time it had not been compromised, but days before the final vote thousands of emails were leaked, though the damage was mitigated by a number of restricted reporting measures deployed in relation to the French media.

Russian election hacking I also found – to my horror, I might add – had also already been deployed in the UK. In 2015, the general election campaign was targeted by Russian hackers, who GCHQ believe were state-backed and former minister Chris Bryant said in February 2017: "There is now clear evidence of Russian direct, corrupt involvement in elections in France, in Germany, in the United States of America, and I would argue also in this country." GCHQ deployed measures to counter the 2015 attack, carried out by APT28 who are also known as Fancy Bears. According to the limited details of their report, the GRU had planned to target every Whitehall server, including the Home Office, Foreign Office and Ministry of Defence, and every major TV broadcaster, including the BBC, Channel 4 and Sky. Additionally, in April 2017, the Commons Public Administration and Constitutional Affairs Committee concluded foreign states had attempted to target the Brexit referendum. While the committee report focused on a denial of service attack on the Register To Vote site, it also made clear: "The US and U.K. understanding of 'cyber' is predominantly technical and computer-network based. For example, Russia and China use a cognitive approach based on an understanding of mass psychology and of how to exploit individuals." Russia went on to successfully hack the Westminster emails of members of the UK parliament in June 2017, leading to a public declaration that "bribery risks" had become a very real threat.

It took me a short while to get to grips with the big concepts in all of this but, in essence, specific state data can be washed and released through back channels like Wikileaks, aiming to negatively impact individual candidate campaigns, and denial of service or phishing attacks can work more crudely towards a similar aim. The exploitation aspect, I discovered, is central to big data's inherent value and the basic premise of a hybrid assault. You see, using big data, companies such as Cambridge Analytica often conduct what's called an Ocean personality assessment – normally used in psychology – and the more expansive the data held, the more intricate your individual profile can be. With the right data, it can then be targeted at people you know too. A basic profile, as Michael Kosinski found in his research, can predict your behaviours just based on social media likes alone. An advanced profile, based on what websites you visit, what news you read, your job, your politics, your purchases, your medical records, would mean such a company knows you much better than you know yourself. This allows the people who pay for such services to target you at an individual level with news, information or social media posts which are tweaked to make sure they have the biggest psychological impact on you. Fake news and alternative facts are a central part of this and that includes hacked data dumps which can cause discredit. The Russian terms pokazukha, which means something like a staged stunt, and zakazukha, which refers to the widespread practice of planting puff pieces or hatchet jobs, are both terms which are relevant in the broader context of all of this. Fake news had to come from somewhere, and there it was, all along.

Further, using such psychometric profiles, the simplistic creation of AI driven bots on social media can also push selected messages into more common public view, with the added bonus of the Social Media Echo Chamber ensuring the activity is shared between the appropriate, self-selecting recipients too. This can also keep much of the activity out of sight – because it only hits certain groups – and is the core reason the authorities were so late in responding to the threats during elections. It was only in March 2017, after it was too late, that the Ranking Democrat member of the House Intelligence Committee, Adam Schiff, told CNN the committee was investigating whether the Donald Trump campaign coordinated with the Russians to spread fake news through trolls and bots online and sway the election.

"We are certainly investigating how the Russians used paid media trolls and bots, how they used their RT propaganda platform to disseminate information, to potentially raise stories, some real some not so real, to the top of people's social media," Schiff said.

In many ways, a little historical digging makes sense of not only bots, but a lot of the alternative outlets spewing conspiracy theories. The Russian state was sponsoring 'Web Brigades' as far back as the 1990s, paying around eighty Rubles a comment for people to spam the internet with false information – not to convince people, but to confuse them. To create distrust in all media. They were also paying high-profile bloggers, which made me think about sites like

Info Wars and Prison Planet in an even darker light. If you set this against Trump's decrying of the mainstream media as Fake News while promoting certain outlets, it is not hard to see the apple hasn't fallen too far from the tree.

In 2013, Russian reporters investigated the St. Petersburg Internet Research Agency, which employed around four hundred people at the time, and found the agency covertly hired young Russians as "Internet Operators" paid to write pro-Kremlin postings and comments. Twitter Bot armies of over twenty-thousand artificial accounts were also uncovered. The group's office in Olgino, a historical district of Saint Petersburg, gave rise to the now well-known terms "Trolls from Olgino" and "Olgino's trolls," both of which are synonymous with both bots and human accounts which spread propaganda. Internet Research Limited, the company behind the Olgino operation is considered to be linked to Yevgeniy Prigozhin, head of the holding company Concord and a "chef" working for Vladimir Putin. Documents published by broadly benign hackers from Anonymous International, appear to show Concord is directly involved and researchers have cited e-mail correspondence in which specific orders were given to the army and, in turn, reports were returned on the completed missions. According to journalists, Concord organised banquets in the Kremlin and "cooperates" with the Russian Ministry of Defence.

There are also things called Dark Posts, predominantly used on Facebook, which are only ever seen by the intended recipients and which disappear straight afterwards. According to reports as far back as 2015, these dark posts – which are known generally as unpublished posts – are not the same as targeted adverts but they do share common properties. For example, both allow you to promote posts to specific people. While targeted posts allow you to aim at an audience based only on parameters such as gender, relationship status, education, and so on, dark posts allow you to use keywords. The main difference is that dark posts publish without showing up on your own wall so, only the target sees it. It's not hard to see how this is deployed so effectively by groups using big data to hone down who they are aiming for and even the most basic advertisers have an understanding of this. One I found wrote of dark posts: "Using text that highlights their interests, your community members will feel like you're speaking directly to them." The thought of this amount of power in the wrong hands, well, it doesn't take a lot of imagination to see what has happened and the additional benefit to using dark posts, in particular in regulated election campaigning, is clear: no one will really know, so there's no accountability. I suspect the spends on dark posts are in no way declared and, subsequently, the Electoral Commission is not only outgunned in terms of powers but clueless.

Explaining bots while giving evidence to the Senate Intelligence Committee in April 2017, former FBI Agent Clint Watts highlighted the reason the bot accounts are so effective as a delivery mechanism, explaining: "Whenever you're trying to socially engineer them [voters] and convince them that the information is true, it's much more simple because you see somebody and they look exactly like you, even down to the pictures." Watts went on to say the bot campaign came via a "very diffuse network" which often competes with its own efforts "even amongst hackers, between different parts of Russian intelligence, and propagandists — all with general guidelines about what to pursue, but doing it at different times and paces and rhythms." This makes a great deal more sense when set against the Concord investigation.

Artificial Intelligence, much of which was developed by people like Robert Mercer, was originally thought to be primarily a Twitter issue, but Facebook has also now recognised that the creation of these bots – false profiles – has infected their platform. They have gone as far as acknowledging how this impacted on both the US Presidential election and on the UK's Brexit referendum. As of the late spring 2017, Facebook directly attributes the growth of its false accounts problem to government interference. "We recognize that, in today's information environment, social media plays a sizable role in facilitating communications – not only in times of civic events, such as elections, but in everyday expression," they said in their latest security report. "In some circumstances, however, we recognize that the risk of malicious actors seeking to use Facebook to mislead people or otherwise promote inauthentic communications can be higher."

In advance of France's election campaign, the company also shut down around thirty-thousand suspicious accounts posting high volumes of material to large audiences, saying: "We have had to expand our security focus from traditional abusive behaviour, such as account hacking, malware, spam and financial scams, to include subtler and insidious forms of misuse, including attempts to manipulate civic discourse and deceive people."

What had become clear to me in a very short space of time was that all of the strands of the hacking web interact to create a whole – a viral organism dependent on each of its elements to work effectively, mutate, and spread. We, people, are little more than the host keeping it alive: like any good infection, it relies on us to continue to exist. This is a natural progression, I suppose. A computer virus for all intents and purposes engineered by a malicious enemy to attack humans rather than machines. The next generation of chemical warfare, if you like, designed to work on Dopamine, Oxytocin, Serotonin, and Endorphins and, so far, it has proven highly effective. Big data provides the key to the delivery system and the route to infection, hence the commodity value.

What was also apparent is the organism relies on the interactions of key figures across the world – ones who share a common goal. Among them are many who show some signs of having fallen to a much older, cold war technique: provokatsiya. The full explanation of the term is often given as: "Taking control of your enemies in secret and encouraging them to do things that discredit them and help you. You plant your own agent provocateurs and flip legitimate activists, turning them to your side." In some cases, it can extend to creating extremists and terrorists where none exist, effectively creating a problem in order to solve it, and the Russian services have been known to deploy such tactics since the Tsarist period. As with all classic money-laundering operations, however, the trick to successful data-laundering to these ends would be to establish a legitimate looking front, so it would make sense to deploy provokatsiya in this context, in order to integrate that business as quietly as possible. In my view, this would be especially effective somewhere cash has been successfully cleaned for years. A market you had an understanding of.

In March 2017, it was revealed that almost eight hundred million dollars of money from Russian criminal operations was laundered in the UK as part of a global scheme to clean up to eighty billion in illegal funds. One source, while discussing how the financial sector is so complex this could easily go unnoticed, said: "If you are on the back end you are kind of playing Whack-a-mole, trying to pick this up."

So there I was in the perfect place, Britain, playing Whack-a-mole. But this was no longer about following the money – finances had become secondary. The thing to follow was the most valuable commodity of all: the data itself.

ELEVEN:

Behind the labyrinthine network of data companies, I discovered an even deeper connection between Trump, Brexit, and Russia. By the time I found it, my investigation had already uncovered those first signs of broad, international data laundering, apparently being used to manipulate democracies and the markets with the state-backing of Russia. I'd also stumbled across the first clear example of the complex machinery in practice while investigating crime and immigration in Sweden. The public figures, limited companies, and other groups involved in the UK arm of this operation – which clearly relied on hacking, psychometric targeting, propaganda, and disinformation – were left exposed by the very same thing they had been using as a weapon: big data.

Extraordinarily, it turned out, these parties had also received a somewhat unveiled warning from the Information Commissioner's Office (ICO) ahead of the UK's snap general election in June 2017. When I kicked over this particular stone, the final piece of investigative work ended up being referred to the Electoral Commission (EC) – as it appeared Leave.EU may have had further undeclared donations of services within their complex company structure, taking them well beyond those crucial permissible campaign limits. It was also sent back to the ICO, due to the complex issue of what they call 'sugging' across multiple companies.

The Information Commissioner's Office is the United Kingdom's independent body set up to ensure information rights are maintained in the public interest. They keep a national register of data controllers – people authorised to handle our data – and uphold the laws set out in the Data Protection legislation. Their powers are similar to the Electoral

Commission in terms of demanding compliance through orders and agreements, issuing substantial fines, or instigating prosecutions. They are just as flawed as the EC too, in terms of inadequacy in situations like this one – circumstances which affect the direction of a whole nation. The data protection regulations themselves were set to change in 2018 and, though this enhancement was an initiative of the European Union, the government – the full Conservative majority under Theresa May before June 2017 – had committed to implementing the new framework. The General Data Protection Regulations was the title of the new law, which was set to replace the Data Protection Act 1998 on the 25th of May 2018. Though a much stronger framework, this wouldn't have addressed the central weaknesses in effectively responding to an act of war with a fine.

The ICO itself holds information on every single company handling "controlled data" in the UK – basically everything which falls under the regulations – and, in the wake of revelations about the use of 'big data' in the Trump and Brexit campaigns, issued some starkly worded guidance for political parties ahead of the 2017 general election. Having read the document, which did cause some raised eyebrows, I initially approached the ICO with three specific questions, largely arising from things I'd found out while looking into the background of Brexit. I wanted to know if Vote Leave (not Leave.EU) was ever fined or reported over spam messages sent by US company UCampaign via their app; was there an official, ongoing inquiry into Cambridge Analytica or SCL Elections – the UK parent – and, if so, what was the official comment of the ICO. I also wanted to know where one company is restricted to transfers of data within the European Economic Area (EEA) and they transfer data to a non-restricted company (who can transfer data anywhere in the world), was this legal? I wasn't really anticipating the reply that I received.

The ICO responded with what turned out to be an unprecedented press release, headed "Information Commissioner warns political groups to campaign within the law," which confirmed just how serious the situation really was as we approached Theresa May's contentious general election. The ICO, it turned out, had also written to all major political parties, reminding them of their obligations when contacting potential supporters during the election campaign. The Commissioner's Office went as far as inviting every party to a briefing session, to hear details of the updated guidance on the use of personal data in political campaigning, which included data analytics and associated technologies. The ICO briefing was scheduled for the 4th of May 2017, the same day as local elections across the United Kingdom, and the Commission later told me that each of the parties had sent delegates. After June's election, it was revealed that the Conservative Party used potentially illegal surveys during their campaign.

Elizabeth Denham was appointed UK Information Commissioner in July 2016, having previously held the position of Information and Privacy Commissioner for British Columbia, Canada and, also, Assistant Privacy Commissioner of Canada. By December 2016 she had led the office to issue its largest ever fine to telecommunications company TalkTalk, a record four hundred thousand pounds for poor website security which led to the theft of the personal data of nearly 157,000 customers. The ICO said the website's security was so poor the attack succeeded "with ease."

Denham said at the time: "TalkTalk's failure to implement the most basic cyber security measures allowed hackers to penetrate TalkTalk's systems with ease."

"Yes hacking is wrong, but that is not an excuse for companies to abdicate their security obligations. TalkTalk should and could have done more to safeguard its customer information. It did not and we have taken action," she added. The two British hackers were caught thanks to one of them discussing selling the data on.

Denham also raised concerns in late 2016 when the data-sharing between Facebook and WhatsApp became an issue following acquisition – WhatsApp had been co-opted to share the address books and message records of the encrypted messaging service users to allow greater precision in targeted messaging. Denham wrote in the Guardian, saying: "If those two sets of data were put side by side, Jenny's personal, private information suddenly wouldn't seem quite so private." To say she was alive to the dangers of large datasets, such as those used by Cambridge Analytica, would be an understatement. In her statement on the ICO's political intervention ahead of the election, Denham said: "Engagement with the electorate is vital to the democratic process. But, if a party or campaign group fails to comply with the law, it may face enforcement action as well as reputational damage to its campaign. People have a right to expect that their information will be used in line with the law and my office is there to uphold that right."

The ICO made it clear to me the new guidance was issued in response to an "increase in complaints from members of the public about the promotion of political parties, their candidates, and their views during political campaigns." Specifically, the Commissioner's Office had received complaints about "the use of surveys to gain support for campaigns now or in the future" and also "concerns that their personal information has been shared between national and local organisations." The employment of surveys is broadly cited by controversial company Cambridge Analytica, who use the data they gather to form psychometric profiles which guide targeted messaging, or simply to expand the amount of data, such as contact details, they hold. It was these tactics that were successfully deployed in both the Brexit and Trump campaigns and both campaigns are linked to Russia, hacking, and the use of disinformation to drive voter behaviour.

The ICO guidance explicitly covers viral marketing, stating it must comply with the same rules as direct marketing and cannot dip around consent to the use of data by simply asking people to pass it on. Leave.EU, the campaign of Arron Banks fronted by Nigel Farage, trading under the name Better For The Country Limited, was fined fifty thousand pounds by the ICO for sending five-hundred-thousand unsolicited text messages asking people to support Brexit between May and October 2015 – a year before the referendum took place. The ICO, though I specifically asked, made no comment on the official Vote Leave campaign's use of American app provider UCampaign which, by their own admission, used phone book access via the application to send unsolicited messages to the relatives of hundreds of thousands of voters. The ICO database shows no registrations for UCampaign, the company behind it, Political Social Media LLC, Vote Leave, Vote Leave Limited, or Get Change Limited. Both of these activities would fall well within the definition of viral marketing set out in the guidance.

In terms of the survey data gathering, such as that deployed by Cambridge Analytica, the ICO specifically define this practice as "sugging." They made clear using surveys to collect data (whether ultimately used by the company conducting the survey, or sold on to others, or intended to gather the information for use in marketing) falls within direct marketing. Even open source data, they said, requires adherence to data protection legislation and this would include social media likes and posts. There is no access to collection and retention of this data which escapes the legal protections.

As I'd already established through the documents I had been shown, Leave.EU and Cambridge Analytica worked together during the Brexit campaign, despite the fact comments have been made attempting to distance themselves from this. I'd also already obtained an exclusive insight which uncovered that the Electoral Commission was, in fact, investigating Leave.EU for undeclared and potentially illegal donations of services by Cambridge Analytica, also known in the UK as SCL Elections, during the EU referendum. Though the ICO refused to confirm whether they were investigating these companies in tandem with the Electoral Commission, with my own investigative work revealing a broader picture of Russian-linked data laundering, I found the ICO's public access database held invaluable information on these companies. It appeared both were structurally designed to engage in sugging and to facilitate transfers of data within and outside of the EEA. The ICO state that sugging attracts a maximum fine of £500,000 as it is a breach of the Privacy and Electronic Communications Regulations (PECR).

Leave.EU, the company behind the unofficial Brexit campaign, registered with the ICO on the 29th of February 2016 and this registration expires in 2018. They set out their headline reason for processing data as being to: "Enable us to promote our goods & services" and state they hold personal, family, lifestyle, social circumstances, and financial details. In the sensitive class of information, they are registered to hold political interests and racial/ethnic origin data and the company is authorised to share what it holds with affiliate groups, central government, suppliers and service providers, financial organisations, and the Electoral Commission.

Despite being a company established specifically to support the domestic Brexit campaign, the register for Leave.EU shows: "Personal information is traded as a primary business function" and adds the information may be shared with business associates, advisers, other associates, and "traders in personal data." The UK based company entry also states: "It may sometimes be necessary to transfer personal information overseas" though this is restricted to within the EEA.

This didn't strike me as a company established purely for political campaign purposes and it certainly didn't sound benevolently patriotic. Subsequently, I started to dig more.

Cambridge Analytica, I found, was slightly different. The company was first registered in November 2015, and the registration was set to expire in late 2017. The address listed for them was at the Cooperation Trust Center, Wilmington, Delaware, though it also gives a UK representative, Jordanna Zetter, based in London. She is, it would appear, an Operations Executive at SCL Group. Listed as a "data analytics" company, they state they carry out marketing, advertising, and PR functions, as well as undertaking research. They hold the same classes of primary data as Leave.EU but the sensitive information is much deeper and that starts to tell the true story – Cambridge Analytica holds records on people's physical and mental health, racial and ethnic origin, religious or "other similar" beliefs, trade union memberships and "political opinions." The other difference from Leave.EU is that the US company includes retained data from survey respondents and can transfer the data they hold to territories and countries around the world. There is no restriction to the EEA. One of the primary business functions they had listed on the ICO register was to acquire data through surveys – a method first developed by Kosinski, the Cambridge academic, which bears similarities to aspects of Cambridge Analytica's psychometric profiling. This is also the activity which falls squarely within the definition of sugging.

But, I confirmed having seen it elsewhere, Cambridge Analytica is not the principle trading name for the organisation in the United Kingdom, in fact, it is only the US brand which became famous as a result of the Trump campaign. In the UK, the primary business is SCL Elections Limited, and its own registration strengthened the depth of connection to Leave.EU and the businesses – and people – behind it.

SCL Elections Limited registered in November 2015, the same month as Cambridge Analytica, but according to the records trades at a separate London address in E14. The sensitive data classes held are the same as CA but the headline data is expanded to include memberships, employment, and education information. Again the transfer of data is worldwide, not EEA restricted, and the company can share data with business associates. Working with Leave.EU, whose primary business function is the trade of data, this means a legitimate transfer from the UK could reach America or another worldwide territory without the law technically being broken. This also means Leave.EU, via its connection with Cambridge Analytica and SCL, could buy in databases created outside of the EEA area where data is regulated, or simply buy sugged databases created through Cambridge Analytica and SCL surveys hosted outside of the EEA. When you factor in that Steve Bannon has defined links to Cambridge Analytica by way of his former seat on the board, and the company's owner, Robert Mercer, was a key donor to Trump's campaign, this starts to create a pretty grim jigsaw puzzle.

In January 2017, Trump signed an executive order exempting non-US citizens from the privacy shield – a European Union and United States law which defined what data could be shared between businesses on both sides of the Atlantic Ocean and how that data could be used. It was designed so data protection laws could be upheld between the EU's the member states and the US, where information regulation remains much weaker. Wired reported at the time: "The Privacy Shield was developed by EU and US negotiators in 2015 after the previous data sharing agreement between the two groups was struck down by Europe's highest court. In October 2015, the European Court of Justice ruled the Safe Harbour framework was invalid as data being

sent out of the EU was not being properly protected."
The case was pushed through the EU's highest court by
Austrian privacy campaigner Max Schrems and the
court ruled that the European Commission's original
trans-Atlantic data protection agreement, which went
into force in 2000, was invalid because it failed to
adequately protect consumers. It came about in the
wake of the scandal involving Edward Snowden.
Facebook, which found itself in the middle of Schrems'
case, came under the scrutiny of the Irish data
protection authority (DPA) who were compelled to look
into the company's data protection practices. The EUCJ
said the Irish DPA had to decide: "Whether...transfer of
the data of Facebook's European subscribers to the US
should be suspended on the grounds that that country
does not afford an adequate level of protection of
personal data."

In July 2016, the European Commission deemed the
new EU-US Privacy Shield Framework adequate to
enable data transfers under EU law and, on January the
12th 2017, the Swiss Government announced the
approval of the Swiss-US Privacy Shield Framework as
a valid legal mechanism to comply with Swiss
requirements when transferring personal data from
Switzerland to the United States. Only days after the
Swiss agreement, Trump signed his order. Lawyers
continued to argue the Privacy Shield was safe,
however, citing that no presidential Executive Order
can override existing laws written by Congress, and
Congress has already approved the Judicial Redress Act
which granted EU citizens the right to use the US
courts in the case of misuse of data. The act became
law on the 1st of February 2017.

Whether the order the president signed took effect is
one thing. Trump's intent, however, is another matter
entirely, especially given the direct links to data
companies and his White House administration. Even a
few years ago, I discovered while exploring all of this,
both the EU and the US were aware of the capabilities

of data exploitation in circumstances exactly matching the Leave.EU and Cambridge Analytica/SCL scenario and, it appears, Trump took the step to directly interfere in the enhanced protections while being directly involved and beholden to parties potentially benefitting his arrangement.

As I'd found out, the data laundering trade also involves reportedly legitimate purchases of hacked data in exchange for Bitcoin and it was apparent to me the arrangements of international transfer available to SCL and its subsidiary provided a direct channel for the potential use of laundered data in the UK. This left me even more concerned about the discovery relating to when Leave.EU received it's fifty thousand pound fine for the 2015 spam campaign: they claimed they obtained the lists from a third-party supplier. In much the same way, the official Vote Leave campaign would have avoided data protections as they were not registered themselves and nor was the app provider, UCampaign, who would have retained the British data captured by the app in the US.

As far as I could see it, the existence of an effective data-wash was clear: whether it was legally or illegally sourced, it could enter the United Kingdom, or Europe even, and leave it just as freely.

When I started looking behind Leave.EU, the mirroring of SCL's registration became even clearer. Better For The Country Limited registered with the ICO in August 2015 at the same address as Leave.EU, but this company included transfers to countries and territories throughout the world. The company connections were becoming more obscure but, finally, provided the more direct connections which I had been missing. While Leave.EU had not yet posted accounts, Better For The Country Limited last filed showing over one million pounds in shareholder funds. The company was registered with Companies House in May 2015, listing its nature as "other information services." The directorships when I looked, in April and

May 2017, showed the prominent Leave.EU figure Andrew Wigmore, Maria Ming, Alison Marshall, Elizabeth Bilney, the well-known UKIP donor Arron Banks, Ranja Abbot, and Dawn Williams. Bilney I found interesting, also being listed as a director at Banks' flagship alternative media outlet Westmonster, and a new venture 'Big Data Dolphins' alongside Alison Marshall.

Big Data Dolphins was an unknown quantity having only been registered with Companies House in December 2016, giving its nature as "business and domestic software development" and "data processing, hosting and related activities." The ICO registration, I saw, was a mirror of SCL's but was different in that it was shown as having data transfers restricted to the EEA. The shareholders also link to Rock Services, Banks' insurance company, though the majority share (91%) shows as being owned by Deep DD Limited which returns no trace on any company searches I've managed to do.

Also registered at Lysander House, a development in Bristol and the home of most of Banks' businesses, Bilney was listed as an active director of Chartwell Political Limited, a company set up in June 2014 to carry out market research and public opinion polling. The company then showed as owing nearly three hundred and forty thousand pounds. The second director, Bridget Rowe, was listed on the company website underneath a picture of the back of Banks talking to journalists and alongside her was the name James Pryor. Rowe worked in print news, including alongside Rupert Murdoch, and previously worked as the director of communications for UKIP. Pryor had worked on elections all over the world, for the Conservatives at Downing Street, and as a campaign director for UKIP. They claimed to be uniquely able to: "Identify the range of threats that can emerge to destabilise political and election campaigns," and went on to say: "It is well known that 'best intelligence' wins wars, especially Information Wars. The battle for hearts and minds hinges, crucially, on securing, shaping, re-shaping and controlling the Message."

Bilney was, of course, also a director of Westmonster, the 'Breitbart' styled news agency launched by Arron Banks – which was incorporated in January 2017 and lists a major shareholder as Better For The Country Limited. The second major shareholder and director is Michael Heaver, previously communications officer for MEP Nigel Farage and former chair of UKIP's youth arm, Young Independence. The youth group, much like the Sweden Democrats original movement for younger members, is no stranger to controversy. In 2013, the then chairman Olly Neville was fired by the party for supporting same-sex marriage. Another incident occurred on a few days later when the Northwest chairman and prospective Parliamentary candidate for Chester, Richard Lowe, was allegedly compelled to resign because of a lack of confidence over his support for same-sex marriage and other views that, according to reports: "Clashed with UKIP policy." Additionally, during the first UKIP leadership election in 2016, youth members were accused of body shaming and attacking one of the candidates, Lisa Duffy, on a closed Facebook group. The group was shut down after the Huffington Post reported on racism and homophobic attacks being found on the page.

By 2014, Heaver was actively writing for Breitbart, the right-wing alternative news outlet then headed by Bannon and funded by Mercer. Bannon had already launched the site in the UK at that time, specifically to further his "cultural war" and influence the 2015 general election. While Banks and Farage were openly with each other while in the US supporting the Trump campaign, Heaver provided a definite, prior connection between Farage, his official public office, and Bannon.

The background information in all of this is of such a complex nature, I now find it easy to understand how difficult it has been for the world's media agencies to reduce the available evidence to the short, sharp punches needed for headline-led reporting. For example, both Mercer and Trump were both linked to Russia's twelfth richest businessman, Dmitry Rybolovlev because Mercer's yacht was seen docked near the oligarch in March 2017 after Trump's plane was seen next to the oligarch's prior to the US election – though Trump and Dmitry were also connected by a ninety-five million property deal in Florida, a stone's throw from Mar-a-lago.

Rybolovlev himself has a controversial history, associating with criminals in the 1990s before becoming embroiled in the murder trial of a business partner. During his divorce – the most expensive settlement in history – he was also implicated in the April 2016 Panama Papers, with reports on the judgement saying his use of offshore companies in the British Virgin Islands was deemed a "textbook example of the lengths rich people (in most cases men) go to protect their considerable wealth in case of a marital breakup." He was also implicated in the Football Leaks scandal which revealed he and football agent Jorge Mendes set up a secret system to illegally buy players' shares. Using a Cyprus-based offshore investment fund, named Browsefish Limited, Rybolovlev illegally manipulated the price of his own players through third-party ownerships. If you add the Cyprus assessment from the Kremlin Watch report into this mix, the inability of the news outlets to condense stories like this is easily explained.

Arron Banks was also named in the Panama Papers as a shareholder of PRI Holdings Limited which Panamanian-based Mossack Fonseca set up as an offshore company in 2013. The British Virgin Islands, known by the abbreviation BVI, is an offshore British territory and international tax haven which dismissed an anti-corruption summit held in London, in April 2016, by then prime minister, David Cameron. Another shareholder of PRI was Elizabeth Bilney.

Banks himself is also more directly linked to Russia. In his own account of the Brexit campaign, Banks describes meeting "a shady character called Oleg" while at UKIP's annual conference in September 2015. "He was introduced to us as the First Secretary of the embassy – in other words, the KGB's man in London," wrote the UKIP donor, who went on to say he was invited to a private meeting with the Russian ambassador Alexander Yakovenko. "Our host wanted the inside track on the Brexit campaign and grilled us on the potential implications," Banks recorded in his memoir. Though the meeting was two years before I began investigating, I've picked through the Russian Embassy staff lists and found only one Oleg in a position prominent enough to warrant a public listing. Captain Oleg Kornienko is shown on the embassy's website as the Defence and Naval attaché.

Banks' own directorships at Companies House are relatively straight forward. He's an active director at Avista Awards (a food award scheme), Parsons Jewellers, Old Down event catering, Rock Services (his insurance company), and Precision Risk Services – an insurance investigator. However, a variant of the Precision Risk company name also featured in Bank's Panama Papers listings under the PRI Holdings umbrella and was linked back to Gibraltar-based STM Fidecs Management Ltd, which acted as secretary to Banks's PRI Holdings Limited. The Observer reported at the time that STM Fidecs Ltd was the first to register Leave.EU as a wholly owned subsidiary before its ownership passed to Banks.

By this point, as I sat reading through pages and pages of documents and material, the international link between the alt-right and far-right parties was already established. The interference of Russia in western democracy and the substantial and genuine security threat it posed had been, for all intents and purposes, fully confirmed. Even the collaborative use and extent of disinformation and propaganda had also been set out in an undeniable way. As I sat reviewing the ICO's statement on their investigation while going back over the Electoral Commission documents, it was clear that our own independent bodies were deeply concerned about interference in democracy during the general election and were alive to the specific risks we faced. Equally, they didn't have the right teeth to sink into the issue in any way likely to make a difference when up against this web of companies, both national and international, linked directly to Arron Banks – to Brexit – which included agencies specifically geared towards the deployment of tailored political messaging and the collection, use, and sale of intricate personal data.

I could see it all so clearly. Our personal data was being harvested both here and abroad, bought and sold as a commodity, potentially illegally, while also being used for political purposes. This additionally relied on alternative media outlets to drive specific messages, including from parties directly serving in public offices. It was apparent that those who controlled the alternative media outlets also controlled the data – and its use – and all of them were indisputably connected to each other on both sides of the Atlantic. Cambridge Analytica had openly sourced data from survey operations too, using it to build psychometric profiles of electorates. This data had either, in part or in full, been sold on or transferred and subsequently used in the direct viral marketing of political messages. Leave.EU has used this data, working with Cambridge Analytica, and it appeared this fell within the ICO definition of illegal sugging. Robert Mercer, Donald Trump, Nigel Farage, Arron Banks, Steve Bannon, Michael Heaver and Elizabeth Bilney were now inseparably linked to one another and, whether by data acquisition, personal association or through other linear exposure, all of these parties were also linked to Russia – a country directly implicated, at a state-sponsored level, in interfering with elections across the western world.

Watching these puzzle pieces fall into each other was awful, if I'm honest, and it was hard to know where to start. Nonetheless, I took a deep breath and wrote to SCL, asking if they or Cambridge Analytica had ever been investigated by the ICO for data breaches, or if they are currently under investigation. I wanted their official comment on the Electoral Commission investigation into their relationship with Leave.EU, whether they were aware of the sugging definition, and if they were continuing the practice of using surveys to develop databases. I also wanted to know whether they had bought data from, or sold data to, Leave.EU, Better For The Country Ltd, or Big Data Dolphins.

As the growing scale of the international data wash was starting to be exposed, the question started to shift. I wasn't just sat asking what the hell happened anymore, I was asking who else was involved. But I didn't get that answer straight away. Something unexpected happened instead.

It was about eleven o'clock on the morning of the 3rd of May 2017 when I wrote to the SCL Group, the parent company of Cambridge Analytica and SCL Elections, asking the specific questions arising from my investigations. They replied at half-three in the afternoon the day after, Thursday the 4th of May, not from SCL, but from Cambridge Analytica's press email address, answering the questions. This wasn't a standard press office reply, however. The subject line read "Complaint" and the email was copied to the ethics team at the National Union of Journalists (of which I am a freelance member), Byline, and Impress (the new press regulator I work to the rules of). The company wrote: "You have published a number of inaccuracies and misrepresentations about Cambridge Analytica in your Byline blogs entitled "Data Laundering: The New Chemical Warfare" (28 April) and "The Big Data Wash" (3 May)." They went on to list a number of points they wanted addressing, requesting me to "let us know how Byline intends to correct these mistakes" – though there were no mistakes – and also provided answers to the original questions I had asked. It was bizarre and I am not the only person who felt that it was the beginning of a rather litigious effort to have all mention of them they didn't like struck from the record – which seems to be the reason why they set the legal team on the Guardian. I suppose I had two benefits on my side, namely that I know bankruptcy isn't that bad – as long as you can ration food – and I'd already taken on the Met and won where it counted. That's without even starting on the inevitable fact I was only writing the truth.

The specific clarifications requested by Cambridge Analytica actually ended up raising more questions than they resolved, but for the sake of clarity and chronology, the original questions and responses from a company spokesperson were:

1. Have SCL Elections / Cambridge Analytica ever been investigated by the ICO for data breaches / are you currently under investigation by the ICO?

"No and no. CA/SCL has never been investigated by the ICO for data breaches. We are compliant with data laws. Like a range of organisations, we are in touch, with the ICO, to help them with their ongoing assessment into the use of data analytics."

2. What is your official comment on the Electoral Commission investigation in the LEAVE.EU campaign, which appears to centre around donations of services by yourselves.

"We did not do any work (paid or unpaid) for Leave.EU."

3. Are you aware that the practice of data collection by way of surveys for other uses, including the sales of database to others, and viral marketing, falls within the ICO definition of 'sugging'? Are you continuing this practice?

"Whenever we conduct research, we have the explicit consent of each respondent for the use of their data."

4. Do you buy from or sell data to Leave.EU, Better For The Country Ltd, or Big Data Dolphins? Have you bought or sold data from these companies in the past?

"No we have not."

Cambridge Analytica went on to list the points it found objectionable and started by saying it did not use psychometrics on the Trump campaign. This wasn't true. There's a rather brilliant video which was filmed at the Concordia Summit in the United States of America in September 2016. The presentation was given by Cambridge Analytica's CEO, Alexander Nix, and, in the video, he states Cambridge Analytica had profiled all adult Americans and, before leaving the stage, announced one of the remaining presidential candidates was using this new technology. At that time there were two candidates left in US election, Donald Trump and Hilary Clinton. The latter did not use their services. Also, in a broadly reported press release from Cambridge Analytica, Nix is quoted as saying: "We are thrilled that our revolutionary approach to data-driven communication has played such an integral part in President-elect Trump's extraordinary win." Additionally, in their own marketing materials, the company says: "We collect up to 5,000 data points on over 220 million Americans...and predict the behaviour of like-minded people," to which Nix added "if I was to tell you that an individual had voted for a particular party over the last 40 years the same way, you would conclude that is a fairly good indicator...Now imagine if we could overlay thousands of data points that are predictable about behaviour. Of course it works." When later reports started to critique the company's technique, Nix was quoted in March 2017, by the New York Times, as saying: "We bake a cake, it's got 10 ingredients in it. Psychographics is one of them."

So, I had clarified that they had used the method in the Trump campaign, with their own words. It seemed odd, to be honest, they would even challenge it but they had also been busy deleting web records linking them to Leave.EU by this point.

Unsurprisingly, the company spokesperson went on to dispute any connection to Leave.EU, saying they did not work (paid or unpaid) for Leave.EU and did not work on the EU Referendum. Again, this seemed bizarre, given that most of the evidence of the collaboration came from them and the Electoral Commission was specifically investigating donation-in-kind of services made to Leave.EU. Of course, those documents I'd seen, backed up by other reports, showed quite clearly that a working link between Cambridge Analytica and Leave.EU did exist.

Cambridge Analytica also said their psychometric offering was not based on a method developed by a Cambridge academic – they were talking about Kosinski – and added that the Ocean personality model had been around for about 30 years. They also denied any dealings with academic researcher Michael Kosinski of Cambridge University. It was known and accepted the Ocean model had been in existence for around thirty years and the sections of the original articles they were referring to weren't controversial at all. One said: "Scientific research, including that by Michael Kosinski at Cambridge University, has shown that a big data profile can be used to develop targeted marketing or messaging, designed to drive a behavioural response in an individual. The technique is known as either psychographics or psychometrics and has become famous following its use by Cambridge Analytica in the Trump and Brexit campaigns," while the other said: "A basic profile, as Michael Kosinski found in his research, can predict your behaviours just based on social media likes. An advanced profile, based on what websites you visit, what news you read, your job, your politics, your purchases, your medical records, would mean such a company knows you better than you know yourself." In the end, I made one small amendment, to the effect that the data collection by survey bore similarities to Kosinski's work, rather than was based upon it. Still, it all seemed overkill. Cambridge Analytica also stated it does not use Facebook likes, added it has no connection whatsoever with "fake news" or "alternative facts", despite having had Bannon on the board, and said it did not use "bots" on the presidential campaign. I put these weird points on the record in a follow-up article for reasons of fairness, even though the original articles attributed none of these to the company. I think the last point they raised was the one which they knew was a sticking point. They said they had never transferred any data to Leave.EU. By then I had actually submitted the evidence I'd gathered during my investigations to the ICO, the appropriate authority, so they could investigate. That, technically, made me a witness but they knew this as they'd clearly seen the articles.

Rather than put me off, as a result of their response I doubled down and figured I'd carry on, casting the net even wider because I had a good idea where to catch what I was after.

TWELVE:

It was Marine Le Pen's financial links and open investigations which revealed the true scale of Russia's European Union operations.

With an established, complex, international network of the far-right and Russia working together on the manipulation of electorates, through psychometrics and disinformation campaigns, France was thought to be the next domino to fall in their advance on the control of finance and politics. Le Pen was, at the time I started investigating, facing the final round of the French Elections against the subsequently successful and immensely popular centrist Emanuel Macron. Before the election, however, all bets were off and Le Pen, having just stepped down from her role as leader of the far-right Front National in order to broaden her appeal, continued to be openly supported by Nigel Farage, Donald Trump, and Vladimir Putin.

Aside from the things I had already started to expose by inspecting the public registers, Le Pen quickly showed herself to be the weakest link in the clandestine operation's chain – open investigations and clear financial links to Russia were hanging over her and not hard to drill into. The first thing was Sweden was not alone in its strong response to interference in the democratic process. Working with the EU, Facebook – who had already been pressured to employ fact checkers to monitor posts on its network and – took out full page adverts in German newspapers advising people how to spot fake news. The platform then shut down thirty-thousand fake accounts spreading disinformation ahead of the French election campaigns and also teamed up with Google on an initiative to counter disinformation and alternative media sites spreading fake news in favour of Le Pen. Ten days ahead of the first round of votes, Facebook released an official blog confirming their priority was to remove suspect accounts with high volumes of posting activity and the biggest audiences. They even deployed AI to help speed up this process. "We've made improvements to recognize these inauthentic accounts more easily by identifying patterns of activity — without assessing the content itself," Shabnam Shaik, a Facebook security team manager, wrote in the update.

It was looking into all this with Sweden in mind I found Le Pen's Front National was also historically linked to the Nordic country in a different way: via the far-right party I'd studied, the Sweden Democrats. Le Pen' s party had actually helped fund the SD's 1998 election brochure.

The right across Europe had all of those long established connections I'd already picked over and had aligned with Russia and the US white supremacy movement, but Britain's UKIP, under Nigel Farage, appeared to have steered clear of this. In 2014, Farage ruled out an alliance with the Front National but relatively swiftly changed tack, eventually giving public backing to Le Pen. If you look a little more closely at UKIP, however, it was already allied with the Sweden Democrats, having formed an EU parliamentary coalition with them in the same year he declined Le Pen. Along with other groups, the new coalition included one former Front National MEP, Joëlle Bergeron, who resigned from the party after being asked to stand down, having called for voter's rights for European immigrants. She had been a Front National member for forty-two years. This whole period turned out to be hugely significant in terms of the more overt shifts in the right-wing parties across Europe.

After Putin publicly declared his vision of a functioning "Eurasian Union," the Kremlin began systematically building bridges with the EU groups and, at the same time, Marine Le Pen outlined her concept of Europe as independent nation states controlled by a tripartite axis made up of Paris, Berlin, and Moscow. It is not hard at all to start to gather the huge mass of evidence which surrounds Putin's vision and the way in which it capitalised on the more extreme political groups and nationalists. Anton Shekhovtsov, of UCL School of Slavonic and East European Studies, made a statement in 2014, saying "there is no doubt that the Kremlin uses the European far right. As things are, Russia cannot compete with the EU in terms of economy, human resources, capital and IT– it's only chance to dominate is if Europe is reduced to separate nation states. While direct financial backing is difficult to prove, there is little doubt that Moscow is holding the purse strings. Ideally, Moscow would like to be funding mainstream politicians, but this is expensive and difficult. It is much easier to focus on MEPs where restrictions are more nebulous. Though I believe Russia has been paying these extreme right parties handsomely for lobbying its interests in Brussels."

Another expert, Professor Mitchell Orenstein of the Department of Political Science at Northeastern University in Boston, made a prescient call for the EU to be alive to the risks back then too. "I really do not believe Putin's challenge to Europe is being taken seriously enough," he said. "Brussels must begin looking at how these parties are being funded. Putin's position regarding the Ukraine is one thing, but when it comes to the rest of Europe, he doesn't need to resort to land-grab tactics. He can just sit patiently on the sidelines and watch as the far right tries to dismantle the EU once and for all."

Over time, however, this initially more insidious creeping Russian influence became increasingly obvious, from around 2013 onwards. It was then Le Pen was invited to Moscow by the State Duma leader and Putin ally Sergei Naryshkin, where she also met with Deputy Prime Minister Dmitry Rogozin. During the 2017 French election campaign, she visited Moscow again, meeting Putin himself, who Russian media reported to have said: "We attach a lot of importance to our relations with France, trying to maintain smooth relations with both the acting power and the opposition representatives."

2013 was the same year Nigel Farage met Russia's London Ambassador, Alexander Yakovenko – who later met UKIP and Leave.EU donor Arron Banks after the UKIP conference in 2015. Banks, as his memoir clearly said, described his contact as being with the KGB's man in London and they held their lengthy discussion about Brexit over vodka. Even before Banks met Oleg, however, in March of 2014, Nigel Farage named Putin as the world leader he most admired, praising the way the Russian president handled "the whole Syria thing" as "brilliant." Notably, it was after the first Farage meeting with Yakovenko that UKIP's MEPs began to appear with increasing frequency on RT, the Russian state media channel, and Farage went on to be offered his own show after Brexit. Farage was also 'knighted' on the channel in March 2017, though the clip went wrong when the little girl dressed up as the Queen asked why he didn't like foreigners.

It was against the development of this backdrop that, in January 2016, James Clapper – then the United States Director of National Intelligence – was instructed by the US Congress to conduct a major review into Russian clandestine funding of European parties over the previous ten years. The ground work by Putin's Kremlin had been going on for a decade and the review arose amidst Washington's significant concerns over Moscow's exploitation of European disunity, which they – rightly – believed was aimed at undermining NATO, blocking missile defence programmes, and reversing economic sanctions which came about after the annexation of Crimea. At the time, one senior government official from the UK told the Telegraph: "It really is a new Cold War out there. Right across the EU, we are seeing alarming evidence of Russian efforts to unpick the fabric of European unity on a whole range of vital strategic issues." A year later, when Russia's advance had started to claim overt successes, these British officials were nowhere to be seen and this comment was resigned quietly to history.

Clapper himself resigned ahead of Donald Trump's inauguration in November 2016, by which time Brexit had caused a significant shock across the EU and troop movements had begun escalating on Europe's Eastern borders. By February 2017, the Baltic states, Poland, Romania and Bulgaria were accommodating soldiers from across the NATO member states and more than seven thousand troops had been deployed in the countries bordering Russia. The UK was acting as the lead nation in Estonia, the home of original Capstone experiment, where eight hundred soldiers were based at the Tapa, around fifty miles from Tallinn. French and Danish forces were also deployed with them. British soldiers had also been stationed in Poland as part of a US-led NATO mission of about four thousand troops supported by the Romanian army – one of the last acts of Barack Obama. To give some idea of the scale of Russian aggression, the official estimates were that Putin had deployed over three-hundred thousand troops to the EU border, along with a whole host of new military equipment. It has also been rumoured that one of the Russian cruise missile systems had covertly been brought within firing range of major European targets.

France's strategic role as a leading NATO nation is crucial and they are, in the wake of Brexit, in line to take the role of Deputy Supreme Allied Commander held by Britain since 1951. It is subsequently logical France would fall within Russia's sights. This makes it all the more alarming that, in 2014, the Front National, while aiming for the presidency under Le Pen, confirmed taking Russian money. The First Czech-Russian Bank, based in Moscow, initially loaned the party nearly nine and a half million Euro (which is over seven million pounds) and a further two million Euro (around one and half million pounds) was borrowed from a company based in Cyprus – the home of Rybolovlev's Browsefish and a country declared a Russian asset by Kremlin Watch. At the time, Le Pen responded to the media coverage saying: "What is scandalous here is that the French banks are not lending," while Russia correspondent Luke Harding, reporting for the Guardian, wrote: "In Soviet times the KGB used "active measures" to sponsor front organisations in the West including pro-Moscow communist parties. The Kremlin didn't invent Europe's far-right parties. But in an analogous way Moscow is now lending them support, political and financial, thereby boosting European neo-fascism." Harding made similar conclusions to the academics and intelligence experts I had discovered, reporting that: "Tactically, Russia is exploiting the popular dissent against the EU – fuelled by both immigration and austerity. But as right-wing movements grow in influence across the continent, Europe must wake up to their insidious means of funding, or risk seeing its own institutions subverted."

Only days before I started to look into Le Pen in May 2017, a joint investigation by French journalists at Mediapart, in collaboration with Latvian colleagues at re:Baltica, revealed Vilis Dambiņš, a director of an intermediary company managing assets related to the family of Alexander Babakov, Vladimir Putin's special representative for relations with Russian organisations abroad, personally met with at least two high-ranking officials of Le Pen's Front National, to discuss options for the party to get a further Russian loan. The second loan, reportedly an application for three million Euro, was made to an organisation called Strategy Bank, which allegedly had its licence revoked, and the loan was never completed. The first loan provider, FCRB who issued the nine and a half million Euro loan, also had its licence to trade removed in 2016 due to "poor asset quality" and a failure to "normalise its work." The bank was fully owned by billionaire Roman Popov, who had, until then, managed to maintain a low profile. However, in July 2016, the Czech central bank filed a legal complaint against the financial management of ERB bank, also owned by Popov. As a result, anti-corruption police launched an investigation into the suspicious syphoning of funds.

First known as the European-Russian Bank, it was set up to fund Czech-Russian trade but, according to insiders, primarily served as the source of finances for Popov and his influential countrymen. The inquiry was triggered when a portion of the bank's finances simply disappeared. According to sources: "Money was flowing from the ERB bank through bonds, mostly fictitious ones." ERB responded to the probe via its website, saying it was in a "good condition" and also in the Czech press, saying it was all part of "the anti-Russian rhetoric that has long been used in the EU countries and partially also in the Czech Republic." The pattern of response was now quite familiar to me, and it was not restricted to Russian firms alone but also to anyone who is linked to them, whether directly or indirectly. It all formed part of the broader disinformation and confusion narrative.

Le Pen's finances do not improve on closer inspection. She has also been personally subject to a European Union investigation of her funding which resulted in an adverse finding.

The European Anti-Fraud Office (know as OLAF) is the only EU body mandated to detect, investigate and stop fraud with EU funds. In July 2016, OLAF concluded an investigation concerning the misuse of parliamentary assistance allowances by Marine Le Pen in her official capacity with the Front National. The unit recommended to the European Parliament they recover a rather large sum of almost three-hundred-and-fifty thousand Euro. The specific details of the allegation against Le Pen were that she used funds allotted for parliamentary assistants to pay the salaries of her personal assistant, Catherine Griset, and her bodyguard, Thierry Legier, for work unrelated to her EU role. As a result, and in an effort to recoup the funds, the parliament began withholding half of Le Pen's stipend effective from February 2017 and suspended her expense allowances and half of her housing allowance in March. Le Pen, of course, denied any wrongdoing yet invoked her immunity as an MEP, refusing to attend questioning by the investigating magistrates. She also asked the EU's General Court to suspend the recovery action while awaiting a primary ruling on a legal request to have the investigation findings thrown out. The General Court rejected Le Pen's case in April 2017, having already waved away similar requests from three other Front National members.

Numerous other party MEPs were targeted in the same inquiry and also faced salary sanctions. The Parliament is seeking to recover a total of over one million Euro and French investigators, probing a fake jobs scam, raided the party's headquarters outside Paris in March 2017. The French authorities carried out the warrants as they attempted to determine whether the Front National appropriated European Parliament funds to pay for twenty assistants who were presented as parliamentary aides while working for the party in other domestic capacities.

Exploring these broader allegations against the Front National, OLAF provided me with a broadly worded response, telling me: "OLAF is investigating suspicions of fraud and irregularities concerning the use of parliamentary assistance allowances by MEPs belonging to the Front National."

"The OLAF investigation is examining possible breaches of the Statute of Members of the European Parliament and its implementing measures, potential conflicts of interest and possible misuse of EU finances. However, as the investigation is on-going, OLAF is not in a position to confirm or deny the alleged involvement of any specific persons in this case, nor make any other comments," their statement said. "This is in order to protect the confidentiality of on-going and possible ensuing investigations, subsequent judicial proceedings, personal data and procedural rights."

"The OLAF investigation is examining possible breaches of the Statute of Members of the European Parliament and its implementing measures, potential conflicts of interest and possible misuse of EU finances," their spokesperson wrote.

Having contacted the European Parliament directly, they were incredibly helpful and sent a comprehensive background to the framework and regulation of MEP expenses. The parliament told me: "Members of the European Parliament are entitled to assistance from personal staff whom they may freely choose. The parliamentary assistance allowance may not be used to cover personal expenses or for grants or donations of a political nature. Members may not either directly or indirectly employ members of their immediate family (parents, children, brothers, sisters, spouses or stable non-marital partners). In general, contracts with assistants must not give rise to any conflicts of interest." They also set out the rules relating to the allocation of financial support and how it can be used: "The maximum monthly amount defrayable in respect of all such personal staff is EUR 24 164 (2017 rate). None of these funds are paid to the MEP themselves. A Member's staff duties must specifically relate to the Member's work as Member of the European Parliament."

The specific rules under which the Front National were being investigated related to the impermissibility of using EU funds to "finance contracts concluded with an organisation." The regulations further prohibited funds from being used for "pursuing political objectives, such as a political party, foundation, movement or parliamentary political group." A list of admissible and non-admissible costs in relation to the assistants has been adopted by the Bureau of the Parliament and clearly mentions as inadmissible expenses: "Any expenses in relation to elections, referenda or any other campaign whether at national or EU-level." These rules, it transpired, also triggered a 2016 investigation into Farage's UKIP.

The Alliance for Direct Democracy in Europe, a UKIP-controlled EU Parliamentary group, was asked to return over one-hundred-and-seventy thousand Euro after officials uncovered a breach of the rules arising from the alliance pouring money into the United Kingdom's 2015 general election and the Brexit referendum. UKIP spent the EU funds on polling and analysis in constituencies where they hoped to win a seat in the 2015 general election, including in South Thanet – a seat contested by Farage. The party also funded polls to gauge the public mood on Brexit, months before official campaigning began. The EU report on the misspending concluded that "these services were not in the interest of the European party, which could neither be involved in the national elections nor in the referendum on a national level. The constituencies selected for many of the polls underline that the polling was conducted in the interest of UKIP. Most of the constituencies can be identified as being essential for reaching a significant representation in the House of Commons from the 2015 general election or for a positive result for the leave campaign." I had previously established that Russia had interfered in the 2015 general election and foreign powers were involved in cyberattacks during Brexit.

The report also concluded there were "a substantial number of activities for which financing ought to be considered as non-eligible expenditure," in respect of spending on polls around the Scottish and Welsh elections in 2016.

Having already uncovered quite a substantial labyrinth of companies which utilise surveys and polling to harvest and trade in data, some of which I'd directly linked to UKIP, Donald Trump, and Arron Banks, the conclusions reached by the EU were set in a much clearer context. The potential data laundering activities and disinformation campaigns used to sway the electorate also tied in with a broader series of links between Farage, Trump, Wikileaks, and Russia, the ongoing Electoral Commission investigation into Leave.EU, and the referrals I'd gone on to make to the ICO in respect of the data laundering and sugging.

Farage responded to the EU report, then as interim leader of UKIP, saying: "We are in an environment where rules are wilfully interpreted as suits. I've understood absolutely the rules. This is pure victimisation."

Speaking to the Guardian after Brexit, Banks repeated much the same line, saying: "We were just cleverer than the regulators and the politicians. Of course we were," adding they "pushed the boundary of everything, right to the edge. It was war." As I'd found, those rules, the mechanisms they were up against were next to useless.

The ADDE as a whole went on to be denied two-hundred-and-fifty thousand Euro in grants for failing to follow the rules and, as a result of the EU inquiry, the parliament told me the group declared itself bankrupt in the wake of it.

Once you start looking, the trail is almost endless. I barely registered this at the time but UKIP had already faced an OLAF investigation which resulted in one of their MEPs being sent to prison for fraud offences – in circumstances mirroring the ongoing Front National investigation. In July 2015, former UKIP MEP Ashley Mote was sentenced to five years in prison having been found guilty of several fraud-related offences committed to the detriment of the European Parliament's budget. The court case was triggered by an OLAF investigation carried out in 2010, which focused on the expenditure of a part of Mr Mote's allowances for hiring parliamentary assistants through a specific service provider. The evidence showed the MEP diverted over three hundred and fifty thousand Euro into private accounts. The EU Parliament sanctioned the investigation and it was referred to police in the UK who discovered more payments arising from false and misleading documents. The court sentenced Mr Mote to five years in prison. Other investigations into UKIP MEPs including Farage have since started to gain pace.

I really wanted to explore the failings which allowed these situations to arise and OLAF kindly provided me with more information about their structure and powers. The unit fulfils its mission, they told me, by carrying out independent investigations into fraud and corruption involving EU funds, so as to ensure that all "EU taxpayers' money reaches projects that can create jobs and growth in Europe; contributing to strengthening citizens' trust in the EU Institutions by investigating serious misconduct by EU staff and members of the EU Institutions; and developing a sound EU anti-fraud policy." OLAF can investigate matters relating to fraud, corruption and other offences affecting the EU financial interests concerning all EU expenditure, as well as some areas of EU revenue, mainly customs duties. Based in Brussels, OLAF has roughly four hundred staff members, more than three hundred of whom are working as either investigators or selectors or in investigation support (forensics, legal services, etc.) The team have diverse backgrounds – some having worked for national police or customs authorities, or as lawyers or judges. The Director-General of OLAF is Mr Giovanni Kessler and the unit is fully independent in its investigative mandate from any other EU or national institution, body or authority. It neither seeks nor receives instructions from any party and, while this is good, the structural defect of it is obvious. OLAF is not, however, a prosecuting body, it only carries out administrative investigations and, when relevant, OLAF sends the information gathered in its investigations (final case reports) to the competent national authorities for their consideration and possible follow-up. This means local agencies can choose not to take action.

The unit can recommend financial, judicial, disciplinary and administrative action to those local authorities where it finds a misappropriation or wrongful retention of EU funds or an illegal diminution of the EU revenues. In such a case OLAF will recommend to the competent authority at EU and/or Member State level to recover the money or prevent the money from being unduly spent. Where they uncover a possible criminal offence in a Member State, OLAF will recommend consideration of judicial follow-up by the authorities in that state. Where they only find a possible disciplinary offence, the unit can recommend consideration of action by the EU Institution, body or agency concerned. Additionally, where they discover a weakness in the management or control systems or in the legal framework, OLAF may recommend that action should be taken by the competent EU Institution, body, office or agency, or authority of the Member State. This latter happened, causing a huge change across the EU for the better just as Britain was stepping away.

Investigating Le Pen had clarified the picture that the Russian-sponsored far right was united in its focus on the destabilisation of the European Union and, in the face of limited capabilities and responses from the authorities, was capitalising on exploiting its advantage over the electorates through underhand financial and political means. Through pushing the rules to the very limits, as Banks described. Accusations of European interference in the UK's snap general election, bizarrely made by UK Prime Minister Theresa May, were subsequently alarming in the face of clear evidence to the contrary. At the time I felt it was indicative of either a wilful blindness, an abject failure by our domestic security services, or something more sinister – May was either doing the same or was in on the gag. Donald Tusk, President of the European Council responded, calling for moderation by May, saying: "The stakes are too high to let our emotions get out of hand because at stake are the daily lives and interests of millions of people on both sides of the Channel." I agreed with him.

The final round of France's campaign took place on Sunday the 7th of May 2017 and the result may have changed the world forever. Macron won despite a huge, if somewhat predictable, leak of emails. In the wake of his election, the EU and NATO started to change gear straight away, and Russia was called out as an enemy within weeks, along with the UK and US.

Le Pen was formally charged with misspending on her staff in June 2017.

THIRTEEN:

It was only weeks since Sweden but, sitting back, I knew the far-right had aligned internationally, working in a complex network to undermine democracy and the stability of western powers. Collaborating across multiple fronts, they were deploying state of the art techniques to hack data, emotionally control electorates, and spread disinformation. Over a period of years, they had gained control of political discourse and, subsequently, beneficial economic outputs through an almost indecipherable maze of personal and company connections. Seeing it all come together was like watching a slow motion car crash and the situation was exacerbated by a dawning realisation all of this raised more questions than it answered, especially when the changing face of terrorism was considered. The greatest unanswered question which leapt out at me was: has this global operation also played an active role in terror attacks aimed at the democracies they are targeting? There is still no firm answer, but the red flags were up, even as I first pondered the darkness of it.

In 2000, almost all terror attacks across the world involved the use of bombs. Non-complex, explosive devices. And, between 2006 and 2013 the number of terrorist attacks across Europe dropped significantly, including in the highest volume category – separatist violence. During the same time period, the number of arrests increased, as countries introduced updated surveillance and counter-terrorism strategies. The largest increase in arrests related to religious terrorism offences, though there was a disproportionately large increase in this group when contrasted against the other categories of terror. I suppose I may always wonder if this is connected to the same theory Manne

Gerell raised with me – about implicit bias and the new underclass – but that's a question for greater minds.

While there was clearly an argument to be made that efforts of the authorities and the airline industry restrictions on liquids had an impact in reducing bombings, the fact remains bomb-making materials are still broadly available across Europe. As my investigation found in Sweden, ex-military explosive stock is readily accessible and in active use, and the Brussels bombing underlined the point. 2015, however, saw a significant shift in the style of attack – the method turning to the use of vehicles to mow down pedestrians. When you start to probe these new attacks, set in the context of the development of a global operation which psychologically targets people to drive its own agenda with an extensive disinformation network (which has also claimed to be ISIS in cyber-attacks) the significant change in the terror pattern takes on a different tone. This can also be held up to scrutiny against the quick responses of Alt-Right media sites – and even Donald Trump – who have presumptively claimed incidents as being terrorism often within minutes of the attacks taking place, all of whom use the events to drive their own viral messages through their complex channels. These narratives have been exploited to the advantage of far-right political parties, often during active campaigns, and many of those parties, I'd established, were clearly linked to Russian destabilisation operations.

The lesser known of the vehicle enabled incidents took place in Nantes on the 22nd of December 2014 following another in Dijon, the day before.

Three days before Christmas in 2014, Sébastien Sarron ran over pedestrians at the Christmas market in the French city of Nantes using a van, then attempted suicide with a knife. Ten people, including the suspect himself, suffered non-fatal injuries and one person died. French Interior Minister, Bernard Cazeneuve, went on record to say the attacker was unbalanced.

While there were some reports circulating at first which claimed Sarron had shouted "Allahu Akbar," police swiftly stated a notebook in his van contained "incoherent suicidal phrases" and set out his fears of "being murdered by the secret services." Sarron was an alcoholic French farmer, drunk at the time of the attack, and committed suicide in his prison cell in April 2016.

In Dijon, the day before, another man was arrested after a vehicle-ramming attack, driving into pedestrians in five areas of the city within the space of half an hour. Two people were seriously injured. The forty-year-old driver was known to the police for minor offences, committed over the course of twenty years, and had repeatedly been treated for: "Serious and long-established psychiatric issues." The local prosecutor said the incident was not linked to terrorism. The New York Times reported speaking to the city prosecutor in the aftermath, who said the driver had become "very agitated" at home after watching a television program about the plight of children in Chechnya."

The next attack took place on Bastille Day, the 14th of July 2016, in Nice. French investigators identified the perpetrator – killed during the incident – as Mohamed Lahouaiej-Bouhlel, a thirty-one-year-old man of Tunisian nationality. Originally born in the North African country, he held a French residency permit and lived in Nice where he married his French-Tunisian cousin, with whom he had three children. His parents continued to live in Tunisia and stated after the attack they rarely heard from him since the move to France in 2005. Lahouaiej-Bouhlel's father told investigators and reporters the attacker underwent some psychiatric treatment before he moved to Nice and, according to his wife's lawyer, was repeatedly reported for domestic violence. Looking briefly into his background, he was known to French police for five criminal offences including threatening behaviour, violence, and petty theft. François Molins, the prosecutor leading the inquiry into the possible involvement of organised terrorism linked to Islam, has publicly made clear there was no link to the religion, except in a very short period before the attack. Discussing the motives, he referred to the deceased suspect as: "A young man completely uninvolved in religious issues and not a practising Muslim, who ate pork, drank alcohol, took drugs and had an unbridled sex life."

There is another oddity in this case in that, while Lahouaiej-Bouhlel regularly sent small sums of money to his family in Tunisia, only days before the attack he persuaded friends to smuggle bundles of cash worth around one-hundred thousand Euro to his relatives. The whole attack, in truth, does not feel right and I had a horrible intuition, even at the time, he had been paid to commit the atrocity – I remember calling a good friend, also an ex-cop, and talking it through in this really uncomfortable *so who was it then?* way. We had almost the same conversation nearly two years later when Andrei Karlov, Russian Ambassador to Turkey, was assassinated by Mevlüt Mert Altıntaş, an off-duty Turkish police officer. The killing took place at an art exhibition in Ankara, Turkey on the evening of the 19th of December, following several days of protests over the Russian involvement in Syria and Aleppo.

Reacting to the assassination, Trump accused the trigger man of being "a radical Islamic terrorist," while the Russian Duma responded by saying: "The culprits in this monstrous provocation, both the executors and those who guided the terrorist's hand by instigating Russophobia, ethnic, religious and confessional hatred, extremism and fanaticism, must face their deserved punishment." In addition, Turkey's despotic President Erdoğan responded with a video message in which he said "Turkey-Russia relations are vital for the region and those who aimed to harm ties were not going to achieve their goals." The Turkish Foreign Ministry also made clear they were not prepared to let "this attack cast a shadow on the Turkish-Russian friendship."

Islamic State groups, who have repeatedly shown they will claim almost any attack in their name to spread their message, have never taken responsibility for the murder.

I suppose what set the alarm bells ringing in my head, though it made much more sense in the wake of what I started investigating in Sweden, was the moment Vladimir Zhirinovsky, leader of the right-wing nationalist Liberal Democratic Party of Russia, started making claims the killing was: "A false flag operation by the West." Frantz Klintsevich, the deputy chairman of the Russian Defence and Security Committee, also reportedly said the assassination of Karlov was a "true provocation," adding: "It was a planned action. Everyone knew that he was going to attend this photo exhibition. It can be Isis or the Kurdish army which tries to hurt Erdogan. But maybe – and it is highly likely – that representatives of foreign Nato secrets services are behind it." Klintsevich was the person who previously promised a "harsh and unambiguous" response to any planned expansion of NATO membership, and said Russia would "aim our weapons, including the nuclear ones" at any countries seeking to join the alliance. This was rather pointedly aimed at Montenegro, who finally joined NATO in May 2017, but that membership finally came in the wake of a Russian assassination attempt on the country's Prime Minister.

Two Russian intelligence officers spent months overseeing the recruitment and equipping of a small force of Serbian nationalists to attack the Montenegro parliament building, disguised as local police, and kill Milo Djukanovic. The plot was only foiled hours before it was due to take place and Nemanja Ristic, one of the plotters wanted by the authorities, had been photographed not long before the incident standing next to Sergei Lavrov, Russia's foreign minister. When the sensational allegations were made public, with the full support of the UK security services, Lavrov was simultaneously making a speech criticising NATO as a "Cold War institution," saying it was the expansion of Western unity which had been the cause of instability across Europe over the last thirty years. I must confess, I didn't know much about Lavrov at the time, but I kept his name on file, just in case. As things developed, I'm glad I did.

Looking back over all this a few years down the line, knowing the breadth of the international disinformation network and who it was working for, what happened in the immediate aftermath of the Nice terror attack made more rational sense. Social media was virally attacked with false claims of hostage situations, a double attack – with some accounts showing images of the Eiffel Tower exploding – and claims of a further attack in Cannes. This was accompanied by almost endless images of wholly unrelated persons being named as missing persons, victims, and suspects. Marine Le Pen came out almost straight away too, condemning immigration and government policy in response to the attacks, attracting a lot more voter interest than usual due to the artificially amplified public mood.

On the 19th of December 2016, another truck was deliberately driven into a Christmas market, this time at Breitscheidplatz in Berlin, leaving 12 people dead and 56 others injured. The truck's original driver, Łukasz Urban, was found shot dead in the passenger seat. The suspect, Anis Amri – a failed asylum seeker from Tunisia – was killed in a shootout with police near Milan four days later.

Amri fled from Tunisia to escape imprisonment for stealing a truck and arrived for the first time in Europe in 2011 on a refugee raft at the island of Lampedusa. According to reports he lied about his age, pretending to be a minor, and was sent to the temporary migrant reception facility on the island where, according to Italian security officials, he took part in a particularly violent riot, when the centre was set on fire and several people were injured. He was subsequently imprisoned for four years for this and a robbery offence. In Tunisia, Amri was also sentenced in absentia to five years in prison, reportedly for aggravated theft with violence and his record stated he had been arrested several times for possession and use of drugs. According to his family, he drank alcohol, took drugs and was never really religious. Amri was released in 2015 and it is believed he went to Germany at this point, where he was involved in a bar brawl, drug dealing, and an eventual knife attack over drugs in July 2016. He disappeared after police tried to question him. After he was shot dead in Milan, his autopsy found that he frequently consumed drugs.

While it is on record that Moroccan intelligence warned Germany about a potential attack planned by Amri and the domestic security services did monitor him in Berlin, he showed no signs of planning a terrorist event according to official reports submitted to the German Interior Minister. As a result, national and international right-wing politicians and commentators drove a narrative which blamed the attack on the German Chancellor, Angela Merkel and her policy of accepting an "unlimited" number of asylum seekers and migrants. These groups also condemned the lack of border checks under the EU's Schengen system for allowing the perpetrator to travel freely through several countries after the attack. In essence, this was the same pattern I saw in Sweden and, only days before I travelled there to investigate crime and immigration, that hijacked truck was deliberately driven into crowds along Drottninggatan in Stockholm on the 7th of April 2017.

The suspect, thirty-nine-year-old rejected asylum seeker Rakhmat Akilov from Uzbekistan, was apprehended the same day and admitted carrying out the attack at a pre-trial hearing on the 11th of April. Investigating the incident, Säpo (the Swedish intelligence service) have publicly stated they had received a limited amount of information on the suspect but were unable to confirm it when they followed up on the lead. Due to this, they reportedly deemed him only a "marginal figure," on the fringes of extremist groups.

Akilov arrived in Sweden on the 10th of October 2014 and claimed asylum, saying he needed refuge from "the Uzbek security services which he claims tortured him and accused him of terrorism and treason." Uzbekistan remains closely tied to Russia – it was a Soviet socialist republic for almost seventy years until 1991 and both countries have had diplomatic relations since 1992. During the early years of independence, Uzbekistan stayed within the Ruble zone, not leaving until the winter of 1993 but, ten years later, Gazprom took over control of the Uzbek pipeline network, tying the countries together financially once again. In the same year, 2003, Uzbekistan started exporting gas to a recovering Russian Federation. After the annexation of Crimea in 2014, separatist tensions began to rise but this was somewhat appeased when Russia forgave nearly all of the Uzbek debt to boost relations between the two countries. When Sweden's Migration Board ruled against Akilov's application and he was ordered to leave the country within four weeks, he failed to do so voluntarily and did not appear at the Swedish Migration Agency when called. Due to this, his case was referred to police but he went on the run. The subsequent investigation into Akilov found he was registered at the same address as others with links to fraud and other offences. A number of people living at the property were convicted of false accounting and severe tax crimes. He was also linked to Chechnya and a Facebook group which aimed to expose the "terrorism of the imperialistic financial capitals."

The Swedish far-right was accused of trying to profit from the Stockholm attack, much in the same way as Le Pen, and were caught by the Swedish press producing fake news and circulating fake quotations online. The disinformation included tweets and social media posts from serving officials within the Sweden Democrats.

Among all of the suspects, from France to Germany, to Sweden, the common points were easy to identify: criminal offending histories, limited or no links to terrorism – even under surveillance – and mental health issues. In two cases, there were links to suspicious finances and two direct links to Chechnya. Looking at it in this way, having purposefully avoided the limited references to Islamic State, it was much easier to distill the facts as they really are. Something was not right, off, and it went beyond simple extremism or radicalisation. With almost all the suspects killed before questioning and almost every single connected person arrested released without charge, the evidential links to religious terrorism are almost entirely reliant on internet searches and social media, distorted by disinformation. It was this which set me wondering about something else: with so many people now radicalised online, could we even be sure who was responsible?

In respect of the promotion of extremism and conversion to radicalised ideology online, some claims of responsibility for Islamic State attacks and other activity reported to have been the work of ISIS have already been traced back to the Kremlin-linked hacking group APT28. In April 2015, France's TV5 Monde network was knocked off the air for around eighteen hours in the aftermath of a cyberattack which also led to the hijack of the agency's website and Facebook page. The hackers, who identified themselves as the "Cyber Caliphate," also leaked documents they claimed were the identification cards of French soldiers involved in anti-ISIS operations. Initially, the hack was attributed to sophisticated online operatives ideologically aligned to the Islamic State. However, French investigators later announced the attack was carried out by Russian hackers. Sources close to both the investigation and TV5 Monde's president also told France 24 "the finger of blame" pointed at the Russian state, confirming a report by L'Express. This conclusion was further supported by the findings of security vendors FireEye and Trend Micro.

FireEye's security experts said: "The website which published leaked information was hosted on the same IP block as other APT28 infrastructure and used the same name server and registrar that FireEye has seen APT28 use in the past." According to the cyber security experts, the computer malware and scripts featured in the attack were typed on a Cyrillic keyboard and timestamps showed the code was compiled, during office hours, in Moscow and St. Petersburg. The threats against the families of French soldiers serving overseas and other jihadist propaganda also contained numerous grammatical mistakes, echoing the story which surrounds Guccifer and the DNC leaks. The Russian hacking group, the reports said, also "targeted the computer systems of Nato members, Russian dissidents and Ukrainian activists."

President of FireEye, Richard Turner, said: "What we already suspect is that the group is sponsored by the Kremlin. We now also believe that ISIS was a decoy and APT28 was actually responsible for the attack on TV5 Monde. Russia has a long history of using information operations to sow disinformation and discord, and to confuse the situation in a way that could benefit them."

"The ISIS cyber caliphate could be a distraction tactic. This could be a touch run to see if they could pull off a coordinated attack on a media outlet that resulted in stopping broadcast and news dissemination. We have been watching APT28's infrastructure very closely and have seen them target other journalists around the same time as the TV5 Monde attack," he added.

Though the thought was deeply unnerving, if state-sponsored actors could hack under this guise for this purpose, it was a credible threat that they may be hosting and managing false Islamic State radicalisation operations too. This changes the meaning of terrorism as we have known it for several years and, combined with the clear advantage certain parties were exploiting in the wake of events, tends to provoke the taking of a more critical view of all these incidents. There can be no exception to this, even in the United Kingdom.

On the 22nd of March 2017, a terrorist attack took place in Westminster. The attacker – fifty-two-year-old Briton Khalid Masood – drove a car into pedestrians on the pavement along the south side of Westminster Bridge and Bridge Street, injuring more than fifty people and killing six. After the car crashed into the perimeter fence of Parliament grounds, Masood abandoned it and ran to New Palace Yard where he fatally stabbed and killed a police officer. He was then shot by another armed officer and died at the scene. Though the attack was instantly attributed to Islamic terrorism by right-wing figures and media outlets across the world, police have found no link with any terrorist organisation.

Born Adrian Russell Elms, the deceased suspect later changed his name to Adrian Russell Ajao, then to Khalid Masood after he converted to Islam. Police said he also used several other aliases, including Khalid Choudry. He dropped out of school at sixteen and by eighteen was described as a heavy cocaine user. In 2000, he was sentenced to two years in prison for grievous bodily harm after a knife attack in a public house, which took place in Northam in Sussex. He was sentenced to a further six months in prison in 2003 for possession of an offensive weapon following another knife attack in Eastbourne. As well as these two prison terms, Masood had convictions for public order offences going back to 1983. His background matched the French and German suspects and his profile was otherwise atypical, as most jihadi terrorists are under thirty while he was over fifty.

While an ISIS-linked news network reported that Islamic State did celebrate the attack as their own, analysts monitoring their activity online said claims of responsibility appeared to be part of a broader effort to mask losses in Iraq and Syria, and specifically cited: "The lack of biographical information on the attacker and lack of specifics about the attack suggested it was not directly involved." Government and security services in the UK agreed. Towards the conclusion of the initial investigation, Neil Basu, Deputy Assistant Commissioner of the Metropolitan Police and Senior National Coordinator for UK Counter-Terrorism Policing, announced investigators believed Masood acted alone, adding: "There is a possibility we will never understand why he did this."

Westminster clearly fitted the obvious exception pattern of the other events and is the only attack, with the exception of the Turkey assassination, which had any direct connections to a political target. All of these incidents have, however, helped drive the disinformation narrative, feeding right-wing politicians and false reports such as those which led me to Sweden in the first place, the very same investigation which exposed the previously missing links in the chain which definitively connect Russia and the far-right. The change in the pattern of terror incidents and the surrounding information suggested something very drastic had changed not just in the method, but in the suspects too: petty criminals, drug users, often with mental health issues and who could not be directly linked to terrorism. I found myself asking again and again if there was something else to it.

False flags have been broadly admitted in the past – actions used to justify another end – and large payments of cash, such as those made in Nice, are not associated with the acts of radicals. In fact, and more to the point, Da'esh has been losing financial ground for years. By February 2017, Alessandro Pansa, Director General of the Department of Information Security for the Italian Council of Ministers, publicly announced: "ISIS has significantly retreated. Its sources of revenue, primarily smuggling oil products and antiquities, are at the edge of drying out." Russia, however, which appeared to be at the heart of everything else we were witnessing, was no stranger to deploying black operations tactics. Together with the Dagestan military offensive, it was a false-flag bombing which led the Russian Federation into the Second Chechen War.

In September 1999, Russia saw apartment bombings which killed almost three hundred people and injured more than one thousand. Explosions happened at Buynaksk on the 4th of September, Moscow on the 9th and 13th and Volgodonsk on the 16th. An explosive device similar to those used in these bombings was also found and defused in an apartment block in the Russian city of Ryazan a week later. On the day after the last devices were found, Vladimir Putin ordered the air bombing of Grozny, which marked the beginning of the Chechen offensives.

According to the Moscow City Court, the bombings were acts of terrorism organised and financed by the leaders of the armed group, the Caucasus Islamic Institute, yet thirty-six hours after this announcement, three FSB agents were arrested by the local police for planting the Ryazan explosives. The incident was, however, officially declared to have been a training exercise and the agents were released on Moscow's orders.

Prominent figures Yury Felshtinsky, Alexander Litvinenko, Boris Berezovsky, David Satter, Boris Kagarlitsky, Vladimir Pribylovsky, and even the secessionist Chechen authorities have always maintained claims the 1999 bombings were a false flag attack, coordinated by the FSB in order to win public support for a new full-scale war in Chechnya – a move which boosted the popularity of former FSB director

Putin. The pro-war Unity Party succeeded in the subsequent elections to the State Duma and helped Putin attain the presidency within a few months. The MP Yuri Shchekochikhin filed two motions for a parliamentary investigation of the events, which were rejected and a public commission to investigate the bombings was rendered ineffective by the government's refusal to respond to its inquiries. Notably, two key members of the Kovalev Commission, Sergei Yushenkov and Shchekochikhin, have since died in apparent assassinations and Litvinenko's death is probably the most famous execution of a spy in history – he was poisoned with radioactive material in London. The British public inquiry concluded the FSB killed him, and "probably" did so on the direct orders of Putin himself.

Nervously drumming my desk, I found myself thinking it was entirely possible the changed face of terror in Europe was the darker side of the global destabilisation operation I'd been sticking my nose into, this hybrid offensive. In many ways, it made sense, not least because the public reactions helped the disinformation and far-right narratives become more mainstream and embedded in national politics and media reporting. Russia was obviously no stranger to false-flags to achieve its goals, the apartment bombings showed that but, once I started looking, the darkness began to layer. For example, Ukraine took Russia to the International Courts of Justice in The Hague for a face-off in March 2017, having lodged a forty-five-page indictment in the same January. The Ukrainian government was asking the United Nations' highest court to fine Russia for "intervening militarily in Ukraine, financing acts of terrorism, and violating the human rights of millions of Ukraine's citizens." The indictment accused Russia of violations of the International Convention for the Suppression of the Financing of Terrorism 1999 by: "Supplying money, weapons, training, and other support to separatists in the self-proclaimed Donetsk and Luhansk People's Republics in eastern Ukraine," and demanded compensation for "terrorist acts committed on its territory, including the shelling of civilian areas and the shoot down of Malaysian Airlines flight MH17."

Olena Zerkal, one of the deputy foreign ministers of Ukraine told the court: "Russian Federation tactics include support for terrorism and acts of racial discrimination, as well as propaganda, subversion, intimidation, political corruption and cyberattacks."

Malaysia Airlines Flight 17 (MH17) was travelling from Amsterdam to Kuala Lumpur when it was shot down over eastern Ukraine on July 17th 2014, killing almost three hundred people on board. The Dutch-led team of detectives from Australia, Belgium, Malaysia and Ukraine, who spent more than two years investigating the incident, presented their initial findings in September 2016, saying that "audio intercepts, witness statements, and forensic evidence show the missile launcher, a Buk SA-11, arrived from Russia after separatists requested additional support against Ukrainian airstrikes." According to a report by the Telegraph, they added that "it fired the missile that brought down MH17 from a field about ten miles south-east of the crash site on the afternoon of July 17 before returning across the border next day."

Wilbert Paulissen, head of the Central Crime Investigation department of the Dutch National Police, told reporters: "MH17 was shot down by a 9M38 missile launched by a Buk, brought in from the territory of the Russian Federation, and that after launch was subsequently returned to the Russian Federation." Some witnesses also submitted evidence to the investigation claiming the weapon was, in fact, supplied and crewed by the Russian army's 53rd Air Defence Brigade, which was stationed in Kursk.

Responding to the report on behalf of Russia, Maria Zakharova, a spokeswoman for the Russian Foreign

Ministry, said: "The Dutch Prosecutor's findings confirm that the investigation is biased and politically motivated."

The further I looked into the links between Russia and terrorism, the worse the picture got, and then I discovered Russian security services had been sending its own extremists to Syria to fight with the Islamic State, in a state-sanctioned effort which started in 2012.

Initially an exercise which appears to have been designed to minimise domestic terror attacks around the winter Olympics, by December 2015 almost three thousand Russians had left the country to join wars in the Middle East. Alexander Bortnikov, director of the FSB, confirmed this during a meeting of the National Anti-Terrorist Committee and official data appears to show more than ninety percent left Russia after the summer of 2013. One senior analyst for International Crisis Group, an independent body aimed at resolving conflicts, Ekaterina Sokiryanskaya, told Reuters reporters that "Russian is the third language in the Islamic State after Arabic and English. Russia is one of its important suppliers of foreign fighters."

The news agency had been investigating the situation and found several people willing to come forward. One had been a wanted man in Russia, a member of an outlawed Islamist group, hiding in the forests of the North Caucasus, dodging patrols by paramilitary police and "plotting a holy war against Moscow." In December 2012 the FSB found him and said if he agreed to leave Russia, the authorities would not arrest him and would facilitate his departure. "A few months later, he was given a new passport in a new name, and a one-way plane ticket to Istanbul" Reuters wrote, adding: "Shortly after arriving in Turkey, he crossed into Syria and joined an Islamist group that would later pledge allegiance to radical Sunni group Islamic State."

While the FSB declined to comment on the investigation, Dmitry Peskov, speaking on behalf of

Putin, told reporters: "Russian authorities have never cooperated or interacted with terrorists. No interaction with terrorists was possible. Terrorists get annihilated in Russia. It has always been like that, it is like that and it will be in the future."

While there was not decisive or definitive evidence available and there is still a long road for the world to travel in that respect, I realised we were already facing a very credible question. What if the Islamic State, as it's currently understood, is only as real as the Cyber Caliphate? In part, it was this which inspired me to start looking beyond the borders of the European Union and the United States.

FOURTEEN:

Within the somewhat expansive structure of Arron Banks' complex business network, I discovered a rather plain looking diamond.

Parsons Jewellers in Bristol had been in the same family for generations when it hit trouble and was eventually bought by the man behind Leave.EU and Westmonster. In his autobiography, the same one which had proven useful time and time again as regards Russia, Banks outlined his desire to turn the outfit into a "brand."

According to the Parsons website, Banks sources his gems from a series of mines he owns in South Africa, under the company name Kophia Diamond, and is listed as a director alongside Jonathan Ian Banks and James Pryor. Jonathan has a law firm registered to Banks' primary offices in Bristol, and Pryor – ex-UKIP and a former Margaret Thatcher communications guru – is the same person connected to the other Banks linked company, Chartwell Political. While there was no website for the mining operation, Pryor's email address was listed as the contact address for any queries. Banks himself is further linked to the region by lobbying and mining companies unearthed in the Panama Papers and he spent part of his childhood in South Africa, but other contemporary evidence was not hard to come by. On the 25th of January 2015, ahead of the small state of Lesotho's last election, Leave.EU's Andy Wigmore and James Pryor were both present in the country, "burning the midnight election oil." Helpfully, Wigmore posted a photograph of them both – with that caption – on social media, along with pictures of him and Arron visiting mining operations at various points in time. At least one of Banks' mining operations is located in Lesotho, where early general elections were held in June 2017 following a no-confidence vote in the incumbent prime minister – who led in coalition after a military coup caused the 2012 election to fail and a snap election to be held in 2015. The political landscape was clearly complex and I wrote to Wigmore and Banks, asking how the coming election could affect their mining interests in Lesotho but there was no reply. While there was no indication as to exactly what involvement they had in the 2015 election campaign beyond the photograph, Wigmore, along with both Arron and Jonathan Banks and James Pryor, were pictured with the King of Lesotho on the 11th of June 2014, during an apparent trip to visit their mining facilities. Wigmore's Instagram in general shows he is no stranger to political celebrity – he can also be found pictured in the infamous gold lift at Trump Tower and with Lord Ashcroft, among others.

Banks, in his autobiography, describes Pryor as his "fixer in Africa" and states both Pryor and Wigmore worked together for the conservatives in the late 1980s. Banks goes on to say he bought not one but two mines in Lesotho and visits them periodically but makes clear Pryor is on hand there most of the time, to keep him updated. I also asked Wigmore and Banks what connections they have with the king but there was no reply.

Having a look back through online records, I saw Banks was shown in the Panama Papers as the director African Strategic Consulting Ltd ("lobbying"), African Strategic Resources Ltd ("mining"), and African Strategic Capital Ltd ("wealth management"). Of course, there was no indication of illegality in this structure but it did raise some questions so, I asked Wigmore and Banks what lobbying, if any, the consulting group had done. There was no reply so, I also started to look for clues elsewhere, revisiting Banks' other operations. On the Chartwell website, I found that Pryor listed his previous experience as including assistance to the Basothu National Party (BNP) in Lesotho, though it was not clear in which election. The party was facing accusations in advance of the 2017 campaign from incumbent Prime Minister, Pakalitha Mosisili, who said the BNP's founder, Lesotho Leabua Jonathan, was a "lackey of the British who turned a blind eye to his atrocities to undermine Lesotho's independence." He stated a vote for them would be tantamount to returning the country to the "dark era" of nationalist rule.

"Chief Leabua, supported by the English, was not ready to accept defeat," he said. "He declared a state of emergency and suspended the constitution instead. Basotho entered a dark era in which their basic human rights were violated. A lot of people were killed, while some Basotho were literally buried alive in places like Lipeketheng at Hlotse in Leribe district. Those were the acts of the nationalists."

"Last year, we celebrated 50 years of Lesotho's independence and we have now begun another journey. Like I said, we started the first journey on a wrong foot under a nationalist regime. We cannot afford to repeat that mistake by starting another 50-year journey under a government of nationalists," he added.

Chief Malapo of the modern BNP responded with a now internationally familiar, Trumpesque narrative, saying "Ntate Mosisili is a pathetic liar. He believes he can fool every Mosotho with his distorted information and propaganda." He may as well have said "fake news."

I asked Wigmore and Banks if there was any financial support given by donation to any of the Lesotho political parties in the 2017 race but there was no reply.

The BNP's history, I discovered, was colourful, fractious, and deeply tied to Russia. After trips to the People's Republic of China and the Eastern Bloc in May 1983, Basotho Prime Minister Leabua Jonathan announced that China and the Soviet Union would be establishing embassies in the kingdom. The South African government responded angrily to the announcement and reminded Jonathan of a promise he made in 1965 not to allow an embassy of any communist country in Lesotho so long as he was Prime Minister. Vincent Makhele, the Basotho Minister of Foreign Affairs, visited Moscow in September 1984 for discussions with officials in the Soviet government. In a sign of increased KGB presence in Lesotho, staffing levels in the embassy in Maseru were increased and in May 1985 the Soviets appointed their first resident ambassador to Lesotho. In December 1985, Makhele returned to Moscow and signed a cultural and scientific co-operation agreement (along with a technical and economic agreement) with the Soviets. These inroads in Lesotho suffered a setback when Jonathan was overthrown during January 1986, in a military coup which was led by Justin Lekhanya. As a result, the Russian embassy in Maseru was closed in August 1992 and the Russian Ambassador to South Africa has also been allocated to cover Lesotho since. The two countries have maintained a history of bilateral agreement, however. Predominantly with Russia providing scholarships, including to senior government officials. In the summer of 2014, around the time of Banks' group meeting with the king, Russia began to deliver humanitarian aid to Lesotho.

Lesotho's illegal mining operations are also an increasingly violent affair and, in March 2017, police arrested four people in connection with the massacre of fourteen illegal Basotho miners on Gauteng's East Rand. The bodies were found following other, unrelated shootings around illegal mine shafts near to Benoni, with six corpses found along the railway line and the rest on the banks of a stream nearby. Police believed this was a clear body dump and not where the killings took place. According to reports, the area had become the: "Epicentre of a battle between gangs for control of tonnes of precious metal in disused mine shafts." In a briefing, the national police commissioner, Lt-Gen Khomotso Phahlane, revealed that four men —

all of them Basotho nationals — had been arrested, three of them being caught on the run in Lesotho. "Several firearms, which we suspect may have been used in the killings, have been recovered with those who were arrested in Lesotho. We are working with our Interpol counterparts to have them brought back to South Africa along with the weapons," he said.

One witness to the murders anonymously told reporters: "Zimbabweans, Malawians and Mozambicans were digging and they came up through the hole during the early evening with their gold rocks. The Basotho were waiting for them. They were armed and ready to shoot. When they came out the hole, the Basotho shot them, stole their gold and dumped their bodies by the railways."

One 2017 joint report between the South African government and the United Nations estimated that "Turf wars between international crime syndicates are behind the deaths of more than two hundred illegal miners murdered in the killing fields of South Africa's mines over the past four years." It was released before the Benoni murders.

Ahead of the 2017 election, the Construction and Mine Workers Union accused diamond mines of coercing their workers into signing advance voters' applications in violation of their rights. They have lodged a joint call with the Transformation Resource Centre, asking the Independent Electoral Commission (IEC) to intervene and assure the miners were protected. In a strongly worded attack, they made plain it was a criminal offence to "force workers to provide the IEC false information about employment" or to "prohibit workers from voting" on Saturday the 3rd of June 2017. Tskioane Peshoane of the TRC accused the government of condoning the contravention of the electoral act by foreign companies. I asked Wigmore and Banks if they were aware of the Union's concerns, whether it affected their own operations, and if they had any concerns of their own. There was no reply.

Aside from mining – which includes, I discovered, the ownership of shares in a Niger uranium operation – and politics, Banks had also focused a lot of efforts on charity work in Lesotho, along with other projects. In 2013, a proposed microlending facility, was to be bankrolled by the British businessman to: "Enable Basotho women to diversify business interests and explore opportunities they could not pursue before" according to Thesele Maseribane, the Minister of Gender, Youth, Sports and Recreation. On signing the memorandum of understanding, Banks was apparently "committed to providing further funding to establish the financial institution behind the plans." At the time, Lesotho was implementing a three hundred and sixty-million-dollar contract signed between the country's Government and the United States Government through the Millennium Challenge Corporation – an independent US foreign aid agency which states it is: "Helping lead the fight against global poverty." Another of Banks's charities, Love Saves The Day, has been linked to suspected money laundering in Wigmore's native Belize.

As a foreign business opportunity with development funding flowing in and a host of measures taken by the government to make the country a more attractive investment prospect, it isn't hard to grasp Bank's broader interest in Lesotho, but how he got there might not be such a mystery.

I was talking to a contact about all this and the discussion of Lesotho reminded them of a conversation a friend once had over dinner with Pryor. The friend – a former broadsheet correspondent – went on to explain "Pryor effectively told me that they work on elections in dodgy places, sometimes taking on work passed on from Lynton Crosby that was considered too sensitive for Crosby." Sir Lynton Keith Crosby, to give him his full name and title, is an Australian political strategist who has managed election campaigns for right-of-centre parties in several countries. Crosby has been described as a "master of the dark political arts" and "The Wizard of Oz," and, in 2002, he was described as: "One of the most powerful and influential figures in the nation." His most famous tactic, for political clients losing arguments, has been dubbed *The Dead Cat Technique*, which involves throwing something so horrible at winning opponents everything up until that point is instantly forgotten. Theresa May employed Crosby's services in the snap election of 2017, in the middle of which not one but two terror attacks took place – one a bombing in Manchester and the second a vehicle enabled attack at London Bridge. May suffered heavy losses in the final vote, losing her majority, but was able to mitigate this to some degree as other parties suspended campaigning in the wake of both attacks during the short campaign.

With the Leave.EU crew running Lesotho campaigns and funding election activity in the UK at the same time – and having discovered the connection between them and May went beyond a "Conservative/UKIP" alliance logo on social media dark posts – I became certain more deceased felines were being kept on ice, ready to be thrown on the table.

FIFTEEN:

Faced with these undeniable connections between Trump, Brexit, Russia, and the far-right – including France's Marine Le Pen, I made a very personal decision to go all in and see how far I could get. It was already looking bleak, of course. Alongside Russia were the alt-right and a monstrous disinformation network – shady collaboration incorporating the deployment of Wikileaks, other hacking operations, and psychometrics company Cambridge Analytica. And all of them were engaged in ongoing interference with Western democracy. The extent of this murky, cloak and dagger operation was, however, becoming increasingly easy to root out.

On the 12th of January 2017, Arron Banks posted a picture of Andrew Wigmore in Mississippi. The caption read: "Andy over in the US this week with Gov. Bryant. & our good friends from Mississippi!" I knew this because an American researcher had contacted me via Twitter and set out some information which would have taken a lot longer to find otherwise. I call Wendy Siegelman the Queen of Charts, such is the quality of her work.

In April 2008, then Mississippi Governor Haley Barbour welcomed a delegation headed by Russian Federation Senator Mikhail Margelov and the US-Russia Business Council (USRBC) President Eugene Lawson to Jackson. USRBC is a trade association based in Washington, DC, which represents around three-hundred companies with operations in the Russian market. The Council's mission, it says, is to expand the US-Russian commercial relationship and lobby for an economic environment in which businesses can succeed in a "challenging Russian market." The council also provides "significant business development, dispute resolution, government relations, and market intelligence services." The membership is cartel-like, being made up of major interests such as Alfa-Bank, Boeing, Cargill, Citigroup, Coca-Cola, Ford, LUKOIL, Procter & Gamble, along with other well-known businesses, banks, law firms, and accountants. A career Foreign Service Officer, Daniel Russell was appointed CEO in 2013. He had served as Deputy Assistant Secretary of State responsible for relations with Russia, Ukraine, Moldova, and Belarus and for international security and arms control issues in the US State Department's Bureau of European and Eurasian Affairs. He also held the role of Chief of Staff to the Under Secretary of State for Political Affairs, William Burns, from 2008 to 2009; as Deputy Chief of Mission in Moscow from 2005 to 2008; and as Deputy Chief of Mission in Almaty, Kazakhstan, from 2000 to 2003. With a CV like that, it was far from a flight of fancy to believe Russell may have been a spy.

At the time the delegation visited Barbour, a Russian investment by SeverCorr was in its first phase in the state and had brought four-hundred-and-fifty high-paying new jobs to Mississippi. The salaries were nearly ninety thousand dollars on average, compared to the state's median income of under forty thousand, according to reports. Mississippi listed over five billion dollars of exports in 2007 and the state's exportation to Russia alone grew fifty-two percent between 2004 and 2007. Over that period, many of the sectors the state government had been targeting for growth benefitted from the increase – for example, non-traditional Mississippi exports of computers and electronic products skyrocketed by more than five-thousand percent and Governor Barbour made a public statement that Mississippi looked "forward to a long and thriving relationship with Russia."

At a delegation luncheon sponsored by SeverCorr, said to have been arranged to "enable state business leaders to take a closer look at Russia economically and politically," USRBC's President, Eugene Lawson, underscored the idea SeverCorr's investment in Mississippi should send a signal to other Russian companies – and the Russian government – that the US was open to (and welcomed) foreign investment. As Lawson pointed out, not one Russian investment in the US had been turned down by the US foreign investment review process, which is conducted by the Committee on Foreign Investment in the United States (CFIUS). Senator Margelov, meanwhile, emphasised the importance of mutual cooperation in his own remarks, suggesting the two countries put aside the "negative rhetoric". which had emerged in Duma elections and that year's US presidential campaign which saw Barack Obama enter the White House, ousting the Republicans. Margelov suggested the US needed to take advantage of "a new generation coming of age in Russia that is not bound by Cold War stereotypes." He also asserted: "Today's global realities demand pragmatism and an "equal partnership" between the US and Russia."

Margelov had worked as an interpreter in the International Department of the Central Committee of the Communist Party of the Soviet Union. He also taught Arabic at the Higher School of the K.G.B and was Senior Editor in the Arab section of the TASS News Agency. He was a spy. Between 1990 and 1995, he was employed by a number of US consulting companies dealing with investment projects and, in 1995, became project director for the publicity campaign of Grigory Yavlinsky and the Yabloko party. In 1996, he was the chief co-ordinator for advertising in President Boris Yeltsin's re-election campaign, after which he went on to head the President's public relations department and was later a director of the Russian Information Centre (Rosinformcentr), a government agency covering events in the Northern Caucasus. From May 1998 to September 1999, he held a managerial position at RIA Novosti news agency, then spent January to March 2000 as a consultant to Vladimir Putin's Electoral

Headquarters, in charge of contacts with foreign media. In 2009 Canada refused an entry visa for Margelov, by then the Kremlin's special representative to Africa. The reason, according to Canadian sources, was Margelov's connection to the Soviet intelligence services.

The Mississippi delegation also enjoyed private discussions with both Governor Barbour and his deputy, Phil Bryant. Parties from the USRBC attended a dinner at Barbour's private residence and Phil Bryant, then the Lieutenant Governor, hosted a private dinner at his home too.

Hayley Barbour, I discovered, had founded a lobbying company called BGR Group in 1991. In 2013, the firm was paid almost fourteen million dollars and its three largest clients were the Republic of India, Ukraine Chevron Corporation, and the State of Kazakhstan. In April 2015, the Government of South Korea retained BGR for public relations and image building. The firm also employed various former political figures.

Barbour was the governor of Mississippi between 2004 and 2012, having previously served under Ronald Reagan before becoming head of the Republican National Committee for a number of years. During his stint as governor, his BGR monies were held in a blind trust arrangement but this arrangement had always attracted media coverage. His filings with the Mississippi Ethics Commission showed continued payments from BGR and withdrawals from the trust which had a market value of nearly three-and-a-half million dollars according to its trustee, the president of the Bank of Yazoo City, Griffin Norquist. Correspondence between Barbour and the trustee from 2008 and 2009 – filed with the Ethics Commission – show Barbour pulling nearly two hundred grand out of the trust in 2008, seventy-five thousand dollars of it for an income tax payment, and over two hundred and fifty thousand out in 2009 with an unspecified portion of it being for taxes. His state salary was listed at just over one hundred and twenty-two thousand dollars a year, so the tax designations of these withdrawals indicate a significant second income which no one knew about. According to Norquist, as of December the 31st 2008, the aggregate market value of assets in the trust was almost three and a half million dollars.

BGR Group represented Alfa Bank, one of the USRBC members, from at least 2004 until 2015, during the period Barbour was holding the public office of governor. Lobbying Disclosure Act papers which I found on the internet – a much better system than the UK's absolute refusal to discuss lobbying except during scandals – show BGR received almost six million dollars from the Moscow bank over the period, for lobbying activity related to "Bilateral US-Russian Relations." The people behind the Russian financial organisation are very closely linked to Vladimir Putin according to the infamous assessment of Christopher Steele, a former British spy.

Alfa-Bank is one of the largest private financial houses in Russia as regards total assets, total equity, customer accounts, and loan portfolio. Under International Accounting Standards, in December 2014, the assets of Alfa Banking Group — which comprises Alfa-Bank as well as subsidiary banks and financial companies — totalled over forty-three billion dollars. By the end of 2014, Alfa-Bank served over one-hundred-and-sixty thousand corporate customers and over eleven million private individuals. Alfa-Bank has over eight-hundred branches in Russia and abroad, including a subsidiary bank in the Netherlands, as well as financial subsidiaries in the United States, United Kingdom, and Cyprus. According to the bank's website, in February 2014, Putin held a meeting with one of its owners, Petr Aven, at his residence in Novo-Ogarevo. Putin and Aven discussed the: "Situation in the banking sector and current performance of the bank." Aven also sits on the Board of Directors at LetterOne Group – also known as L1 Group, established in 2013 to invest in international projects in energy, telecommunications and technology. L1 acquired assets from German utility business E.ON in October 2015, in a deal worth over one-and-a-half billion dollars, which saw the Luxembourg-based group gain Norwegian oil and gas resources. The group also had significant interests in BP and the North Sea. By 2015, Aven was named as one of the richest people in the world, with a personal worth of around five billion dollars. The group made fourteen billion dollars alone from selling TNK-BP to Rosneft in 2013 and bought up student housing in the UK and shares in Uber before assessing additional investments.

In May 2017, Aven and his fellow Alfa Bank owners, Mikhail Fridman and German Khan, filed a defamation lawsuit against BuzzFeed for publishing the unedited and unverified Trump–Russia dossier of Steele, which alleged financial ties and collusion between Putin, Trump, and the three bank owners. However, Alfa Bank also came to the notice of the media and the FBI when computer experts found its servers communicating with the Trump organisation before Donald was elected. A detailed analysis showed a series of DNS lookups between the Alfa Bank server in Moscow and a server owned by the Trump organisation, described as being set up in a peculiar fashion – it designed only to accept communications from a small number of other unique IP addresses. A private channel, in other words. From May the 4th until September the 23rd 2016, the Russian bank looked up the address to the Trump corporate server almost three thousand times – this was more traffic than from any other source. In fact, Alfa Bank alone represented eighty percent of the lookups. Indiana University computer scientist, L. Jean Camp, told reporters: "The conversation between the Trump and Alfa servers appeared to follow the contours of political happenings in the United States. At election-related moments, the traffic peaked."

"There were considerably more DNS lookups, for instance, during the two conventions," Camp added.

According to CNN: "Publicly available internet records show that address, which was registered to the Trump organisation, points to an IP address that lives on an otherwise dull machine operated by a company in the tiny rural town of Lititz, Pennsylvania."

The Trump organisation claim it was a marketing server, however, Richard Clayton, a cybersecurity researcher at Cambridge University, commented on a series of objections to evidence of communication between the servers, saying "I think mail is more likely, because it's going to a machine running a mail server and [the host] is called mail." Others have also dismissed claims of the communication logs being faked to damage Trump due to an impossibility in recreating random traffic volume.

I did more research and found Listrak is the Lititz-based company. It is regularly hired to send emails on behalf of stores, hotels and other businesses. Apparently rapidly growing, the company sends more than two billion marketing emails a month to generate interest for its clients. Listrak Chief Executive Officer Ross Kramer told reporters the FBI came to the Listrak office before the November election and, though he declined to provide details on the FBI visit, he said "it was very cordial, and we've given them everything they need." Kramer added Listrak was retained by a Florida company, Cendyn, which specialises in marketing for the hospitality industry and was working on behalf of Trump hotels.

What I subsequently found really odd was a statement from Cendyn, which said: "A thorough network analysis conducted by Cendyn at the request of the Trump organisation determined an existing banking customer of Cendyn, completely unrelated to

Trump, recently used Cendyn's 'Metron' Meeting Management Application to send communication to AlfaBank.com." The explanation defied all logic, in particular when the second highest number of DNS hits coming from Alfa Bank was aimed at Spectrum Health, which belongs to the family of Trump team stalwart Betsy DeVos.

Devos issued a completely different denial, saying the lookups related to "Voice over IP traffic." To me, the pattern looked like a simplistic data transfer, with transmission periods from seconds to over an hour on a regular basis and a number of secretive, though benign, hackers have arrived at similar conclusions. One, for example, stated: "When Spectrum connected to Trump Tower, Trump Tower's next connect time was significantly longer, indicating Spectrum had modified a large chunk of records [which] had to be synced to Trump Tower, then pushed on to Alfa Bank. This detail was important in identifying that replication was in use. In this scenario, Trump Tower was functioning as a center-point, a data distribution center if you will."

Less covertly, Christopher Davis, who runs cybersecurity firm HYAS InfoSec, told reporters "I've never seen a server set up like that. It looked weird, and it didn't pass the sniff test." Davis won the prestigious FBI Director Award for Excellence after tracking down the authors of one of the world's nastiest botnet attacks. Another internet cyber-security pioneer, Paul Vixie, told Slate: "The parties were communicating in a secretive fashion. The operative word is secretive. This is more akin to what criminal syndicates do if they are putting together a project."

Then, four days after New York Times journalists started following the story, on September the 27th 2016, the original server, mail1.trump-email.com, was switched off and the Trump organisation created a new hostname, trump1.contact-client.com. This simply enabled communication to the very same Alfa server via a different route. The new server's first communication was, in fact, with Alfa Bank and experts have made clear "when a new hostname is created, the first communication with it is never random. To reach the server after the resetting of the host name, the sender of the first inbound mail has to first learn of the name somehow. It's simply impossible to randomly reach a renamed server."

This is where things started to come full circle from Mississippi to Russia, again. Jeffrey Birnbaum of Barbour's BGR rejected allegations of communication between Trump's team and the Russian bank, on behalf of Alfa, saying: "Neither Alfa Bank nor its principals, including Mikhail Fridman and Petr Aven, have or have had any contact with Mr. Trump or his organisations. The assertion of a special or private link is patently false." By the time I started to find all this out, the Sunday Times had called the Bank's parent company, Alfa Group, "one of the most controversial business empires on the planet."

Alfa Bank financed one of the companies involved in building Iran's Bushehr nuclear power plant, according to corporate documents and lobbying disclosure records. In the mid-2000s, according to its own public reports, Alfa Bank provided financing to Atomstroyexport, a state-controlled Russian company which was a major player in Iran's developing nuclear energy program. The relationship included "loans and other client services." At the time Birnbaum – of BGR – dismissed reports of Alfa having deeper links to Iran's nuclear ambitions as misguided, saying: "Just because Alfa Bank had a line of credit with an entity that did business with Iran does not make Alfa a financier of Iran's nuclear program." Communicating through BGR, the bank's CEO added that contact had ended "after 2008 U.N. sanctions." At the time, there was no problem with the plant from a US foreign policy perspective. In fact, during 2007, while Alfa was financing Atomstroyexport, Secretary of State Condoleezza Rice endorsed the plant as a proper component of Iran's civilian nuclear program and, in 2010, Hillary Clinton told the UN "Our problem is not with their reactor at Bushehr. Our problem is with their facilities at places like Natanz and their secret facility at Qom and other places where we believe they are conducting their weapons program."

Alfa's other owner, secretive oligarch Fridman, even freely enjoyed the privilege of visiting the White House twice, in May 2010 and again in May 2011. Each time, according to White House logs, Richard Burt, a former top diplomat who negotiated the 1991 START I nuclear treaty with the Soviet Union, accompanied him. According to Burt, Fridman's goal was "to strengthen ties between the United States and Russia and to discuss Russian ascension to the World Trade organisation."

Burt has longstanding connections with both BGR Group and Alfa. He was previously executive chairman of Diligence LLC, a corporate intelligence operation which employs former spies, and now holds an advisory role at Aven and Fridman's investment operation, Letter One.

In 2005, BGR and Diligence became ensnared in scandal when, working as a BGR contractor, it was alleged they attempted to obtain corporate records of an Alfa rival from the auditor KPMG. As a result, KPMG sued Diligence and the latter settled the case by paying KPMG over one-and-a-half million dollars. Another rival, IPOC Growth Fund, also sued Diligence and BGR Group in a case which was settled in 2008. Ed Rogers, BGR chairman, was an early owner of Diligence and, according to reports, the company was actually set up inside BGR's Pennsylvania Avenue office.

In the first two quarters of 2016, Burt's lobbying firm received over three hundred and fifty thousand dollars for work he and a colleague did to garner support for a proposed natural-gas pipeline opposed by the Polish government and the Obama administration. The Nord

Steam gas connection would have allowed more Russian gas to reach central and western European markets – bypassing Ukraine and Belarus and extending Putin's leverage over Europe. Burt's lobbying work for New European Pipeline AG began in February 2016 when Russian state-owned oil giant Gazprom still owned only a fifty percent stake in the company. In August, however, five European partners pulled out and Gazprom now owns one-hundred percent. The Swedes, of course, were specifically concerned about details of the discussions around Nordstream being relayed from the Riksdag to Russia when the property scandal involving the Sweden Democrats and Putilov erupted.

During the same period, Burt says he also helped shape Trump's first major foreign policy address, recommending the man who is now president take a "more realist, less interventionist approach to world affairs. In the subsequent speech, Trump said "I believe an easing of tensions and improved relations with Russia — from a position of strength — is possible," adding: "Common sense says this cycle of hostility must end. Some say the Russians won't be reasonable. I intend to find out."

It was obviously incestuous, to say the least, but when you look at the 2016 development of Alfa Bank's L1 portfolio things become even clearer. LetterOne's new L1 Health unit, which was to be based in the US, was announced in mid-2016 and was already working to identify investment targets, aided by an advisory board which included not only Burt, but Diageo Plc Chairman Franz Humer, a former chairman of the world's largest manufacturer of cancer drugs, Roche Holding AG.

"Innovations in technology, biology, and genomics are changing the way we think about health-care treatments," Fridman said of the project, adding: "This enables us to look at health care in new and unique ways."

One of Trump's flagship policies was always the removal of so-called Obamacare and, server or not, it is now clear Trump was never far removed from Alfa Bank in any case. All of this, however, also led me right back to Arron Banks' January 2017 photo of Phil Bryant – by then the Governor of Mississippi years after his private dinners with the Russians and Barbour – with Leave.EU's Andy Wigmore.

Bryant had been close to Vice President Mike Pence for years, through the Republican Governor's Association, but his direct ties to Donald Trump were even clearer. By the end of the presidential election campaign, Bryant had swapped allegiance from Ted Cruz to become broadly referred to as one of the most reliable Trump surrogates. He also set to work raising two million dollars for Trump's campaign in short order. Bryant subsequently enjoyed a close relationship with Trump, including visits to Trump Tower in New York, and commentators noted the then Presidential candidate often made a "B-line to Bryant even in a crowded room of VIPs." According to one source: "Trump even ditched his Secret Service detail to get on an elevator with Bryant in Trump Tower, then gave Bryant a personal tour of his war room."

This also put Bryant in direct contact with Jeff Sessions.

While being interviewed by reporters in late 2016, Bryant had to cut one interview short, saying Sessions' Chief of Staff, Rick Dearborn, had been meeting with Ivanka Trump to "work out calendars" and needed to update his itinerary. Rick Dearborn is now the White House Deputy Chief of Staff for Legislative, Intergovernmental Affairs and Implementation, having been the executive director of the Presidential Transition Team for Trump. He had spent more than twenty-five years working on Capitol Hill before this and, during that time, also worked on President George W. Bush's Energy Agenda. Dearborn worked as Chief of Staff for Jeff Sessions when the latter was a senator –

from 2004 until 2016 when he joined the Trump team. He was, I'm told, the second Sessions staffer to land a senior role in the Trump White House.

One of the central issues in the investigation into Donald Trump and his relationship with Russia relates to Carter Page – a man whose CV largely consisted of doing financial business with Russia until Trump. Page was somewhat mysteriously hired by the Trump campaign as a foreign policy advisor, despite holding no qualifications for such a role. During the election, it became public knowledge the FBI was investigating Page's ties to Russia and, after Trump's success, Page travelled to Moscow for "unknown" reasons. In February 2017, it was discovered he had "been colluding with Russian intel officials during the election." Spy agencies, including GCHQ, were not specifically targeting members of the Trump team but happened to gather evidence through what CNN reported as "incidental collection." Their accidental intelligence was then passed to the US as part of a routine exchange under the so-called "Five Eyes" agreement between the US, UK, Australia, New Zealand and Canada. Page's own direct connection to Jeff Sessions is not in doubt and, importantly, sources have also been publicly clear: "The Page connection was Rick Dearborn, Sessions' chief of staff, who hired Page because Dearborn knew nothing about foreign policy but needed to put together a foreign policy staff for Trump's Alexandria, Virginia, policy shop and he happened to know Page."

Russian agents have not held back from commenting on Page either, highlighting his ambitions in the energy sector. "He got hooked on Gazprom," Victor Podobnyy, an officer of the SVR (Russia's foreign intelligence agency) said. "It's obvious that he wants to earn lots of money."

Page, it appears, shared a mutual interest with Burt. Christopher Steele's controversial intelligence dossier went further, alleging Page met with the head of

Russian oil giant Rosneft, Igor Sechin – a man described as one of President Vladimir Putin's key deputies. According to the report, Page and Sechin discussed lifting sanctions imposed on Russia as a result of its annexation of the Crimean Peninsula and "support of pro-Russian insurgents in eastern Ukraine."

Flicking through the pages and pages of research, I noted that, in January 2017, BGR was hired by the Ukrainian government to: "Support and help open lines of communication between key Ukrainian officials and US government officials, journalists, non-profit groups and others." In truth, I wondered if Ukraine had simply decided to spy on the US's Russian link directly. Without a doubt, however, I could see there were no degrees of separation between any of these men. This is where the second round of Russian connections manifested, in the form of Nigel Farage.

The distinctly shadowy advisor to Donald Trump, Steve Bannon, and equally controversial Trump-appointed Attorney General, Sessions, had already known Farage for several years. In 2012, Bannon invited the UK politician to New York and Washington where he was introduced to Sessions. This was two years before Breitbart launched in London. Sessions himself was, at the time I was doing this snooping, embroiled in a fresh ethics row after President Trump's firing of the FBI Director James Comey, right in the middle of the Russia inquiry. Extraordinarily, the Attorney General had to remove himself from the investigation after undisclosed meetings between him and Russian officials were made public. Those very same officials were photographed inside the White House shortly afterwards and Sessions' name went on to become synonymous with the other subjects of the unprecedented collusion allegations, Paul Manafort, Michael Flynn, Carter Page, and Roger Stone. But there, right in the middle of all this, was a British politician I'd linked to the far-right and Russia already.

Visiting the Republican National Committee in mid-2016, Farage met a Bryant aide, John Barley Boykin, who suggested Farage visit Mississippi. The following day a formal invite from Bryant was sent to Farage. On the 23rd of August 2016, Farage arrived in Mississippi with Leave.EU's financial backer Arron Banks. According to reports, it was actually Bryant who asked Farage to speak at the Trump rally and it was Steve Bannon who telephoned Farage to discuss what he would say. When Farage and Trump subsequently met the next day, Donald Trump was so impressed with the speech he wanted to personally introduce Farage to the stage. Sessions was present at the rally along with another Russia Inquiry figure, former mayor of New York, Rudy Giuliani. Russian oil company Rosneft is a client of Rudy Giuliani's law and consulting firm, Giuliani Partners, and Alfa Bank has previously hired Rudy Giuliani as a paid speaker. Investigative journalist Grant Stern has written: "Circumstantial evidence strongly indicates that President Donald J. Trump and his campaign associates brokered a massive oil privatization deal, where his organisation facilitated a global financial transaction to sell Russian Oil stock to its Syrian War adversary, the Emirate of Qatar." The Emirate of Qatar was another Giuliani client.

Aside from this monstrously deep web of US business links to Russia, along with speeches by British politicians, my investigations had already established more substantial collaborative efforts between the so-called "Bad Boys of Brexit", the Trump campaign, and Russia. Yet, the Leave.EU connection was relevant at the time for one further reason: Roger Stone. During the 2016 campaign, Stone was accused by John Podesta of having prior knowledge of Wikileaks publishing his private emails which had been obtained by a hacker. In fact, before the leak, Stone tweeted: "It will soon the Podesta's time in the barrel," and five days prior to the release he did it again, writing: "Wednesday Hillary Clinton is done. #Wikileaks." Breitbart News, the

Mercer and Bannon disinformation channel, also published a subsequent denial by Stone, in which he claimed he had no advance knowledge of the Podesta e-mail hack or any connection to Russian intelligence. The thing was, I had already established a link between Russia, disinformation, Wikileaks, Trump, and Brexit, and found clear evidence from intelligence agencies that Wikileaks was known as a Russian operation.

It transpired that Stone was a gift that kept giving the more I looked into him.

During a speech on the 8th of August 2016, Stone said: "I actually have communicated with Assange" and referred to an "October surprise" coming via the Wikileaks site. He also stated that, while he had never met or spoken to the site's founder, the pair had a "mutual friend" who served as an intermediary. The same day the speech was given, Stone was tweeting about a dinner he had with Nigel Farage, who was, of course, seen visiting Assange in March 2017 and had always refused to give reasons for the meeting.

In May 2017, Farage changed tack and told Germany's Die Zeit newspaper he visited the Ecuadorian Embassy for "journalistic reasons, not political reasons" before cutting the questions short, saying: "It has nothing to do with you. It was a private meeting." What set him off, according to the reporters, was when they directly asked if he was working for Russia. In response to questions about his 2013 meeting with Yakavenko, Farage began ranting "I think you are a nutcase! You are really a nutcase! Brexit is the best thing to happen: for Russia, for America, for Germany and for democracy." For me, Farage's response clarified pretty much everything. This car-crash interview came shortly after Wikileaks had dumped material aimed at influencing voters in France to vote against Emanuel Macron and side with the far-right candidate Marine Le Pen – whose deep financial and political ties to Russia I'd already exposed. Farage was, as I've set out, openly supporting Le Pen during her campaign, and was backed up by Leave.EU and Banks' alternative media site Westmonster. By this time, that deep relationship between Farage, Russia, and Julian Assange, most openly displayed through RT and UKIP's activities, was bathing in the disinfectant of sunlight.

I took the time to sit and review everything I'd uncovered so far and decided there was nothing so easy as a simple financial trail which would expose this global mess. Those days of investigative journalism were clearly dead, along with stories compacted to fit headlines and column inches. We were dealing with such a complex problem I still think the whole truth may never be known, especially if the assertions of Christopher Steele – that the cover-up operation began on Putin's orders as soon as Trump won – are to be given credit. I realised it was also more complicated than a question of exposing diplomatic gain. Those days were gone too. This power play had gone directly for political and financial dominance on a scale which condemned the diplomatic wrangling of independent nations to the past, rendering countries standing as lone entities impotent. I could see this was the true reason the EU had been targeted – structurally, it could potentially defeat this axis along with NATO, which is why divide and conquer was crucial.

Almost idly, I called the Ecuadorian Embassy, to ask how many times Nigel Farage had visited Julian Assange. They hung up as soon as the question was asked.

SIXTEEN:

While I was busy trying to unravel all of this, the world was plunged into chaos on Friday the 12th of May by a massive cyberattack which crippled the United Kingdom's National Health Service – as well as a number of other large infrastructure organisations across many nations, including Spain's Telefonica, Fedex in the US, and – reportedly – some Russian organisations.

The source of the attack was pretty clear from the outset and its timing was no coincidence, yet a bewildered media, in reality unequipped to report on the complexities of cyber warfare, scrambled to push focus onto the impact of the hack while adding base-level explainers on Ransomware to a confused and scared public. Extraordinarily, British Home Secretary, Amber Rudd, was also quick to make a statement the attack was not "targeted" and, across the British parties – by then all electioneering – the focus shifted immediately to arguments about public spending. The election flux was a huge weakness and it was exploited with ruthless efficiency. In short order, both Wikileaks and the infamous, former NSA IT contractor Edward Snowden also began to lay the blame at the door of the United States' National Security Agency, as the attack allegedly involved the use of Eternal Blue – a spying tool designed to exploit a weakness in Microsoft Windows remote access capabilities. Amidst all the noise, however, it seemed obvious to me the culprit was sitting in plain sight.

Ransomware is a type of virus or malware which, when activated, encrypts the contents of a computer (or computers) so the user or owner can't access anything. It's called Ransomware because it offers the opportunity to have the data restored in exchange for a payment – normally in the cryptocurrency Bitcoin. It makes for an effective Denial of Service (DoS) attack and there are no guarantees systems will be restored even if payment is made by the victim. This attack used a version of the software called Wanacryptor 2 or "Wannacry," which would normally infect a computer through the standard route of opening an attachment in an email or via an infected browser cookie. However, the software also integrated the capabilities of a previously stolen tool from the NSA, Eternal Blue, which allows an infected computer to search for and infect other vulnerable computers on internal or external networks. The software exploited a mechanism within Windows which Microsoft released a patch for after the theft had occurred, though older versions of the system were still wide open as this support had finished. Vehicle manufacturing plants, power plants, and rail services were among the other institutions and companies shut down as a result of the attack and experts rightly predicted the software would continue to attack vulnerabilities over the following days.

The spread was hindered when a young computer blogger discovered the software communicating with an unregistered domain name (http://iuqerfsodp9ifjaposdfjhgosurijfaewrwergwea.co m) and by registering the domain name himself – what's known as sink-holing – the software stopped interacting. It appears the lack of ability to communicate with the domain made the software decide it was in sandpit mode – meaning not actively deployed. The domain itself was human generated keyboard garbage – named by swiping a hand across keys – and, because it was sink-holed on the day of the attack, the original registration details weren't accessible to anyone looking. I know this because I was one of the people looking.

While the Ransomware itself was freely available on the internet and not traceable in any useful sense, Eternal Blue proved to be a different matter. On the 8th of April 2017, a group of hackers known as The Shadow Brokers released a lengthy, rambling statement in what appeared, to me, to be deliberately broken English, which commenced with "Dear President Trump, Respectfully, what the fuck are you doing? TheShadowBrokers voted for you. TheShadowBrokers supports you. TheShadowBrokers is losing faith in you. Mr. Trump helping theshadowbrokers, helping you. Is appearing you are abandoning "your base", "the movement", and the peoples who getting you elected."

The group's reappearance came only days after Trump's unexpected intervention in Syria with airstrikes targeting a Russian-Syrian airbase and a spokesman for Vladimir Putin responded to those strikes stating the US had violated international law "under a false pretext", and the country's UN deputy ambassador, Vladimir Safronkov, warned "extremely serious" consequences could follow the strike. The prime minister, Dmitry Medvedev, also said the action had "completely ruined relations." The Shadow Brokers' statement mentioned Syria repeatedly and also cited disgruntlement at the rumoured removal of Steve Bannon from the National Security Council. They also went on to make further statements about Trump's supporters, saying they: "Don't care if you swapped wives with Mr Putin, double down on it, "Putin is not just my firend he is my BFF." Don't care if the election was hacked or rigged, celebrate it "so what if I did, what are you going to do about it"," adding that they supported "the ideologies and policies of Steve Bannon, Anti-Globalism, Anti-Socialism, Nationalism, Isolationism."

On the topic of Russia, they openly aligned themselves with the Federation too, saying "for peoples still being confused about TheShadowBrokers and Russia. If theshadowbrokers being Russian don't you think we'd be in all those US government reports on Russian hacking? TheShadowBrokers isn't not fans of Russia or Putin but "The enemy of my enemy is my friend." We recognize Americans' having more in common with Russians than Chinese or Globalist or Socialist. Russia and Putin are nationalist and enemies of the Globalist, examples: NATO encroachment and Ukraine conflict. Therefore Russia and Putin are being best allies until the common enemies are defeated and America is great again." These were both Russian narratives I had become very familiar with.

At the end of the statement, the core message of which was an echo of almost all non-state actor and alt-right narrative which I'd already linked directly to Russia and its disinformation, the hacking group gave a password to a darkweb site where the NSA tools were freely available.

The original NSA hack took place in August 2016 and drew significant commentary, including from Edward Snowden who tweeted: "Circumstantial evidence and conventional wisdom indicates Russian responsibility," which he interpreted – according to the New York Times – as a "warning shot to the American government" in case it was thinking of imposing sanctions against Russia in the cyber theft of documents from the Democratic National Committee.

"No one knows, but I suspect this is more diplomacy than intelligence, related to the escalation around the DNC hack," Snowden said, around the time Julian Assange's Russian outfit Wikileaks stated they had files to release and Stone was making his speech and having dinner with Farage.

Personally, I find Snowden curious. At first, being a whistleblower myself, I fully supported what he did but now I find his residence in Moscow increasingly uncomfortable. Russia has extended his leave to remain until 2020, with Putin himself commenting on the refusal to extradite Snowden in his Oliver Stone interviews, saying: "No, under no circumstances. Because he's no criminal." I can't say one way or another whether I trust Snowden, but knowing people the way I do from policing, I'm only too aware that circumstances change people – make them pliable. Especially when others have some element of control, which manifests as control over destiny in Snowden's case. This is something clearly included within the meaning of kompromat. I suppose my feelings about Snowden distill down to the factor of unknown risk, which you must always approach as high one because it's unquantifiable.

In January 2017, a report jointly compiled by the NSA, CIA and FBI concluded Russia's intelligence services had indeed conducted hacking attacks against organisations involved with the 2016 US presidential election, with the most high-profile target being the Democratic National Committee (DNC). By then, I had investigated far enough to have identified the hacking group APT28 as being directly attributable to the Russian intelligence services and to other operations which also involved significant elements of disinformation. I knew they had previously claimed to be ISIS, again using flawed language patterns and this little side note stuck, thankfully. James A. Lewis, a computer expert at the Center for Strategic and International Studies, mirrored my concerns about the group's use of English, saying: "This is probably some Russian mind game, down to the bogus accent...some of the messages sent to media organisations by the Shadow Brokers group [were] delivered in broken English that seemed right out of a bad spy movie."

After the attack, I took a more focused look at the Russians and re-confirmed that Russia's military intelligence, the GRU, is known to operate under the name APT28 – which is also known as Fancy Bears. I found it was also known that a second group with strong links to the FSB, the modern version of the KGB, existed under the name APT29, or Cozy Bear. Security experts believed the groups have been supporting operations to influence the domestic politics of foreign nations, including by leaking stolen information, since at least 2014 and attacks on the World Anti-Doping Agency, the DNC, the Ukrainian Central Election Commission were among those attributed to them. Security company FireEye had previously documented that APT28's software is Russian made, saying: "The malware is built during the working day of the GMT + 4 time zone, which includes Moscow and St. Petersburg, and the developers used Russian language settings until 2013." They also highlighted the group has extensive Zero Day attack capabilities – meaning they have deep pockets – and have shown they can take on multiple targets at the same time, which is indicative of state-backing. "For example, operations might involve setting up thousands of web domains, and dealing with the massive amount of information they are stealing likely involves the use of trained linguists to understand and evaluate it. All of this means that ATP 28 is likely to involve hundreds of staff directly, if not thousands indirectly," said Jonathan Wrolstad, a senior threat intelligence analyst working at the company FireEye.

On the 11th of May, the day before the worldwide cyberattack began, technology media outlets reported interception of a spear-phishing attack by Romanian security services. The attack involved the sending of a barrage of emails, including some purporting to be from a NATO representative, to diplomatic organisations in Europe, including Romania's Foreign Ministry of Affairs. The message came from a fake address at the hq.nato.intl domain currently used by NATO employees. The cyberattack was attributed to APT28.

The emails carried APT28's malware which exploits Zero Day capabilities, also initially thought to have been stolen from the NSA, and, I found in the case of the Romanian Foreign Ministry, the infected code was hidden in a word document entitled "Trump's_Attack_on_Syria_English.docx" According to cyber security companies, Romania was one of the worst countries affected during the 12th of May ransomware attack. A NATO spokesman said, at the time of the spear-phishing attack being discovered: "As is common practice, whenever we detect spoofed email addresses, NATO alerts the responsible authorities in Allied countries to prevent attacks from spreading. The hacker group APT28 – which is also called Fancy Bear or Pawn Storm – is well known to the cyber defense community and we track its activities closely."

While I am a man who broadly accepts coincidence, I don't accept it exists in such a state of consistency as to make an identifiable pattern. APT28 and the Shadow Brokers were operating the same software and the same narrative and, I quite reasonably believed as a result, were the same people. It would, of course, make sense them for them to dump the tools on the internet for all too, to muddy the waters by introducing yet more plausible deniability.

The 11th of May was also the same day US spy bosses and the acting FBI chief told the Senate intelligence committee they did not trust software from Kaspersky and, as a result, were reviewing its use across government. The officials cited concerns the Russian-made Kaspersky system could be used by the Kremlin to attack and sabotage computers used in American government institutions. The unanimous agreement on this, as well as a consensus Putin interfered in the US election, came from Daniel Coats, the Director of National Intelligence, Michael Pompeo, Director of the CIA, Michael Rogers, Director of the NSA, Andrew McCabe, Acting Director of the FBI, Vincent Stewart, Director of the Defense Intelligence Agency, and Robert Cardillo, Director of the National Geospatial-Intelligence Agency.

"Only Russia's senior-most officials could have authorized the 2016 US election-focused data thefts and disclosures, based on the scope and sensitivity of the targets," said Coats, adding: "Russia has also leveraged cyberspace to seek to influence public opinion across Europe and Eurasia. We assess that Russian cyber operations will continue to target the United States and its allies."

Though Kaspersky's CEO denied any wrongdoing in an open forum, during a Q&A session, one Redditor asked him why Kaspersky had paid Michael Flynn, Trump's disgraced National Security Advisor fired for his Russian ties. Eugene Kaspersky said it was: "A standard fee for a speech Flynn gave in Washington, DC," and added: "I would be very happy to testify in front of the Senate, to participate in the hearings and to answer any questions they would decide to ask me."

Also on the same day, President Trump signed an executive order commanding a review of the United States' cyber security capabilities.

The President was initially set to sign the order shortly after his inauguration in January and held a press conference on the issue, but the action was delayed. Scott Vernick, a data security lawyer in Philadelphia, said at the time the draft made no mention of the role that FBI, CIA and other major law enforcement agencies have in protecting the nation from hackers. The version of the document finally signed just before the worldwide cyberattack contained significant changes, however, placing responsibility for cybersecurity risk on the heads of federal agencies rather than the White House. A full report on cyber security concerns regarding critical infrastructure was mandated within six months. (The FBI had been completely excluded from the original draft and in the final version greater responsibility for federal cybersecurity was also given to the military – a move which was rejected by the Obama administration.)

White House homeland security advisor, Tom Bossert, discussed the new executive order with reporters, saying: "A lot of progress was made in the last administration, but not nearly enough. The Russians are not our only adversary on the internet."

The change of tack in respect of the FBI's role came only days after Trump's controversial dismissal of its Director, James Comey, who had publicly confirmed the scale of the President's conflict with the agency. Former Director of National Intelligence, James Clapper, told reporters in the days following the dismissal: "What's unfolded now, here, the leader...of the investigation about potential collusion between Russia and the Trump campaign has been removed. So the Russians have to consider this as a, you know, another victory on the scoreboard for them."

"I think in many ways our institutions are under assault," Clapper told CNN, adding "Both externally, and that's the big news here, is Russian interference in our election system. And I think as well our institutions are under assault internally."

On the topic of Comey, the President himself said: "When I decided to just do it I said to myself, I said, you know, this Russia thing with Trump and Russia is a made-up story, it's an excuse by the Democrats for having lost an election that they should've won."

It was patently obvious, looking at all of this together the cyberattack was not random, as Amber Rudd had so carelessly suggested. It could easily be directly traced to Russia in two ways and in less immediately obvious ones too. The accompanying Russian narrative, backed externally by public figures with close ties to the country, was to blame the US Intelligence Services, which would cause (and did start to cause) international distrust and discord. The upshot was some damage to the "Five Eyes" agreement and the other transatlantic alliances which rely heavily on intelligence co-operation to assess and mitigate threats. Nobody else stood to benefit but Putin's Russia. Meanwhile, the Trump administration was desperately seeking to cover up its own clear Russia links and, in doing so, was lashing out at the same security services and law enforcement agencies investigating it – all of whom were additionally affected by the burdens and provisions relating to his revised order on cyber security. I also picked up another anomaly while forensically picking through the mess and discovered the cyberattack, somewhat suspiciously, hit Russia more times on the first day than elsewhere yet caused the least disruption. In a country so well known for false flag attacks and disinformation, this was hardly surprising to anyone who had been paying attention – such tactics are old as the Tsars. Curiously, I noted, Putin very swiftly told the media: "Malware created by intelligence agencies can backfire on its creators." It was about as subtle as a brick, but Russia has never needed to practice finesse because it can afford to simply say: *what are you going to do about it?*

The attack also came at the time NATO had convened for the STRATCOM summit in Prague. Hosted by European Values under the extraordinary circumstances. The whole aim of the gathering was, as I found out, to discuss response options to Russia's mass efforts to destabilise its member nations by hacking, attacking democratic processes and spreading disinformation. Subsequently, I was less than surprised when media reports began to surface, claiming the culprit was North Korea. The main source was the Russian cyber security firm Kaspersky Lab – the same company the under-fire US security services had deemed as posing a risk to government agencies through their Kremlin links. Meanwhile, Snowden and Wikileaks continued to push the story of NSA's stolen Zero Day tools line. Rather than sit back and lap it up, as many newspapers did, repeating the Kaspersky line and letting it drop, I carried on investigating. As a result, I swiftly discovered it was thought North Korea was not, in fact, responsible for the attacks and also had it confirmed that Russian intelligence services have their own Zero Day hacking capabilities which exploit the defects in Microsoft Windows. With the assistance of expert Richard Hummel, Principal Analyst, Production & Analysis at FireEye – the company who had been tracking the hacking activity of Russian intelligence services for some time – the truth started to paint a very different picture.

"At this time, multiple potential attribution scenarios for the WannaCry activity are viable. We are continuing to investigate all potential attribution scenarios," Hummel told me. According to FireEye, financially-motivated cybercriminals are typically responsible for ransomware operations, with many such actors operating independently worldwide. "However," Hummel said, "as of yet, none of these actors have been identified as a strong candidate for attributing the WannaCry operation."

Numerous open-source reports alleged potential North Korean involvement in the cyberattack but, based on FireEye's initial analysis, the code similarities cited between the allegedly North Korea-linked malware and WannaCry were "not unique enough independent of other evidence to be clearly indicative of common operators." The link to North Korea was, at best, tenuous, arising only from lines of code in a version of WannaCry which actually pre-dated the one used in the worldwide incident. When I asked more specifically if the DPRK theory stood up to scrutiny, Hummel told me: "We often encounter cases in which malicious actors have reused code taken from publicly-available tools or other actors' tools. Based on our reverse engineering thus far, the similarities that are being cited between WannaCry and tools associated with the Lazarus group are not unique or significant enough to strongly suggest a common operator."

"For both these reasons, we consider the possibility that WannaCry is attributable to the Lazarus group to be unproven at this time and not necessarily stronger than other attribution scenarios. The primary alternative explanation is that non-state, financially-motivated hackers are responsible for the attackers. However, we are continuing to investigate all possible attribution explanations for these attacks," he added, though the point where non-state meant anything but a deniable asset for Russia had long since passed for me.

"Russia and China appeared to be the two of the more heavily infected regions based on sinkhole data that can be obtained publicly," Hummel continued. "The sinkhole data essentially identifies machines that have been infected and beaconing out to what the community has deemed the "kill switch." If the malware successfully reaches this domain and there is an HTTP web server response, the malware will not encrypt files. If, however, the malware is unable to make a connection then it will proceed with encrypting machines."

Hummel did note a lack of sophistication in the operation and made it clear it was a possibility the culprits may not have anticipated the malware would spread as widely as it did, saying: "One of these aspects is the kill switch functionality." However, while the spread of the attack was halted when the young British IT blogger found a way to stop it communicating, a swiftly released third generation of the malware had already removed the flaw. There was also the Vladimir Putin issue, whereby the Russian President had told that world forum in China malware created by intelligence agencies can backfire on its creators, and it held true, even days after the attack began, that the impact in Russia – despite the alleged spread – was largely non-disruptive and infections were localised relatively quickly. It appeared they already knew how to kill it domestically and helped do just that in a very short space of time.

"Another aspect is that identified ransom payments have been reported to be relatively low thus far, suggesting the operators' payment system may not have been equipped to handle the outcome," Hummel added, helpfully. I'd been sticking my nose into this aspect too, and also saw, across the technical and intelligence community, the low 'ransom' demand and lack of withdrawal activity in the Bitcoin wallets receiving payments had raised suspicions of the financial element being little more than a distraction. To give a bit of context, my sister-in-law (for all intents and purposes) fell victim to a ransomware attack in 2016. In a standard financially motivated attack, she was forced to pay 1 Bitcoin, at the time around one-and-a-half thousand pounds, to retrieve access to her one-woman-band company files. In the worldwide attack, ransom had dropped to only hundreds of dollars on high-profile targets, which led me to suspect from the outset this wasn't a financial scam at all but a further element to muddy the waters in a deliberate decoy.

I may not be hugely technical, but I do have some skills and, following the attack, I used a series of publicly available cyber threat mapping tools and botnet trackers with which I identified a correlation between the locations of computers infected with a peer-to-peer (P2P) worm virus called Sality and the distribution of Wannacry. I wanted to explore how the virus infected computers if it wasn't by spear-phishing. Hummel reviewed the possibility that the Ransomware was using an existing virus network to piggy-back and spread. "At this point, we haven't ruled out any attack vector as we are still researching initial entry into networks. Sality is a worm and has the ability to download additional payloads but we have not found any evidence to suggest that it is being used as a vehicle to distribute WannaCry at this time," he said.

"Sality and other worms like it are heavily distributed and often very difficult to remove as it infects every binary on an infected machine and then auto-propagates. Thus, seeing similarities in distribution or infection patterns isn't out of the question, but doesn't mean it is the vehicle being used," he added.

As with any virus, there are two ways for it to contaminate the first computer before it spreads – essentially a "patient zero" must exist. One way to enter a network would be through an infected email document or browser cookie, through the technique known as spear-phishing, or another would be through the exploitation of a "zero-day" defect which allows a computer to be directly infected through its operating system by hackers. Zero Day defects are unknown to software developers until the attack happens, and are so named because they provide no time for a software patch to be released addressing the weakness. The Wannacry hack also used a network weakness in Windows software, developed as the Eternal Blue espionage tool by the NSA, to spread across any available connections once loaded onto a single networked machine.

"We are still investigating the original entry point, but some theories that have been circulating include email, RDP, and direct SMB exploitation. The only spreading technique we have confirmed is that SMB was used to compromise some machines. We believe the particular incidents we have observed are lateral movement or a pivot from a previously compromised device and as such are still searching for the initial intrusion vector," Hummel said.

In the days preceding the attack, I discovered there was no apparent clue in data traffic which could identify a likely source. Hummel was clear though, telling me: "Based on the evidence and inclusive research into the original entry point, characterising a potential distribution vector would likely be misleading."

Prior to the worldwide outbreak, FireEye was instrumental in stopping the spear-phishing threat targeted at NATO, along with other European Defence and Security Agencies. One of the victims of that Russian attack was, of course, the Romanian Foreign Ministry. When the experts asked me how I knew, I pointed them back to FireEye's own technical documents on their identification of the Russian attack and how they coincided with Microsoft's security updates – the software giant released two patches to shut down the Zero Day defects exploited by the GRU. Being attentive like this does raise eyebrows, but it also gets answers. "The two recently patched APT28 0-days were used to target European Defense and Security entities. The vulnerabilities were in Microsoft Office and Microsoft Windows," Hummel confirmed.

"The APT28 vulnerabilities were not related to ShadowBrokers," he added, making clear that the NSA were not the only intelligence service to have developed and deployed cyberattack software.

After the noise of the Ransomware attack died down and the North Korea line was quietly dropped for a while, more evidence started to emerge of a new cyber weapon in the Russian arsenal. Across the world, alarming reports came in that Russian government-linked hacking groups had devised "a cyber-weapon" called CrashOverride – a malware program which had the potential to disrupt electrical systems. It had already been tested too: it was deployed against Ukraine to shut-down one-fifth of Kiev's power grid in December 2016.

"With modifications, it could be deployed against US electric transmission and distribution systems to devastating effect," commented Sergio Caltagirone, director of threat intelligence for Dragos, a cybersecurity firm who issued the report. "It's the culmination of over a decade of theory and attack scenarios," Caltagirone warned, adding: "It's a game changer."

Dragos named the hacking group responsible for Ukraine, "Electrum" – every company does this for corporate branding reasons – and state they have determined with high confidence it used the same computer systems as the hackers who first attacked the Ukraine electric grid in 2015. That attack, which left a quarter of a million customers without power, was carried out by Russian government hackers according to German intelligence services who agreed with private sector assessments. "The same Russian group that targeted US (industrial control) systems in 2014 turned out the lights in Ukraine in 2015," said John Hultquist, an expert who investigated both incidents for iSight Partners, now owned by FireEye. "Whether they're contractors or actual government officials, we're not sure," he said, but added: "We believe they are linked to the security services."

Dan Gunter, another senior threat expert for the firm Dragos, explained my own concerns quite neatly, saying: "What is particularly alarming...is that it is all part of a larger framework...like a Swiss Army knife, where you flip open the tool you need, and where different tools can be added to achieve different effects."

"This speaks to a larger effort often associated with a nation-state or highly funded team operations," he added.

Once this came out – only just over a month after the Wannacry attack – the North Korea rumour started to resurface.

The BBC reported on the 16th of June 2017 unnamed security sources had informed them the UK's National Cyber Security Centre (NCSC) believed: "That a hacking group known as Lazarus launched the attack." The Lazarus group I'd discussed with FireEye is the name attributed to state-linked North Korea hackers by some experts in the cyber security industry.

The British state broadcaster's report speculated: "Private sector cyber security researchers reverse engineered the code but the British assessment by the NCSC – part of the intelligence agency GCHQ – is likely to have been made based on a wider set of sources." The article also quoted Adrian Nish, who they say led the cyber threat intelligence team at BAE Systems. According to the report, his team saw overlaps with previous code developed by the Lazarus group.

"It seems to tie back to the same code-base and the same authors...the code overlaps are significant," Nish said.

Having looked at the background of this in the first place, I already knew North Korean hackers had been attributed responsibility for previous financially motivated attacks, including a 2016 hack on SWIFT payment systems which netted eighty-one million dollars from the central bank of Bangladesh. The BBC even quoted BAE representative Nish as saying: "It was one of the biggest bank heists of all time in physical space or in cyberspace." However, the May 2017 Ransomware attack, which primarily hit European Telecoms, Manufacturing plants, Transport Networks, the NHS, and other such networks, saw those incredibly low ransom demands – at around three hundred dollars – which was notably unusual and also resulted in a payment total of only around one hundred and fifty thousand dollars to three Bitcoin wallets which have been left completely untouched. The report also repeated a line first used by the poorly briefed Home Secretary, Amber Rudd, that the attack was random rather than targeted. I could see there were issues, with all of this. Firstly, from a strategic point of view, the attack benefitted two parties above all others. Trump and Putin. Secondly, there was at the time insufficient evidence to attribute the attack to North Korea based on an assessment of old code in the Ransomware providing the link alone. I contacted the experts I originally spoke to at FireEye, who told me on the morning of the fresh report nothing had changed in their assessment. It struck me as a bit peculiar so, partly because of the lack of substance in the BBC report, I called the NCSC, who are part of GCHQ. Their only reply, as I anticipated, was that they could "neither confirm nor deny" the report.

The thrust of a declaration such as this is not to comment but not to dissuade anyone from believing the veracity of the report – in this case indicating

North Korea and their state-backed Lazarus hackers were potentially linked to the May attack using Wannacry. However, there was only a "moderate level of confidence" in the assessment. In the case of the intelligence agencies, a moderate confidence level generally means they have credibly sourced and plausible information, but not of sufficient quality or corroboration to warrant a higher level of trust. It meant that, at the NCSC, there was no difference in the information they held to what I'd uncovered as regards the code. Essentially, there was that previous programming link but also doubt as to what it actually meant. As a result, I was able to believe, with a high level of confidence, that FireEye was right and nothing had changed over the four weeks since the attack.

I had, of course, been in touch with industry experts from the start of the outbreak and, while I have no doubt there was North Korean language code in the previous versions of the ransomware and some of the delivery mechanism tools, it was my understanding those similarities in earlier versions were not significant enough to attribute Wannacry version 2 to Lazarus. Also, once the sandpit defect was identified, the software was rapidly adapted twice to remove the so-called kill-switch facility. There was no known North Korean code in those updates either. I had also read the most recent US-CERT bulletin from the NSA and the FBI, which confirmed older programming indicated previous versions of ransomware used North Korean code and deployment methods (they referred back to the Sony attack in 2014) but added nothing to change the view I'd established on the recent software itself. In fact, the most recent bulletin focused on DDoS attacks, rather than DoS, and system vulnerabilities completely unrelated to those used in the Wannacry attack.

Having been one of the few people to look at the bigger picture and take the time to understand the complexities of the attack itself, I remained deeply unconvinced as regards the original source of the

North Korea finding too. With it having been called by Kaspersky – and largely due to the public declarations of the US intelligence community about the firm being a Russian asset, along with the concerns the US Intelligence Community raised over the Kaspersky software posing a risk to US Government systems due to potential exposure to Kremlin access – it was clear something was off. In light of other reports, including other Joint Assessment Reports and a CIA declassified report I'd gotten hold of, it appeared highly probable the assessment of Kaspersky was more than feasible, which threw doubt on everything they said and continued to. Lazarus themselves also appear to be a professional outfit with a broadly successful history and rapidly developing technology and finances. Their last, highly targeted, heist in 2016 was the multi-million dollar Bangladesh central bank attack so, it was subsequently a safe assumption they would have developed well beyond the Sony days and this did not sit well with the low-value Bitcoin demand – or the value of the ransom payments achieved – that lowly hundred and fifty thousand. Those Bitcoin wallets had also, of course, been left untouched. Broadly, the concern I'd followed with interest was the whole ransom aspect of the attack being nothing more than a ruse. None of it sat within the North Korean pattern and didn't fit the clumsy privateer theory some had put forwards. Sitting alongside the Wannacry issue were those growing concerns over other cyber weapons, such as CrashOverride – the Russian tool which had been linked to Russia's cyber intelligence operations like APT28/29 (Fancy Bears and Cozy Bears). Through my own network of contacts, the broader issue under discussion had turned to whether the Wannacry episode was, in fact, a weapons test, with the final payload swapped out and the code seeded to deliberately point elsewhere. It made sense really, the thought Russia was simply testing the delivery mechanism for weapons like CrashOverride, gauging the spread and impact. This is also largely supported by low levels of collateral damage in Russia – the outbreaks were, of course, "localised" with only minor disruption – and this was followed almost immediately by Putin's statement in China that intelligence agency led programs sometimes are accompanied by accidents.

APT28 and 29 subsequently dovetailed back into BBC's rehashed scenario for two further reasons. Firstly, there was still this question of access points. They were running the active spear-phishing operation exploiting Windows vulnerabilities in the run-up to the attack and they got caught out partially because they used a NATO email and it was picked up by the Romanian embassy. The initial entry point for Wannacry, despite its network spread, almost certainly involved some degree spear-phishing and payload adaptation to existing worms like Sality had been all but ruled out. There remained some questions over Zero Day access but, taking into account all the facts available, spear-phishing through emails or cookies appears more likely and Wannacry only needed access to one networked computer to then self-propagate due to the Eternal Blue (or similar) capabilities. Secondly, the involvement of the Shadow Brokers was still highly questionable. My own theory was they were also a deniable asset of APT28/29 and, in part, their broken language pattern was helpful yet again – it was also a feature repeated in the story of the Guccifer 2.0 hack of the DNC (which was Russia) and also in the North Korean code. Poking around, as I do, I found more evidence of this.

Beau Woods, deputy director of the Cyber Statecraft Initiative at the Atlantic Council, told CNBC that the Korean language used in some versions of the WannaCry ransom note was: "Not that of a native speaker, making a Lazarus connection unlikely."

By this point, even Kaspersky's worldwide staff had started to throw doubt on the claims of North Korean responsibility. Asia research director, Vitaly Kamluk, said it was not conclusive evidence. "It's unusual," he added.

Meanwhile, the Shadow Brokers had resurfaced again, threatening to auction data on nuclear systems belonging to Iran, North Korea, and Russia, as well as other stolen US intelligence tools. It was more than enough for me to dismiss the BBC report as spurious. What I concluded, based on the evidence as a whole, is the May 2017 cyber-attack was simply a very pointed, if not partly accidental, warning shot arising from a weapons test and it clearly came from two of the most powerful men in the world – the attack's usefulness to both Donald Trump and Vladimir Putin was impossible to disregard as a coincidence, especially in the broader context of what I was investigating.

In June 2017, the Westminster emails of the UK parliament were breached and a second worldwide attack, using a different Russian payload – a non-recoverable version of the Petya Ransomware – was launched, initially targeting Ukraine's infrastructure. After this, NATO finally came out and publicly reminded the world they would be prepared to trigger Article 5, as they had discussed several years before in Wales, if the attacks continued. It was Russia, without a doubt and I had been right to resist the lazy, mainstream view all along.

As far as I was concerned, Putin and Trump – along with others – had already spear-phished democracy but, unlike with Wannacry or Petya, the Ransomware they'd installed in our institutions could not be fixed by anything as simple as a software patch.

SEVENTEEN:

Returning to my primary investigation, I knew Trump had been communicating with Russia for a prolonged period, but one single meeting left him personally exposed in doing so for the first time. I remember thinking he was rowing the last lengths of the river to impeachment single-handed.

On the 10th of May 2017, Russian Foreign Minister Sergei Lavrov met President Trump and US Secretary of State, Rex Tillerson, at the White House. Initial reports stated they discussed cooperation on a range of issues and policy areas, with a central focus on the hacker's favourite topic, Syria. Lavrov went on afterwards to give a confirmation Trump and Putin would be meeting in July, during the first few days of the G20 summit. This was the same Lavrov, of course, who was linked to the Montenegro events which almost saw the prime minister assassinated before the country joined NATO.

One Russian news agency reported the White House meeting was not simply a polite gesture, with the General Director of Russia's International Affairs Council, Andrei Kortunov, issuing a statement saying: "Regardless of the importance of the Secretary of State's role, US foreign policy is created by the president. I think that Trump has a certain message for Putin that he wants to send personally, through Lavrov." Russia's Foreign Minister himself also pressed the point it was necessary to agree on some areas of policy in advance of the leaders' meeting, in order to ensure "concrete, perceptible results" when the heads of state got together. He also outright refused to discuss Russia's alleged interference in the US elections, referring to them as "bacchanalia." Undeterred journalists at the conference did, however, press the Russian Foreign Minister on the dismissal of FBI

Director James Comey, asking if it "would influence Russian-American relations." Lavrov responded with a joke, saying: "Was he fired? You're kidding!" On the evening of the meeting, Putin made a statement that Comey's dismissal was "America's domestic affair and Russia has nothing to do with it," which struck me as an oddly significant statement.

Lavrov dedicated most of his own press conference to Syria, highlighting Washington could contribute towards the creation of de-escalation zones in the country – reminding journalists both superpowers have a "mutual understanding about the location of the zones and how they will function."

"For the US the most important thing is to defeat terror. Here we are in perfect harmony," he said.

According to Lavrov, he and Trump did not discuss the unilateral sanctions introduced by the Obama administration in late 2016 but added: "Washington understands the seizure of property belonging to Russian diplomats was wrong," indicating they did. He was referring to the seizure of diplomatic compounds by President Barack Obama in December 2016, who had declared the compounds were being used by Russian personnel for intelligence-related purposes. Obama had also expelled thirty-five Russian nationals, declaring them "intelligence operatives." Following Trump's meeting with Lavrov, Trump's administration began to negotiate the handing back of the property to Russia.

Trump also stated, after seeing Lavrov, he was "pleased with the meeting" and, according to an official White House Press Service statement, the president impressed the need for Russia to "rein in" Assad. "He also raised the possibility of broader cooperation on resolving conflicts in the Middle East and elsewhere," the statement added. Trump went on to visit the Middle East, where he pretty much declared war on the Islamic State and then, bizarrely, sided against Qatar in a dispute with Saudi Arabia, despite having almost ten thousand troops stationed in the allied country. The dispute swiftly extended to border crossings and began to disrupt Qatar's gas exports – the country purchased a large stake in Russia's Rosneft in December 2016 in a deal worth billions. As a result of the Saudi crisis, however, Qatar became diplomatically closer to Russian allies Iran and Turkey.

RT's propaganda network was quick to leap into a commentary on the new Gulf crisis, explaining the advantages of the situation: "This may help Russia on the European gas market. Qatar's tanker fleet is barred from using regional ports and anchorages, posing a threat to the country's LNG supplies. Traders are worried Saudi Arabia and allies would refuse to accept LNG shipments from Qatar, and that Egypt might even bar tankers carrying Qatari cargo from using the Suez Canal, despite Cairo's obligation under an international agreement to allow the use of the waterway. If LNG supplies are disrupted, Europe will have to buy more gas from Russia."

"Gazprom is building new pipelines in Europe – Nord Stream-2 and Turkish Stream, but the Russian energy major is facing opposition on the continent," the Kremlin-managed channel added.

This clearly makes sense from a Russian position, because it brings a range of benefits and leverage. However, Trump's angle took me a little while longer to get my head around – until I revisited Carter Page. Christopher Steele's Trump-Russia Dossier describes the huge Rosneft Oil company sale to Qatar but adds a second party, a secret buyer in the Cayman Islands. Investigation work in the US has uncovered that Trump hosted a Qatari state-run business owned by the QIA, the buyer of Rosneft shares in the deal, in the Manhattan Trump Tower for many years. Carter Page, who acted as a gopher in the transaction, was working directly for Trump at the time. Having flatly denied meeting any Russian officials in 2016, Page later contradicted himself as it emerged he met Sergey Kislyak, the Russian Ambassador, during the Republican National Convention. Though Russia always denies the claims, Kislyak is described as a spy and a recruiter of spies by top intelligence officials.

Kislyak was also in attendance at the White House meeting along with Lavrov and, as was originally reported by the Washington Post, during the discussions Trump "went off-script." What they meant was he began to give specific, classified information on the Islamic State threat related to the use of laptop computers on aircraft. Intelligence officials subsequently told reporters US agencies were: "In the process of drawing up plans to expand a ban on passengers carrying laptop computers onto US-bound flights from several countries in conflict zones due to new intelligence about how militant groups are refining techniques for installing bombs in laptops." As a measure of the seriousness of the threat assessment, services were at the time also considering the banning of passengers from several European countries, including Britain, from carrying electronic devices in the cabin on flights destined for the United States. Washington had, allegedly, informed its allies of these plans. While a president does have legal powers to declassify information, the leak of this specific intelligence had serious ramifications – not least because the meeting with Lavrov and Kislyak came only one day after he fired FBI Director Comey.

Trump's national security adviser, General Herbert Raymond McMaster, also present during the meeting, initially gave a statement which said: "No intelligence sources or methods were discussed that were not already known publicly" before declining to comment further. However, it then emerged the classified intelligence President Trump disclosed had been provided in strictest confidence by Israel and, according to sources – current and former American officials familiar with the information itself – the disclosure threw a further diplomatic spanner in the works of an episode which had already drawn the reliability of the White House into question. Israel has long been one of the United States' most strategically important allies, operating one of the most complex and highly active espionage networks in the Middle East. As a result of Trump's disclosure, it was feared the incident could inhibit the critical intelligence relationship amidst clear risks information could be passed to Iran – a close ally of Russia and also Israel's main threat actor.

One former director of the National Counterterrorism Center, Matt Olsen, spoke on ABC, stating Trump's disclosures posed: "A real threat to future sources of information about plots against us."

"Russia is not part of the ISIS coalition. They are not our partner," he added pointedly.

Other US officials have since come forward and told reporters: "The intelligence provided by the spy was so sensitive that it was shared only with the US and was conditioned on the source remaining secret."

General McMaster responded by making clear he was not personally concerned the incident could hinder US Intelligence relations with its partners. "What the president discussed with the foreign minister was wholly appropriate to that conversation and is consistent with the routine sharing of information between the president and any leaders with whom he's engaged," he said.

Sean Spicer, now the former White House press secretary, also declined to answer questions as to whether the White House had made efforts to contact Israel and discuss the disclosure. Dan Shapiro, the Former US ambassador to Israel, also told ABC the: "Careless handling of sensitive information by Trump and his team would inevitably cause elements of Israel's intelligence service to demonstrate more caution."

In a statement emailed to The New York Times, Ron Dermer, the Israeli ambassador to the United States, approached the issue rather politely, in my view, writing: "Israel has full confidence in our intelligence-sharing relationship with the United States and looks forward to deepening that relationship in the years ahead under President Trump."

Despite the White House downplaying the discussion and Israel's rather erudite reply, in yet another bold as brass statement, Putin stepped in and announced via Kremlin aides he was: "Prepared to provide a transcript, not audio recording, of the Trump and Lavrov meeting."

Giving context on the significance of a specific leak of classified information, John Sipher who served in the CIA for almost thirty years, including a Moscow posting in the 1990s, later running the agency's Russia program, commented: "The Russians have the widest intelligence collection mechanism in the world outside of our own."

"They can put together a good picture with just a few details. They can marry President Trump's comments with their own intelligence, and intelligence from their allies. They can also deploy additional resources to find out details," he added.

While all of this was spilling out, it also became public President Trump had asked the F.B.I. director James Comey to shut down the federal investigation into his own administration's Russia links – initially focused on disgraced national security adviser Michael Flynn – before deciding to dismiss the leading law enforcement official. "I hope you can let this go," the president told Comey, according to a memo shared with close senior colleagues, one of whom read parts of it to a New York Times reporter. "I hope you can see your way clear to letting this go, to letting Flynn go, he is a good guy. I hope you can let this go," Trump is alleged to have continued.

Michael Flynn was dismissed after he privately discussed US sanctions against Russia with the country's ambassador to the United States, Kislyak, during the month before President Trump took office, contrary to public denials by Trump officials. In a statement, the White House denied the Comey memo's version of events, though they were already under the shadow of allegations of repeated untruths and Trump had also intimated, in tweets, he may have recorded Comey and any such tapes may be leaked. In response, on the 16th of May 2017, Representative Jason Chaffetz, the Republican chairman of the House Oversight Committee, demanded the FBI turn over all memoranda, notes, summaries and recordings pertaining to Trump and Comey. Such documents, he wrote: "Raise questions as to whether the President attempted to influence or impede [the FBI]."

Flynn's communications with Kislyak were interpreted by some senior US officials as an inappropriate – and potentially illegal – signal to the Kremlin on sanctions issues and the significant investigation was triggered with Comey at the helm. Sally Yates, former Acting Attorney General dismissed by Trump over his immigration measures, also told the Trump administration Flynn was compromised. She later told an inquiry hearing she was ignored and the Trump Administration team had misled the American public over the truth.

Yates pulled no punches, informing a Senate committee about illegal conduct and stood by her evidence afterwards, telling reporters: "We had just gone and told them [the White House] that the national security adviser, of all people, was compromised with the Russians and that their vice-president and others had been lying to the American people about it."

In March 2017 it was also reported Attorney General Jeff Sessions, the long-time friend of Farage along with Bannon, had spoken twice to Ambassador Kislyak, once in July 2016 and once in September 2016. At the time,

Sessions was still a US senator sitting on the Senate Armed Services Committee. During Sessions' Senate Judiciary Committee confirmation hearing in January, he was questioned under oath about "possible contacts between members of President Trump's campaign and representatives of Moscow" and expressed he had no knowledge of any such contact. The New York Times had also reported that Kislyak met with Michael Flynn and another Trump team member, Jared Kushner, in December 2016 to "establish a line of communication" with the Trump administration. This was in addition to the significant number of officials within, or close to, the Trump administration who, I had discovered, were connected with Russia in a vast number of direct and indirect ways.

Even without spies in the White House Trump was, by then, leaking like a sieve and his next effort ended up leading me straight back to the cyberattack, in a way. Via submarines.

In a show of force aimed at North Korea in the wake of their continued missile tests, Trump sent the USS Carl Vinson aircraft carrier to the area, where it joined the advanced submarine the USS Michigan in waters off the Korean peninsula. On the 24th of May 2017, Reuters reported that US President Donald Trump told his Philippine counterpart about Washington's deployment of two nuclear submarines to waters off the Korean coast. According to the official transcript made during the call between Philippine President, Rodrigo Duterte, and Trump, the US President said the US Navy had "a lot of firepower over there...We have two submarines — the best in the world. We have two nuclear submarines, not that we want to use them at all."

As I know a few useful people, I contacted an experienced naval source with a history of extensive service on submarine operations who provided me with a grim – but colourful – explanation of the risks

Trump exposed military personnel and naval operations to.

After having them read the public stories, then Trump's leaks, I asked my source for their initial reaction to Trump's intentions and the former high-ranking naval officer told me: "It's difficult to tell, with a character like Trump, but I don't recall Obama doing this. One thing about Trump is that it is totally possible he's telling the truth or is so stupid that he actually made a blunder."

"Personally," they added, "I think he's done it on purpose. A carrier group always has a minimum of one boat with it, but nuclear boats are top-top secret. This includes stationing and deployment."

What I couldn't understand, without specific detail, was if the Trump leak really significant and if it could give anything away. My source was clear on this, telling me: "As I said, a submarine deployment with a carrier group is normal, even two boats on station is (possibly) normal – though this would be for continuity and sheer firepower."

"If TLAM [*TLAM is the acronym for the Tomahawk missile system*] strikes are planned, it would make sense to be ready to saturate your objective with Hi-Ex cruise missiles rather than risk a miss," they continued. "Think continuity. What Trump is not saying is that there are probably two more boats hanging around, waiting to deliver more TLAM payloads when required."

Perhaps all Trump was doing was letting North Korea he had serious firepower which could be deployed against them, but I found it curious. If submarine deployments are so secret, I couldn't quite grasp why the world was allowed to see the USS Michigan docked in Seoul.

"Power projection," the source told me. "We did it all the time: look at my nuclear submarine, it's fucking awesome! A boat is a serious asset." Though they then dipped questions about the Michigan's nuclear capabilities, my source did add that it "carries some mega stealth and comms intercept kit."

Still curious, I pressed them on whether a leak as generic as Trump's could assist an enemy.

"Yes and no," they told me. "Yes because they could shape their maritime tactics." I thought this was simply about restricting a dragnet search area, but the source told me it was that and more. "Your comms are no longer safe, local GSM networks are capable of being tapped. Emails may – or may not – be intercepted. You get the picture." Effectively, submarines are a naval boat doubling as a spy, they explained.

The response options for an enemy are almost limitless, they continued. "You could go for a full deployment of ASW (Anti-Submarine Warfare]) tactics, or no deployment at all. Deny the US any opportunity to run rings around your own maritime forces."

"Sometimes denial is better," they said. "It's not just bluffing, you actually don't sail from port, leaving all your mega-assets safely at home and blockading the waters around it, to stop the US or someone else snooping around your latest kit." I supposed the question then became what tactics could these US boats Trump exposed find themselves facing. "US boats are seriously good, so you'd throw the kitchen sink at it," my source told me. Specifically, I asked them what a likely Russian response would be and the reply was blunt. "I can't speak for those sneaky bastards, but the best way to catch a submarine is with another submarine, so deploy your boats, with your surface and air forces, and dragnet."

The objective of such an action surprised me too.

"If it's boat to boat, you're trying to get a firing solution on your opponent ASAP, constantly trying to turn inside each other to get the best angle. But there is no chance you would fire." The end game was very different than that I'd anticipated. "All you are doing is forcing your opponent to surface, where you can embarrass the fucker or make them withdraw," the source said.

"The enemy is trying to get a firing solution on your highest value asset, which is?" they turned the conversation and asked me. I guessed at nuclear warheads but was wrong. "Two massive nuclear reactors. It causes massive political and military ridicule. Point scoring."

Following the worldwide cyberattack, which targeted Windows, a number of articles had been reporting Trident submarines run the vulnerable version of the operating system. For me this raised questions as to whether they could be infected by the Wannacry Ransomware, or worse – though it's a grim thought, if Russia can hack to turn the power off, they can surely switch other things on. The one silver lining came from my source who, though they clearly would not divulge operating system specifics, told me a submarine could be switched over to manual after shutting the systems down.

None of it made me feel better. As well as having spies in the White House, Trump was telling people where to dragnet his submarines and potentially hijack their systems. I wasn't faced with much of a choice, as far as I could see, so I took everything I had gathered and turned it into a seventy-page statement of evidence which I sent to the UK and EU parliaments, STRATCOM, NATO, and the FBI via their London field office. For good measure, I made the full statement public via Byline. I was hoping, I suppose, somebody, somewhere, would act.

EIGHTEEN:

After reading back through the evidence I had submitted to the authorities, I realised just how important my lengthy discussion with Steve Komarnyckyj – a PEN award-winning poet and writer for Ukraine's Euromaidan – had been. Komarnyckyj had worked on the Index On Censorship for two years when we started talking through Byline and he had been focusing on the methodology of Russian-led hybrid conflicts, including the deployment of non-state actors and Russia's use of multiple narratives. His personal background was just as fascinating as his work.

"I am a literary translator of mixed Ukrainian and English parentage and grew up in Yorkshire," he told me, by way of introduction. "My partner Susie conceived Kalyna Language Press in part as a means of conveying translated Ukrainian literature to an English audience. However, we want to develop the press so that it publishes translations from other languages and English language fiction and poetry," he explained proudly.

Komarnyckyj began to study Russian activity some time ago, which is perhaps unsurprising given his heritage, but his work led him to look beyond the contentious borders of Ukraine. "I became interested in how Russian soft power can shape the world views of other nations. Ultimately it can be deployed as a weapon of war turning populations against their own states," he said.

This is how Komarnyckyj and I came to make each other's acquaintance – after I'd been busily exploring the mess which links Russia to the far-right across Europe, and to the White House, I was able to broaden the scope of my investigation and found the wealth of evidence (from Capstone to Kremlin Watch) of the live hybrid conflict between Russia and the West.

Komarnyckyj stumbled across the subject in much the same way, he told me.

"When I read about Ukraine in English sources I realised that Russia was putting words into the mouths of English writers and academics. Subsequently, I would meet people who on learning I was Ukrainian would say that Ukrainians were all Fascists etc. It was like talking to dozens of glove puppets operated by Stalin," he said, adding: "Much Western academic discourse and journalism remains polluted by Russian soft power," which confirmed much of what I'd been able to discover on my own.

I wanted to get deeper into Komarnyckyj's unusual background, mainly to find out how a poet ends up with significant experience of a hybrid conflict, so I asked him.

"I am a hybrid myself," he said. "A half-Ukrainian half-English man steeped in both cultures who enjoys Borshch and a bag of chips. However, the negativity towards Ukraine I encountered in England troubled me."

"I and many other Ukrainians fought against the stigmatisation of our culture for years. Russians regard Ukrainian culture as an aberration and believe that Ukrainians are simply self-deluding Russians. Britain I am afraid internalised this view of Ukraine. Worse still it accepted Russia's myth of cultural superiority." This made sense, in many ways, especially when set against the background of the collusion between the far-right right and Putin's Russia. White cultural superiority can be clearly seen in the narratives across the changed face of the West, and it is brutally ugly.

"This notion of Russian cultural superiority is indeed as fatuous as a beer advert," Komarnyckyj added. "Yet it continues to hold sway in Britain. The notion that Dostoevsky and Tolstoy were authors who in some mysterious essentially Russian way reached the parts other writers could not reach. I challenge such views by translating Ukrainian poetry and have won two awards from English PEN along with my publisher Kalyna Language Press. I also lobbied for recognition of the Holodomor the genocide famine inflicted on Ukraine in the thirties."

The Holodomor was a man-made famine in Soviet Ukraine which happened between 1932 and 1933 and killed an estimated seven million to ten million people. The inhabitants of Ukraine, the majority being ethnic Ukrainians, died of starvation in a peacetime, yet the tragedy was only officially recognised in 2006 – by Ukraine along with fifteen other countries – who declared it a genocide carried out by the Soviet government.

More recently, Komarnyckyj told me, he had started to work with voluntary organisations, such as Euromaidan Press, human rights groups and Ukrainian authors to change perceptions of Ukraine in England. "I have not participated directly in the conflict and would like to express my respect for those Ukrainians fighting and dying right now for Europe's freedom," he added.

We turned more directly to the area I'd been investigating, hybrid conflicts. What I had come to call the Alternative War.

"A hybrid conflict is one in which multiple means including military and soft power are used to gain ascendancy over an opponent," Komarnyckyj explained. "The aim is to transform the enemy state into a psychological/political vassal."

"As Vitalii and Dmytro Usenko note, Russians have a much wider of warfare than their western counterparts. They cite the "Social Security Concept" of the all-Russian political party "Truth and Unity Course." This document identifies six priorities for warfare. Many of these would not strike many of us as being means of waging war. They include changing the worldview of the enemy and manipulating history. Russia has also studied Western doctrines laying out how a hybrid war can reach a population beyond the front line." Broadly, Komarnyckyj was not only validating my own findings but adding the benefit of Orwellian language to explain, beyond RT, Breitbart, and Russia's underground markets, the reason we've become so familiar with terms like Fake News.

"It's important to realise that Russia is adopting hybrid war to the service of a mentality which believes in its intrinsic superiority," Komarnyckyj continued. "The USSR as the Usenkos note aimed to create a planet-wide union ruled from Moscow. It shared with both the Tsars and the current regime an aspiration to subdue the world." I couldn't help but wonder if this argument was a little too fantastic but, as I had heard others say it by then, it was no real stretch of the imagination. Besides, Komarnyckyj set it out rather neatly. "Many will argue that such views of Putin are hyperbolic. As I watch politics in the UK and US implode under Russia's destabilisation effort I can only wonder why. Putin controls the President of the United States. What will it take for the west to wake up and realise the danger we are all in?"

According to Komarnyckyj, the priorities of a hybrid war can only be realised by "using non-military means and the humanitarian sphere." He explained a framework he laid out in 2014, which describes some of the mechanisms used to pursue a hybrid war. "1. Agents of influence including politicians, businessmen, corporations with a stake in Russia's localisation program, energy sector etc.; 2. Networks of journalists who may be sectarian Communists or social conservatives; 3. Sectarian left wing sites (such as Counterpunch and Global Research) which exploit a linguistic disconnect to create a sanitised Russia and a conversely stigmatised Ukraine; 4. Political proxies (such as Stop the War and numerous politicians); 5. PR Agencies and consultancies; 6. The Troll army of paid internet commentators, all working to a script." He ticked the well-rehearsed elements off without hesitation and, though we both agreed on adding the huge "bot army" on social media to this list, Komarnyckyj's list also mirrored everything I'd read in the NATO, EU and US Intelligence assessments.

"I would also re-introduce the term Deniable Asset," Komarnyckyj added, "which refers to a tool used to pursue Russia's aims but with no formal link to its military. Western politicians loaned billions to parrot Putin's words. Journalists who trouser cash from Russia Today and praise Putin etc." Again, I found his work mirroring my own, with Wikileaks and some far-right politicians such as Marine Le Pen and Nigel Farage being prime examples.

Darkly, Komarnyckyj also raised the issue I'd long held a personal suspicion over – which had become even more poignant in the light of ongoing terror attacks and the surrounding narratives from Putin-linked figures such as Trump.

"Finally we must consider detached assets," Komarnyckyj told me. "The activist who has drunk in the ideology purveyed from Moscow via that organisation etc. In this context, it's worth noting that there are links between Russian intelligence and ISIS. No direct orders for an attack on the west need be issued by Putin- he just has to wind them up and watch them go." My own research had led me to understand the clear relationship of benefits in kind between conflicts driving immigration and extremism and the resultant anti-immigrant sentiment creating more extremism and conflict. Essentially, this creates a self-perpetuating cycle in which a state such as Russia would have to do little more than sit and watch while its objectives were achieved and security services distracted. The rising number of white extremists targeting Muslims in vehicle enabled attacks is a testament to this and broadly confirms my own thinking on the true source of the changed face of terror in Europe.

Komarnyckyj went on to establish two more concepts, which he argued fell within the use of multiple narratives, attractive to multiple audiences. "For Putin's Russian audience, Ukraine is presented as becoming a "Godless Gay Colony" of the West," he told me, adding: "For the West, Ukraine is presented as a fascist hell hole." The duplicity appeared so obvious I nearly kicked myself for not thinking about in such simple terms earlier. "Kadyrov's persecution of gays is aimed at a religious socially conservative audience stretching from the US bible belt to Afghanistan. Never take Russia and Putin at face value- see the country as a criminal cartel engaging in theatrics and terror to secure its goals," Komarnyckyj added.

While the Alternative War had only just started to be exposed in the West, it had been ongoing for some time right under Komarnyckyj's eyes and there were lessons to be learned. So, I wanted to find out exactly how has this played out in practice in Ukraine. It transpired the tactic has roots much older than the current developments in technology.

"Russia has always viewed Ukrainians and Russians as one people," Komarnyckyj told me. "Many Russians see Ukrainian identity as a kind of blasphemy against the Russian state. Russia has therefore engaged in a hybrid war against Ukraine for centuries. The Ukrainian language was subjected to endless restrictions. Gogol was bribed to rewrite his novel Taras Bulba so that it did not portray Russia as an enemy of Ukraine. These tactics are in accord with the concept of attacking the consciousness of the enemy. Russia's hybrid war seeks to colonise the souls of its foes." But the contemporary development of the technique is clear when set against the evidence now unravelling before us courtesy of the weakest link: The Trump White House.

"In Ukraine as in the US, Russia parachuted its candidate into the presidency. In Ukraine as in the US, he was aided by Manafort, a Republican party fixer. In Ukraine as in the US, the candidate was a Russian style oligarch tasked with establishing a managed democracy," Komarnyckyj said. "A managed democracy is Putin's term for his preferred social model."

"Elections are won by oligarchic political parties by a combination of mass brainwashing using fake news and deniable terror. Critical journalists are murdered by shadowy figures who are never caught. Opposition leaders are gunned down when the cameras are switched off," he added. There was nothing I could deny in this, and nothing I could contradict a word of, but it appeared Ukraine had proved to be a critical sticking point for Russia, exposing a weakness.

"Putin and Russia made a critical error in Ukraine," Komarnyckyj explained. "Because they are blind to the differences between the two nations. Ukrainians have, in the absence of a state developed a ferocious capacity for self-organisation. They have simultaneously understood perhaps better than Russia itself the nature of the current conflict."

"The current war pits popular sovereignty against oligarchic populism- it is being fought within states and between states. Ukraine has its oligarchs but its people aspire towards a democracy where power is granted by the people. When Yanukovych tried to stifle protest in November 2013 he inadvertently mobilised Ukrainian civic society. Ukrainians very quickly developed tactics to overthrow their autocrat," he said.

Undeniably, Russia did have some successes in its advance on Ukraine, though Komarnyckyj informed me this was actually a trap, of sorts.

"Russia's seizure of Crimea was successful because the Peninsula was heavily Russianised. However, its attempt to trigger revolts across Ukraine in 2014 beginning in the Donbas failed. Russia simply does not understand that Ukrainians are not Russians. Putin only succeeded in establishing a heavily armed enclave in the Donbas. It has become a snare in which his ankle is caught."

"A wider invasion though often mooted would be problematic because it would require the mass killing of the people Putin claims to be protecting," he added.

When we started talking about the media and journalism beyond the narrow scope of fake news, more lights began to flick on.

"When Western journalists talk about "rebels" in east Ukraine they are giving credence to a Russian fiction. They might as well argue that Rod Hull's Emu was a real bird. The DNR and the LNR are tools of Russia and completely curated by its intelligence services. These journalists are helping Putin's war," Komarnyckyj told me, adding that "these tactics are in accordance with the concept of attacking the consciousness of the enemy. Russia's hybrid war seeks to colonise the souls of its foes." And there it was, the realisation dawning on me journalism was a weapon – in some cases acting as guardian against this multi-faceted threat but, in many cases, also working for it.

Komarnyckyj had been avidly looking outwardly at the West and I was curious as to what concrete signs he saw of the hybrid conflict elsewhere, beyond my own findings which were solidly based in facts I was comfortable with as being accurate.

"Russia's assault on Ukraine has become a sleight of hand which, like a conjurer's gestures, diverts the audience's attention, it was convenient for western leaders to believe that Putin could be thrown Ukraine like a mad dog might be appeased with a scrap of meat. Equally many of them refused to accept that their countries were under his hybrid attack," he told me. I had seen enough documentary evidence from such a variety of sources I could confirm this without hesitation. "However," he continued, "[Putin's] aims were always much wider than Ukraine. He aspires, like his Soviet predecessors to conquer the world. He believes that transnational and business ties combined with a propaganda blitzkrieg can conquer his foes. The US will become a mirror image of Russia with a managed democracy and a population in thrall to hate propaganda. Europe will splinter into vassal states ruled by weak demagogues like Le Pen." Again, his assessment was flawlessly backed up by evidence.

"I would argue that Brexit was a successful hybrid war operation pursued by means of deniable assets," Komarnyckyj said, banging the very reason I sent the evidence I'd put together to all the various agencies home. "Similarly, Trump's election can be viewed as a triumph for Putin. The war against the West is using bullshit rather than bullets- but it is no less deadly for that. We may find that no British troops die as a result of Putin's attack. But in ten years Britain will no longer be Britain but an oligarchy. The British will be an enclave at the edge of Europe providing a theme park for an international caste of oligarchs." Having established the sheer level of Russian money laundering through the city of London, and the current government's almost inexplicable alignment with the insanity of Trump's White House, this rang wholly true – especially when set against Prime Minister Theresa May's outline of a tax haven state on the doorstep of an increasingly united Europe. Of course, it was also worth repeating that the Conservatives had been aligned in some way with Russian oligarchs since the days of George Osborne.

Komarnyckyj's assessment of the tactics deployed in response to Russia's assault on democracy is very astute and rightly scathing of the wider media. "The war is curiously invisible in the West because it is being pursued by overt rather than covert means," he said. "If an intelligence service bribes a politician to betray their country they are prosecuted. If a media channel pays them for bogus media work, they are praised by an army of trolls and bots on Twitter. They are feted by the oligarchic press (for Putin's Western collaborators include many of our own native oligarchs who share his aims)."

"So, yes, I see signs of the conflict and that in the US and UK Putin is winning," he added.

Since Macron's election, a triumph over Putin's favoured candidate, Le Pen, I had been watching the marked change in the EU stance and, again, found Komarnyckyj and I shared the same view – both in terms of the likely rise of a stronger Europe and the hopeless mess facing Britain.

"Putin has inadvertently created what he most feared: a unified and angry Europe," Komarnyckyj told me. "His successes in the US and UK may ultimately become failures if they galvanise those countries into recognising and targeting their enemy. This may be happening in the US. Alas, the United Kingdom is losing a war it does not even know it is fighting."

Part of my own investigation had uncovered the reality of just how alive Europe and NATO were to the very real conflict, and what active measures they were deploying – including shutting down disinformation channels – but half of the battle, for me at least, had been trying to make people pay attention. Komarnyckyj agreed wholeheartedly.

"In 2014, I outlined a number of initial ideas for defeating Russia's hybrid war," he told me. "I believe that these ideas remain a useful basis for tackling Putin's undeclared war against the west. However, the three initial steps are: 1) To accept that the war is happening. We all have a collective responsibility to see beyond the lies of our foe. Look not at what they say but what they do. 2) To recognise the deniable assets for what they are and target them. Ban Russia Today. Treat the politicians and journalist on its payroll as social pariahs the Lord Haw Haws of the digital age. 3) To develop a plan to counter the threat based on the recognition that it is them or us."

"Sadly we have not reached stage 1 in the UK," he said, explaining that the head of MI6 made a statement recognising the threat last year but worded it in vague terms. "Our politicians are making the problem worse by trying to surf the wave of chaos unleashed by Putin. And Johnson is too large and wobbly, literally and metaphorically, to stay upright on any surfboard. They are actually assisting Putin's efforts to toxify political debate by trumpeting Brexit – a parochial, brain dead policy which will isolate the UK and help splinter the transatlantic alliance."

Before the UK becomes "Russia's North Sea Oblast", as Komarnyckyj termed it, I pressed him on what practical countermeasures need to be taken – in particular considering we were for the moment (and rightly, in my view) – seen as enemies of our EU neighbours. Komarnyckyj did not hold back, saying we urgently need to map Russia's propaganda resources to develop a conceptual framework which breaks the countries resources into categories such as "directly financed media agencies, directly paid agents of influence, Soviet legacy political parties who are still Russian-centric in orientation." He also made clear we needed to collectively shift away from "uncoordinated initiatives towards pooling resources and coordinating actions; move away from reacting to the material produced by the propaganda apparatus to a focus on coordinated action to destroy the apparatus itself; and focus on undermining Putin's virtual world and its hired creators by exposing its – and their – dishonesty."

These moves were well under way in Germany and France already, and Komarnyckyj received them positively, though he placed an emphasis on non-violent action based upon his own experience.

"The strategy must adhere to best practice in terms of being anti-discriminatory. It is likely that the traditional ploy of depicting people negatively will be utilised against any organised campaign. It is also possible that attempts will be made to discredit the campaign by planting agents who will make provocative, inflammatory statements. Indeed, Ukrainian politics has been affected by a number of right-wing parties who may have been sponsored by Russia."

As well as setting out the need for planned action focusing on the structure of Putin's propaganda apparatus, Komarnyckyj told me that any such response: "Must adhere to the principles of transparency, equality, and diversity both as a matter of principle and because this will neutralise several means by which Russia might attempt to discredit the attack on its propaganda apparatus." I agree: we have to fight fire with water, not petrol.

Working as an independent journalist I had been lucky, in that I was able to avoid the trap of editorial slant, but this provided its own struggle because I was effectively competing with the financial backing of billionaires in trying to expose this mess. The situation had set me thinking and I asked Komarnyckyj for his view on the broader involvement of the mainstream media, which isn't directly funded by the public through outlets like Byline.

"There are other elements of the situation in the UK which deserve special mention," he said. "You have an oligarchised media ownership which has assisted Putin's Brexit plans, you face the proliferation of fake and pro-Russian sites- alt-right and hard left- on the Anglophone web, extensive penetration of politics by deniable assets and the Moscow-based press corps who import RU narratives with a gloss of respectability into the western media- in exchange for privileged access."

"The UK needs to tackle its oligarchised media and to introduce sanctions for fake news – journalists need to adopt a code of ethics preventing them from accepting money from subversive fake media channels. We need to educate the public to become resistive to manipulation via social media – and to be intelligent, sceptical consumers of news," he added.

Having carried my own unbreakable ethics through from my time as a police officer and whistleblower, I already saw Byline as a vital frontline resource in this conflict and Komarnyckyj agreed.

"Your work gives a very comprehensive and detailed account of Russia's hybrid operations against the West using open source intelligence and your own investigation. I think it should be widely circulated particularly because you are a British voice on this theme." Nonetheless, we were both painfully aware of the risks of failure. "Britain will not survive unless it rids itself of Russia's deniable assets," Komarnyckyj added.

When turning from the press to the role of academia, Komarnyckyj was less positive.

"The UK and the West must also address the impact of Russian soft power on academic discourse," he told me and didn't pull his punch afterwards. "In the thirties, Russia inflicted a genocidal famine on Ukraine (which involved confiscating everything edible from vast areas) and undertook mass executions from 1930 onwards. Yet Western academia has been manipulated – via a combination of professional ties, the carrot of archival access and the consistency of message emanating from Russia – into arguing that this was in large degree a famine caused by collectivisation. Unfortunately, this reflexively complicit attitude facilitated Putin's attack," he told me. "He knew that the UK would lack robustness to challenge his blatant destabilisation via deniable assets. We are paying a price for our cowardice and allowing him to reinvent Stalin as a great leader. Labour and the left never shed their totalitarian heritage – progressive politics in the UK is crippled by this legacy, fettered by a dead ideology."

On that note, I wanted to know if any of Komarnyckyj's proposed solutions were working on his own front line.

"Ukraine has very quickly worked through steps 1 – 3 from my outline," he told me. "Civic society has been able to develop initiatives to counter Russia's hybrid operations. These include initiatives such as Stop Fake, InformNapalm, Euromaidan Press – these groups tackle disinformation head on and compile intelligence on Russia's war effort via the web. Ukrainians are still facing massively entrenched corruption and have their own populist oligarchs, however, the continuous challenge offered is transforming Ukraine. The population understands Russia and is fighting at every level."

Things here in Britain, Komarnyckyj told me as a dual national, were not going so well, however. "Unfortunately, the UK's 'civic society' and political parties are heavily penetrated by Russia," he said. "Organisations such as Stop the War UK, parties like UKIP, are in effect tools of Putin's hybrid war." My own investigation backed him fully with broad evidence and he added that "the Putin/Milne handshake, the Farage meeting with the RU ambassador illustrate my argument about the move from covert to overt. During the cold war, an agent of influence recruited by the KGB would be prosecuted. During the present conflict, an agent of influence recruited by Russia Today can launch a campaign to bugger up the EU in plain sight. We will pay heavily for our failure to condemn and reject this species of totalitarianism."

"The truth is our greatest weapon," he added, again taking me back to Sweden. "However until we see Russia as it really is rather than through the prism of Russian soft power we are lost."

After speaking to Komarnyckyj, I was actually left with hope. Not because enough had been done, not by a long way, but because I felt some of us were on the right track and the fight back started exactly where things began – in my case anyway – with independent journalism, funded by the direct support of the public: discovering the truth and making it heard. Causing kerfuffle.

I began to believe this is how we could eventually win, by working together. So, I turned my attention towards finishing what I'd started, sitting down with a broadly overlooked intelligence report by the US Intelligence Agencies which confirmed my own findings on Russian subversion in the 2016 Presidential election.

The US Intelligence Community (USIC) was, it transpired, confident the Russian Government directed the compromises of e-mails from "US persons and institutions, including from US political organisations." The disclosures of alleged hacked e-mails on sites like WikiLeaks were, as I had deduced, consistent with the methods and motivations of Russian-directed efforts and these thefts and disclosures were, indeed, intended to interfere with the US election process. The joint statement for Homeland Security and National Intelligence didn't hold back, saying: "Such activity is not new to Moscow—the Russians have used similar tactics and techniques across Europe and Eurasia, for example, to influence public opinion there. We believe, based on the scope and sensitivity of these efforts, that only Russia's senior-most officials could have authorized these activities." Some US states also saw scanning and probing of their election-related systems, which in most cases originated from servers operated by a Russian company. The extent of the efforts to hack voting machines became clearer in May 2017, when contractor Reality Winner was arrested by the FBI for leaking an NSA assessment which showed Russia had managed to get deeper into electoral systems than originally thought.

The detailed report I was reading, which pre-dated the additional information from Winner, included specific information on the coordinated efforts of Russian state intelligence services, hacking under those familiar names APT28 and APT29 – both of whom I had already extensively linked to the ongoing, Russian hybrid operation. The Joint Analysis Report (JAR) was the result of analytic efforts between the Department of Homeland Security (DHS) and the Federal Bureau of Investigation (FBI). The document provided technical details regarding the tools and infrastructure used by the Russian civilian and military intelligence Services, which they refer to as RIS, to compromise and exploit networks and endpoints associated with the US election, as well as a range of US Government, political, and private sector entities. The USIC was referring to the malicious cyber activity by the Russians under the name GRIZZLY STEPPE. Previous reports of this kind had not attributed malicious cyber activity to specific countries or threat actors, however, the JAR made clear: "Public attribution of these activities to RIS is supported by technical indicators from the US Intelligence Community, DHS, FBI, the private sector, and other entities. This activity by RIS is part of an ongoing campaign of cyber-enabled operations directed at the US government and its citizens." Confirming my previous, independent findings, the JAR also stated: "Cyber operations have included spear-phishing campaigns targeting government organisations, critical infrastructure entities, think tanks, universities, political organisations, and corporations leading to the theft of information."

"In foreign countries, RIS actors conducted damaging and/or disruptive cyber-attacks, including attacks on critical infrastructure networks. In some cases, RIS actors masqueraded as third parties, hiding behind false online personas designed to cause the victim to misattribute the source of the attack," the report added.

I was astonished, reading this, to see that two different – but, by then, very familiar – Russian actor groups were confirmed to have participated in the intrusion into the systems of a US political party – the DNC. The first group, APT29, entered into the party's systems in summer 2015, while the second, APT28, entered in spring 2016. Both the GRU and FSB had already been linked by my own investigation to terrorist narratives in the EU and the ongoing hybrid conflict which was targeting democracies across the West, but this was official validation. According to the report, "APT29 has been observed crafting targeted spear-phishing campaigns leveraging web links to a malicious dropper; once executed, the code delivers Remote Access Tools (RATs) and evades detection using a range of techniques," while "APT28 is known for leveraging domains that closely mimic those of targeted organisations and tricking potential victims into entering legitimate credentials." This latter was the same method used to target Macron's En Marche!

APT28's actors, the JAR stated: "Relied heavily on shortened URLs in their spear-phishing email campaigns. Once APT28 and APT29 have access to victims, both groups exfiltrate and analyze information to gain intelligence value. These groups use this information to craft highly targeted spear-phishing campaigns."

"These actors set up operational infrastructure to obfuscate their source infrastructure, host domains and malware for targeting organisations, establish command and control nodes, and harvest credentials and other valuable information from their targets," the report continued, which explained a great deal more about how the Wannacry attack managed to create such a mess and muddied waters as regards the location of a "patient zero." My own trip down the rabbit hole independently verified most, if not all of this, even before reading the JAR – both in the broader context of the world cyberattack, and in the subsequent, unfounded allegations of North Korea being responsible – but I added crucial detail.

In summer 2015, the JAR recaps an APT29 spear-phishing campaign which directed emails containing a malicious link to over one thousand recipients, including multiple US Government victims. They used legitimate domains, including some associated with US organisations and educational institutions, to host malware and send spear-phishing emails. This was the same tactic used with the NATO email and which was caught out in Romania two years later. In the course of the 2015 campaign, however, the report states the group successfully compromised the DNC and at least one targeted individual activated links to malware hosted on "operational infrastructure of opened attachments containing malware." Again, this functioned in a similar way to the Trump-Syria document in the 2017 campaign. The report was unambiguous as to how the spear-phishing operation was used once a person had launched the infected attachment, saying: "APT29 delivered malware to the political party's systems, established persistence, escalated privileges, enumerated active directory accounts, and exfiltrated email from several accounts through encrypted connections back through operational infrastructure." To my surprise, known disinformation actors – associated amongst other things with the spurious 'pizzagate' narrative – began proactively attempting to convince the American public the DNC information was passed legitimately to Wikileaks. This remains untrue, despite being reported on Fox and the Russia-serving right-wing conspiracy theory about the alternative source of the leak will never be repeated by me – due to the distress it has caused a family concerned and out of respect for their requests for it to stop being mentioned. However, the disinformation – designed to cover for known Russian activity – tightened the direct link between the so-called alt-right and the broader state-sponsored hybrid conflict, which I already believed incorporated

Wikileaks as a deniable asset working on behalf of Russia.

The JAR continued documenting the Russian operation, stating it continued in Spring 2016, when APT28 compromised the same political party, again via targeted spear-phishing. This time, the malicious email tricked recipients into changing their passwords through a fake webmail domain hosted on APT28 operational infrastructure – and, again, this was deployed against Macron in France. Using the harvested credentials, APT28 was subsequently able to gain access and steal content, likely leading to "the exfiltration of information from multiple senior party members." The USIC report assesses that the information was leaked to the press and publicly disclosed.

The Russian Intelligence Service groups continued to be actively deployed across Europe, in the UK, and in the US, and the activities the report covered carried on in the US right up until the days before Trump's election – something which was again mirrored in the French campaign.

The JAR was incredible to read: an inarguable statement of Russian responsibility – though I'm still glad I took the long way around to arrive at the same destination. The report was not, however, the only document which exposed the scale of Russia's hybrid operations and how each element had been interacting. Disinformation and its spread was just as important as the more covert cyber-espionage.

I first came across Trend Microsystems when initially looking into hacking – along with the shift in the dynamic of terrorism across Europe – and it was through them I had found out about Russia masquerading as the Islamic State in earlier cyberattacks on France. After I finished reading the NSIC's JAR, Trend released an incredibly detailed research paper on Fake News and disinformation, which exposed how it can be spread by deniable assets, acting through a cash-driven, underground network of privateers. Properly, in my opinion, the cyber security firm opened their June 2017 report by highlighting the true significance of what could have otherwise become a throwaway term.

"Fake news became increasingly common during the past year," they said. "While this concept has many synonyms—disinformation campaigns, cyber propaganda, cognitive hacking, and information warfare—it's just one facet of the bigger problem: the manipulation of public opinion to affect the real world."

"Until society agrees to the norms—whether through government regulation or societal self-regulation—various parties will abuse it to serve their agendas. This results in false information reaching the public—deliberately or by accident. Either way, it results in what we know as fake news today," the authors added, echoing my conversation with Nils Karlsson back at the Malmö Stadhuset.

My own investigations established a clear lack of suitable regulation and ineffective counter-measures, both of which combined to create the environment in which two Western democracies were successfully subverted by Russia. The Trend report made no bones in explaining exactly how useful disinformation is too, specifying how it works within the same sphere of influence as the big data and psychometric tactics utilised by companies like Cambridge Analytica. By "manipulating the balance of how a particular topic is reported (whether that concerns politics, foreign affairs, or something more commercial)," the report said, adding: "The views on that topic can be changed. This can be done either with inaccurate facts or with accurate ones twisted to favor a particular view or side."

According to the analysts at Trend Micro, social media posts also have to attract the target readers of their operation. "To do this," Trend said, "the fake news posts are crafted to appeal to its readers' psychological desires—confirming biases, the hierarchy of needs, etc." In addition, the report set out that some services use crowdsourcing mechanisms to manipulate real users into doing the bidding of fake news promoters. "For example, offer users free likes in exchange for a number of likes produced by the participating user," the report pointed out. "It would be nearly impossible for social media networks to distinguish such manipulated activity from actual or natural user actions."

In their detailed analysis, analysts set out the key benefits to using the underground market, saying it begins with cost. "Legitimate advertising is more expensive compared to the costs of fake news (which is important to smaller, less-funded actors)," they wrote, observing that viral spread through users also gains more traction than adverts. Having explored the existence of the St Petersburg Troll Army, the Kremlin-linked operation which works with bots and humans to spread disinformation and steer public opinion, I found Trend's report complemented what I had already found but expanded upon the costs in detail.

"The pricing models are generally simple: a fixed amount of money results in a fixed amount of actions and manipulations performed on a social media site (likes, favorites, etc.). Some of these services guarantee the quality of these actions as well (i.e., they will use humans instead of bots, etc.)," the report said.

Going beyond social media likes, shares, and comments, however, the Trend research also delves into darker territory. One Russian company, Jet-s, can purportedly manipulate petitions on platforms like change.org – "Its prices vary: RUB 60,000 ($1,065) will turn into 10,000 votes or petition signatures, while RUB 150,000 ($2,664) will give customers 25,000. A vying service, Slavavtope, offers more platforms," the report stated. This clearly would have the ability to drive more significant change than push messaging alone, as these petitions are often used to influence governmental behaviour.

Another Russian site, Weberaser, focuses on taking down and removing undesirable (and ironically, fake) content or information from the internet, or removing top results from search engines. Its services, depending on the complexity of the task and available time, start from three-thousand Rubles (about fifty dollars) if the customer can read Russian or use a machine translator. By the time I was reading this, Cambridge Analytica's parent company, SCL, had recently changed its website, deleting all references to SCL Elections and were upping their public denials of any involvement with Leave.EU. Though the web-archive meant snapshots of their sites were saved for reference, services such as Weberaser remain clearly a useful, if not dangerous, tool.

The services available in these underground markets Trend were discussing extended beyond spreading fake news alone and one factor driving the dark economy appeared to be the same reason deniable assets have always been relied upon in espionage and other state activities: anonymity. Using this underground network it is, Trend highlighted, much easier to hide the true origin of any campaign and protect not only those involved but keep obscured what they are trying to do.

Fake news, Trend identified, is a "means to an objective, not an objective in and of itself," adding: "The parties who commissioned the promotion of fake news sites do so with an objective in mind." I was beyond holding on to any doubt the desire of the people utilising these campaigns and, additionally, the underground network of extra services, had simply been to influence and undermine Western democracies, thus affecting their international policy and military relationships. While the primary motives so far had been political, my own investigations led me to conclude the geopolitical control also led to the control of the money, to the benefit of those responsible. That's a pretty solid objective and is likely to be the ultimate and lasting one. Trend's report largely confirms this view, setting out a stark warning for the future: "Even if political fake news is the most commonly used today, the tools and techniques that enable them are becoming more available. It is inevitable that other motivations—such as profit—will come to the forefront in later years."

Something as innocuous sounding as alternative facts has played a crucial role in all of this – despite being something which initially defied common sense – and Trend's report goes a long way to succinctly explaining the easy psychology of this, saying: "In today's digital era, the attention span of a typical reader is very short. Fake news creators use this to manipulate the public. There's no need for an article to be sensible, complete, or factual; a sensational headline will achieve the objectives just as well."

This made for an excellent, capsule explanation of the alt-right and the broader disinformation which had been combined with the micro-targeting of voters to full, gruesome effect. Taking everything into account – from my own discoveries, Komarnyckyj's view, the JAR, and Trend's report – there was little doubt left in what had taken place. Problematically, as I had accidentally proven, the truth of all of it simply cannot be explained in less than one hundred thousand words, completely contrary to the successful technique Russia had designed and deployed. So, my own responses to the Alternative War – from the articles to the seventy-page statement, to this book – are as much of an experiment as Tallinn once was for Capstone. A weapons test.

NINETEEN:

I suppose, in many ways, I was starting to wrap up loose ends up when I eventually sat down to read "Assessing Russian Activities and Intentions in Recent US Elections," the public version of a highly classified assessment which was provided to President Barack Obama in December 2016 and to additional recipients approved by him at the time. The report was based on information and intelligence which was available to the CIA up until the 29th of December 2016 and, though I was aware of it, I had avoided reading it, intentionally holding it away at arm's length to avoid any taint on what I had been doing. I'll admit, at the end of it all, I was relieved to see it confirmed my own findings.

While the conclusions in the public version of the report were all reflected in the classified assessment, the declassified copy did not (and could not, for obvious reasons) include the full supporting information, specific intelligence, source details and methods used to put it together. This was a protection measure primarily aimed at protecting people who had provided evidence to the authorities and the CIA followed the rules in a way President Trump had not. The report opened by outlining the difficulties faced by the intelligence agencies in the current geopolitical climate – in effect, in the face of a complex hybrid threat from Russia – saying: "The mission of the Intelligence Community is to seek to reduce the uncertainty surrounding foreign activities, capabilities, or leaders' intentions. This objective is difficult to achieve when seeking to understand complex issues on which foreign actors go to extraordinary lengths to hide or obfuscate their activities."

"The nature of cyberspace makes attribution of cyber operations difficult but not impossible. Every kind of cyber operation—malicious or not—leaves a trail," it added.

Intelligence tradecraft has developed over the years into a standard model which combines analysis, probability, and logical reasoning. This is the same standard which was applied throughout my own investigation and includes those assessments of confidence which the NCSC also applied to their North Korea conclusion reported by the BBC. The document also included an analytical assessment drafted and coordinated between The Central Intelligence Agency (CIA), The Federal Bureau of Investigation (FBI), and The National Security Agency (NSA), which drew on intelligence information collected and disseminated by those three agencies. The assessment focused on activities aimed at the 2016 US presidential election, drew on their combined understanding of previous Russian influence operations, and it covered the "motivation and scope of Moscow's intentions regarding US elections and Moscow's use of cyber tools and media campaigns to influence US public opinion." The joint analysis was, however, clear the agencies "did not make an assessment of the impact that Russian activities had on the outcome of the 2016 election," saying "the US Intelligence Community is charged with monitoring and assessing the intentions, capabilities, and actions of foreign actors; it does not analyze US political processes or US public opinion."

Many of the key judgments in the assessment relied on a body of reporting from multiple sources which were consistent with the agencies' understanding of Russian behaviour – meaning they went out and sought open source material too, taking exactly the same approach I had. "Insights into Russian efforts—including specific cyber operations—and Russian views of key US players derive from multiple corroborating sources. Some of our judgments about Kremlin preferences and intent are drawn from the behaviour of Kremlin-loyal political figures, state media, and pro-

Kremlin social media actors, all of whom the Kremlin either directly uses to convey messages or who are answerable to the Kremlin," the report says. The Russian leadership, it adds: "Invests significant resources in both foreign and domestic propaganda and places a premium on transmitting what it views as consistent, self-reinforcing narratives regarding its desires and red lines, whether on Ukraine, Syria, or relations with the United States."

The key findings of the report were starkly worded from the outset but I had already reached the same conclusions and found myself nodding along. "We assess Russian President Vladimir Putin ordered an influence campaign in 2016 aimed at the US presidential election. Russia's goals were to undermine public faith in the US democratic process, denigrate Secretary Clinton, and harm her electability and potential presidency," the report stated. "We further assess Putin and the Russian Government developed a clear preference for President-elect Trump." Where it uses the term *we*, the report refers to the corroborated and agreed opinions of the Central Intelligence Agency, the Federal Bureau of Investigation, and the National Security Agency.

According to the agencies, the level of direct attack deployed in Russia's hybrid assault was unprecedented: "Russian efforts to influence the 2016 US presidential election represent the most recent expression of Moscow's longstanding desire to undermine the US-led liberal democratic order, but these activities demonstrated a significant escalation in directness, level of activity, and scope of effort compared to previous operations."

With moderate (in the case of the NSA) and high confidence (of the CIA and FBI), the report went on to conclude: "Putin and the Russian Government aspired to help President-elect Trump's election chances when possible by discrediting Secretary Clinton and publicly contrasting her unfavourably to him." Moscow's approach, the spies said, evolved over the course of the campaign in reaction to Russia's understanding of the electoral prospects of the two main candidates. When it appeared to Moscow that Hilary Clinton was likely to win the election, the Russian influence campaign began to focus more on undermining her future presidency and the ongoing collection of intelligence between election day in November and the report's publication in December enhanced the USIC's confidence in this conclusion. The influence campaign followed a Russian messaging strategy which "blends covert intelligence operations — such as cyber activity — with overt efforts by Russian Government agencies, state-funded media, third-party intermediaries, and paid social media users or trolls," the agencies said, adding: "Russia, like its Soviet predecessor, has a history of conducting covert influence campaigns focused on US presidential elections that have used intelligence officers and agents and press placements to disparage candidates perceived as hostile to the Kremlin."

The report specifically confirmed the leak activity relating to the DNC hack, saying "Russian military intelligence (General Staff Main Intelligence Directorate or GRU) used the Guccifer 2.0 persona and DCLeaks.com to release US victim data obtained in cyber operations publicly" and this was the channel by which Russia laundered the trail and relayed material to WikiLeaks.

The warning the report gave made grim reading for the Western world, saying "Moscow will apply lessons learned from its Putin-ordered campaign aimed at the US presidential election to future influence efforts worldwide, including against US allies and their election processes." A warning which was proven well-founded in France. "In trying to influence the US election," the intelligence agencies concluded, "we assess the Kremlin sought to advance its longstanding desire to undermine the US-led liberal democratic order, the promotion of which Putin and other senior

Russian leaders view as a threat to Russia and Putin's regime."

Putin had, of course, publicly pointed to the financial web unveiled by the Panama Papers and the Olympic doping scandal – which ruined his own country's sporting reputation – as US-directed efforts to defame Russia. The report suggested he sought to use disclosures to further discredit the image of the United States by casting it as hypocritical. According to the CIA, the Russian President was likely to have targeted Clinton because he had "publicly blamed her since 2011 for inciting mass protests against his regime in late 2011 and early 2012," and because: "He holds a grudge for comments he almost certainly saw as disparaging him." This assertion that the Russian Government developed a clear preference for Trump over Clinton had been repeatedly supported over time and there was no doubt remaining that Trump's Administration had operated in collusion with Russia, whether directly or through deniable assets, for quite some time.

Beginning in June, Putin's public comments about the US presidential race avoided directly praising Trump: "probably because Kremlin officials thought that any praise from Putin personally would backfire in the United States." Nonetheless, Putin publicly indicated a preference for President-elect Trump's stated policy to work with Russia and pro-Kremlin figures spoke highly about what they saw as his "Russia-friendly positions on Syria and Ukraine," at the same time as consistently labelling Clinton's foreign policy as "aggressive rhetoric." It's a point of fact Trump's own foreign policy was highly sympathetic to the Russian Federation and figures involved in shaping his policy had those direct links to Moscow, as I'd established. According to the report, Moscow also saw the election of Trump as a way to achieve an international counterterrorism coalition against the Islamic State in Iraq and the Levant (ISIL), which has come to pass – though this has brought its own questions, not least relating to Qatar, and including a number of serious concerns my own discoveries had raised.

I revisited Trump's counter-terrorism approach on reading the CIA's take and found, on February the 5th 2017, Trump told reporters: "It's better to get along with Russia than not. And if Russia helps us in the fight against ISIS, which is a major fight, and Islamic terrorism all over the world — that's a good thing." However, US national security experts do not believe Russia is committed to combatting the Islamic State. While Washington's top goal is to retake ground and the ISIS self-declared capital of Raqqa, the Russian goal appears to be to ensure Syrian President Bashar al-Assad remains in power.

Jim Townsend, Obama's former deputy assistant secretary of defence for European and NATO policy, told reporters: "Whatever they [Russia] do against ISIS is done to protect themselves or to support Assad. It's a different kind of fight for them."

Colin Kahl, former Vice President Joseph Biden's national security adviser, and Hal Brands, former special assistant to the secretary of defence for strategic planning, had also written: "Russia's overarching goal, and one that it has been fairly successful in achieving, is to fortify the Assad regime in power and thereby protect Russia's strategic position in Syria and the broader Middle East."

Even Republican Senator John McCain, the chair of the Senate Armed Services Committee, has openly said: "The time President Trump spent sharing sensitive information with the Russians was time he did not spend focusing on Russia's aggressive behavior" or putting an end to the "slaughter of innocent civilians and targeting of hospitals in Syria." Another Senator, Ben Cardin, the ranking member on the Senate Foreign Relations Committee, also stated he: "Wouldn't characterize the Russians as allies in the fight against ISIS." Cardin's spokesperson added the latter believes

Russian actions in Syria have "exacerbated the conditions that have allowed ISIS to flourish."

As if there wasn't enough evidence already, looking at this through the CIA microscope it's clear something was out of balance in respect of Russia's true intentions and, subsequently, the Trump narrative. A point which is driven home by the actions of the former USSR in the Aleppo offensive. The benefit to Russia, in terms of a conflict which increases volumes of migration to Europe and fuels the divisive narratives of the far-right parties it supports, is genuinely obvious: destabilisation by assets which are both detached and deniable simultaneously. Meanwhile, because this action exacerbates the problem, terrorism continued unrelentingly and a further attack in the UK – an atrocity at a music concert in Manchester on the 22nd of May 2017 – came during Trump's visit to the Middle East.

Speaking in Riyadh before the bombing, Trump said: "This is not a battle between different faiths, different sects, or different civilisations. This is a battle between barbaric criminals who seek to obliterate human life, and decent people of all religions who seek to protect it."

During his visit, he claimed to have signed the largest arms deal in US history and the Qatar crisis began shortly afterwards. Additionally, those previous patterns I had identified across Europe and the US, pro-Kremlin commentators and media channels were among the first to attribute the Manchester attack to Islamic terror, hours before the police had even established details of the events.

Trump then led a call to the world to unite in the fight against ISIS in the wake of the attack, on May the 23rd – a day before James Comey, the dismissed FBI director investigating his administration, was due to give open evidence about his Russia links – a hearing which was postponed. "This wicked ideology must be obliterated and I mean completely obliterated, and the innocent life must be protected. All civilised nations must join together to protect human life and the sacred right our citizens to live in safety and in peace," Trump said during his press conference with Palestinian President Mahmoud Abbas. The dog-whistling, as this type of provocative propaganda is now referred to, and the distraction were no longer even questionable: these moves were all part of a strategy.

Returning to the CIA's report, the agency outlined Putin had many positive experiences working with other Western political leaders whose business interests made them more disposed to deal with Russia, such as former Italian Prime Minister Silvio Berlusconi and former German Chancellor Gerhard Schroeder. Though it did not go on to specify details beyond this, the report intimated they were already aware of Trump's attempted business deals in Russia, along with his web of divested finances which all circle back to his personal empire.

The CIA also made a shrewd observation that a narrative of contesting the result if it didn't go Trump's way – a mirror of Nigel Farage's rhetoric during Brexit – and public criticism of the US election process as unfair (by Putin, Russian officials, and other pro-Kremlin pundits) almost immediately stopped once the result was known. Continuing along this line would have damaged the overt building of positive relations with Moscow, the report logically concluded. This not only showed just how blatant the true nature of Russian tactics was but also how a U-turn, even as brazen as this, can simply be accepted by people if it is handled correctly. Before the election, pro-Kremlin bloggers had prepared a Twitter campaign, #DemocracyRIP, to be deployed on election night in anticipation of Clinton's victory, according to analysis of their social media activity. This also, almost accidentally, provided one of the final links between Russia and the Leave.EU campaign and Westmonster – both projects of Arron

Banks and Nigel Farage, who ran a similar campaign on Social Media in the wake of the Macron victory in France – confirming the use of strategy came from a common playbook, rather than an elaborate series of coincidences. They had, as I'd established, openly supported the Russian-backed and financed, far-right candidate, Marine Le Pen, throughout the French campaign and still continued to do so, even long afterwards.

The declassified CIA report drew the conclusion the influence campaigns were: "Approved at the highest levels of the Russian Government—particularly those that would be politically sensitive," directly pointing the finger of blame at Putin himself. Moscow's campaign, the agencies said, reflected years of investment in its capabilities, which Moscow has honed in the former Soviet states.

"By their nature, Russian influence campaigns are multifaceted and designed to be deniable because they use a mix of agents of influence, cut outs, front organisations, and false-flag operations," the report added, so close to my own conclusions it caused a shiver to run down my spine. Highlighting the specific example of Moscow's deployment of these tactics during the Ukraine crisis in 2014, when Russia deployed forces and advisers to eastern Ukraine and denied it publicly, the report stated: "The Kremlin's campaign aimed at the US election featured disclosures of data obtained through Russian cyber operations; intrusions into US state and local electoral boards; and overt propaganda." Russian intelligence collection both informed and enabled the influence campaign, the report added, saying: "Russian intelligence services collected against the US primary campaigns, think tanks, and lobbying groups they viewed as likely to shape future US policies. In July 2015, Russian intelligence gained access to Democratic National Committee (DNC) networks and maintained that access until at least June 2016." From the JAR, I knew the access by APT28 and APT29 had gone on right up until the election itself and from my own poking around I had already uncovered a number of connections between Russia, lobby groups like BGR, and Trump.

On the DNC email hack and subsequent leaks, the report states "Guccifer 2.0, who claimed to be an independent Romanian hacker, made multiple contradictory statements and false claims about his likely Russian identity throughout the election. Press reporting suggests more than one person claiming to be Guccifer 2.0 interacted with journalists." This conclusion was, of course, logical and followed previous findings of extensive state-sponsored Russian hacking I'd determined, and the questions around Guccifer being a Russian asset with a fake identity. The content of the DNC leak reviewed in the report was taken from e-mail accounts targeted by the Russian GRU in March 2016 and appeared on DCLeaks.com starting in June. The intelligence agencies stated the GRU relayed material it acquired from the DNC and senior Democratic officials to WikiLeaks – which I already believed with good reason to be a deniable Russian asset. According the analysts: "Moscow most likely chose WikiLeaks because of its self-proclaimed reputation for authenticity." They noted that documents published WikiLeaks did not contain any evident forgeries and, in early September 2016, Putin had said publicly it was important the DNC data was exposed to WikiLeaks, calling the search for the source of the leaks a distraction and denying Russian state-level involvement. Importantly, the report also confirmed the Kremlin's principal international propaganda outlet, RT, had actively collaborated with WikiLeaks. According to the CIA, RT's editor-in-chief visited WikiLeaks founder Julian Assange at the Ecuadorian Embassy in London in August 2013, where they discussed renewing his broadcast contract with RT. This was also reported in Russian and Western media. The Russian media, however, subsequently announced RT had become "the only Russian media company" to partner with WikiLeaks and had received access to "new leaks of secret information." RT, the CIA said, had also routinely given Assange sympathetic coverage and provided him with a platform to denounce the United States – support mirrored by Nigel Farage, who also has those close links with RT and who had also visited Assange, as I separately established.

According to the CIA, the election-related disclosures and disinformation more broadly reflected a pattern of Russian intelligence using hacked information in tailored influence efforts against targets such as Olympic athletes and other foreign governments. Such efforts, they confirmed, have included releasing or altering personal data, defacing websites, and releasing emails. A prominent target since the 2016 Summer Olympics was the World Anti-Doping Agency (WADA), with leaks assessed to have: "Originated with the GRU and that have involved data on US athletes. Crucially, however, the report accurately identified Russia collected information on some Republican-affiliated targets but did not conduct a comparable disclosure campaign. Russia's state-run propaganda machine — which I knew was comprised of its domestic media apparatus, outlets targeting global audiences such as RT and Sputnik and a network of quasi-government trolls — contributed to the influence campaign by "serving as a platform for Kremlin messaging to Russian and international audiences," the report stated. The same pattern was evident in both Brexit and the French election.

State-owned Russian media also made increasingly favourable comments about Trump as the 2016 US general and primary election campaigns progressed, while consistently offering negative coverage of the Clinton campaign. On the 6th of August 2016, RT published an English language video called *Julian*

Assange Special: Do WikiLeaks Have the E-mail That'll Put Clinton in Prison? and an exclusive interview with Assange entitled *Clinton and ISIS Funded by the Same Money.* Starting in March 2016, Russian-linked actors began openly supporting President-elect Trump's candidacy in media aimed at English-speaking audiences. RT and Sputnik consistently cast Trump as the target of unfair coverage from traditional US media outlets which they claimed were subservient to a corrupt political establishment. Again, this narrative was a mirror of both Farage's and Le Pen's respective campaigns and the Russian media hailed Trump's victory as a "vindication of Putin's advocacy of global populist movements", which was also the theme of Putin's annual conference for Western academics in October 2016. Putin's chief propagandist, Dmitriy Kiselev, also used his flagship weekly news magazine program to cast Trump as an outsider victimised by a corrupt political establishment – The Swamp – and faulty democratic election process which aimed to prevent his election because of his desire to work with Moscow. According to the report, Pro-Kremlin proxy Vladimir Zhirinovskiy, leader of the nationalist Liberal Democratic Party of Russia, proclaimed just before the election: "If President-elect Trump won, Russia would drink champagne in anticipation of being able to advance its positions on Syria and Ukraine." This again was a repetition of comments attributed to Putin in respect of the result of Brexit and the misuse of title for Trump provides a huge indicator Russia knew the result in advance.

Conversely, RT's coverage of Clinton throughout the US presidential campaign was consistently negative, focusing on her leaked e-mails and accusing her of corruption, poor physical and mental health, and ties to Islamic extremism. Some Russian officials echoed state lines for the influence campaign – saying Secretary Clinton's election could lead to a war between the United States and Russia – and, in August,

Kremlin-linked political analysts suggested avenging negative Western reports on Putin by airing segments devoted to Clinton's alleged health problems. RT's most popular video on Clinton, "How 100% of the Clintons' 'Charity' Went to...Themselves," had more than nine million views on social media platforms, while the most popular English language video about the then President-elect, called "Trump Will Not Be Permitted to Win," featured Julian Assange and had over two million views. According to the intelligence report, Russia used trolls as well as RT as part of its influence efforts to denigrate Clinton, and this effort amplified stories on scandals about the Democratic candidate and the role of WikiLeaks in the election campaign. The likely financier of the so-called Internet Research Agency – which the agencies defined as "professional trolls located in Saint Petersburg" – was, the report says: "A close Putin ally with ties to Russian intelligence." Again, I'd ascertained exactly the same thing, with the addition of more detail, then added Trend's underground market into the mix. One leading expert cited in the CIA report on the Internet Research Agency claimed some social media accounts which appear to be tied to Russia's professional trolls – as they were previously devoted to supporting Russian actions in Ukraine – started to advocate for President-elect Trump as early as December 2015. Social media trolls, of course, featured heavily in the Brexit and Macron campaigns and had already resurfaced in the UK during the 2017 general election, though many were still mid-transition – bearing mixed US/UK biographies and content. A side-line of my principal investigation had already found since Twitter took steps to allow non-verified accounts to be kept muted, a greater number of these accounts were being human-managed. Additionally, I found it worth noting that, very often, the troll accounts simultaneously support Trump, Brexit, Le Pen and, odd as I thought it was at the time, Scotland remaining a part of the UK.

Russia's effort to influence the 2016 US presidential election, according to the CIA report: "Represented a significant escalation in directness, level of activity, and scope of effort compared to previous operations aimed at US elections." The analysts assessed: "The 2016 influence campaign reflected the Kremlin's recognition of the worldwide effects that mass disclosures of US Government and other private data—such as those conducted by WikiLeaks and others—have achieved in recent years, and their understanding of the value of orchestrating such disclosures to maximize the impact of compromising information." During the Cold War, the Soviet Union used intelligence officers, influence agents, forgeries, and press placements to disparage candidates perceived as hostile to the Kremlin, according to former KGB operatives. Since the Cold War, however, Russian intelligence efforts related to elections have primarily focused on foreign intelligence collection. For decades, Russian and Soviet intelligence services have sought to collect insider information from US political parties which could help Russian leaders understand a new US administration's plans and priorities. Russian Foreign Intelligence Service (SVR) Directorate S (Illegals) officers, arrested in the United States in 2010, were reporting back to Moscow on the 2008 election and, according to the same former KGB operatives, in the 1970s, the KGB recruited a Democratic Party activist who reported information about then-presidential hopeful Jimmy Carter's campaign and foreign policy plans.

The CIA's declassified report concluded: "Election Operation Signals", hybrid conflicts, are the new normal in Russian influence efforts and the intelligence services firmly believe Russian intelligence services would have seen their election influence campaign as: "At least a qualified success because of their perceived ability to impact public discussion." Putin's public views of the efforts suggest the Kremlin and its intelligence services will continue to consider using hybrid operations because of their belief these can accomplish Russian goals relatively easily, without significant damage to Russian interests.

Russia had also sought to influence elections across Europe, the report confirmed, adding the hybrid conflict in the US had not ended with the Trump win. "Russian intelligence services will continue to develop capabilities to provide Putin with options to use against the United States, judging from past practice and current efforts. Immediately after Election Day, we assess Russian intelligence began a spear-phishing campaign targeting US Government employees and individuals associated with US think tanks and NGOs in national security, defense, and foreign policy fields. This campaign could provide material for future influence efforts as well as foreign intelligence collection on the incoming administration's goals and plans."

Even having confirmed nothing was over, the report didn't stop being useful.

After my own significant findings were sent as a statement to international agencies and parliaments in mid-May, the FBI came out at the start of June and declared Nigel Farage a person of interest in their Trump-Russia probe. One source in the Bureau told the Guardian: "If you triangulate Russia, WikiLeaks, Assange and Trump associates the person who comes up with the most hits is Nigel Farage...he's right in the middle of these relationships. He turns up over and over again. There's a lot of attention being paid to him."

While making sure the dubious activity of a public figure came under review by the proper authorities was a clear win for both democracy and independent journalism, Farage immediately took to all media outlets denying any Russia connection whatsoever and decrying the FBI interest as "fake news." In a statement, Farage said: "This hysterical attempt to associate me with the Putin regime is a result of the liberal elite being unable to accept Brexit and the election of President Trump. For the record, I have never been to Russia, I've had no business dealings with Russia in my previous life and I have appeared approximately three times on RT in the last 18 months. I consider it extremely doubtful that I could be a person of interest to the FBI as I have no connections to Russia."

I had clearly set out every reason Farage would be a person of interest to the authorities – in the exact manner specified by the FBI – but some further attention was clearly warranted on the basis of the politician's response, which specifically referred to RT. Thankfully, the declassified CIA document additionally included an extensive annexe of material which was highly relevant.

Annex A of the declassified report was specifically dedicated to RT, the broadcaster which had been tied to UKIP for a number of years. The annexe was originally drawn up in 2012, five years before Farage himself was knighted on the channel in early 2017.

The CIA report introduced RT with a detailed description, saying: "RT America TV, a Kremlin-financed channel operated from within the United States, has substantially expanded its repertoire of programming that highlights criticism of alleged US shortcomings in democracy and civil liberties. The rapid expansion of RT's operations and budget and recent candid statements by RT's leadership point to the channel's importance to the Kremlin as a messaging tool and indicate a Kremlin-directed campaign to undermine faith in the US Government and fuel political protest. The Kremlin has committed significant resources to expanding the channel's reach, particularly its social media footprint." The network, of course, also runs a successful operation in Britain, on which Farage has appeared and the CIA stated "a reliable UK report states that RT recently was the most-watched foreign news channel in the UK" and highlighted that the US incarnation: "Positioned itself as a domestic US channel and has deliberately sought to obscure any legal ties to the Russian Government." As I had established significant ties between Farage, Brexit, Trump, Russia, and the US election, there was subsequently no need for me to limit the scope of the rest of the report, by restricting its definition as being localised to the US.

The CIA assesses, in the run up to the 2012 US presidential election, RT intensified its critical coverage of the United States. "The channel portrayed the US electoral process as undemocratic and featured calls by US protesters for the public to rise up and "take this government back."

"In an effort to highlight the alleged lack of democracy in the United States," the CIA report stated, "RT broadcast, hosted, and advertised third party candidate debates and ran reporting supportive of the political agenda of these candidates. The RT hosts asserted that the US two-party system does not represent the views of at least one-third of the population and is a sham." Much of this content was also recognisable in respect of RTs coverage of UKIP and Farage himself. On the 28th June 2016, for example, Farage appeared on the channel just after the Brexit referendum saying, "Oh, gosh! Who would've believed it? Who would've believed that despite all the threats and bullying from the international community, President Obama, the OECD, [British Chancellor of the Exchequer] George Osborne, the Bank of England... who would've believed the British people would have the courage to say: 'No, no, no, no. We're not listening. We actually want to take back control of our country, our democracy and our lives.' That's what happened." The narrative was almost an exact re-sit of US content aired by RT over a number of years – featured in the CIA report – including a documentary about the Occupy Wall Street movement where the network framed a fight against "the ruling class" and described the current US political system as corrupt and dominated by corporations. RT advertising for the documentary featured calls to "take back" the government. The core message connections were extensive, with the US personified as an undemocratic union of self-interest. Farage has appeared on RT peddling much the same message about the EU with clips dating back to 2011.

Interestingly, the report noted RT runs anti-fracking programming, highlighting environmental issues and the impacts on public health, stating: "This is likely reflective of the Russian Government's concern about the impact of fracking and US natural gas production on the global energy market and the potential challenges to Gazprom's profitability."

Farage, I found, had consistently been for fracking, reaffirmed as recently as 2016 in a BBC appearance, though he and his party have been broadly dismissive of other renewable energy projects which would reduce the UK's reliance on imported fuels. Campaigning in Grimsby in 2015, for example, he claimed, by 2020, people would be paying a "20% surcharge on their electricity bill just to subsidise the renewable industry."

"So I have to say, I think in ten years' time there won't be a renewable industry, we will have rethought the whole thing," Farage added, speaking to BBC Humberside.

By early 2017, the Russian state was seeing heavy lobbying efforts to escalate the reduction of subsidies for renewable energy production and the Russian government has since lowered its target for wind generation between 2021 to 2025 by two hundred and fifty megawatts to just over three gigawatts. In addition, it has also halved its goal for small hydropower plants.

The CIA report also stated: "RT is a leading media voice opposing Western intervention in the Syrian conflict and blaming the West for waging "information wars" against the Syrian Government." Farage had also mirrored this position for some time. The report also referred to the years before 2011, saying "in an earlier example of RT's messaging in support of the Russian Government, during the Georgia-Russia military conflict the channel accused Georgians of killing civilians and organizing a genocide of the Ossetian people. According to Simonyan, when the Ministry of Defense was at war with Georgia, RT was: "Waging an information war against the entire Western world." In 2008, I found evidence of Farage supporting the Russian position in another BBC interview.

Even in 2012, the CIA had captured the truth of RT's position, with the report stating: "In recent interviews, RT's leadership has candidly acknowledged its mission to expand its US audience and to expose it to Kremlin messaging." However, agents recorded the RT leadership "rejected claims that RT interferes in US domestic affairs." The intelligence agency meticulously documented comments by RT's Editor in Chief, Simonyan, who claimed in popular arts magazine Afisha: "It is important to have a channel that people get used to, and then, when needed, you show them what you need to show. In some sense, not having our own foreign broadcasting is the same as not having a ministry of defense. When there is no war, it looks like we don't need it. However, when there is a war, it is critical." The also report stated: "According to Simonyan, "the word 'propaganda' has a very negative connotation, but indeed, there is not a single international foreign TV channel that is doing something other than promotion of the values of the country that it is broadcasting from." She added: "When Russia is at war, we are, of course, on Russia's side," and "RT's goal is "to make an alternative channel that shares information unavailable elsewhere in order to conquer the audience and expose it to Russian state messaging." The annexe concludes that "RT hires or makes contractual agreements with Westerners with views that fit its agenda and airs them on RT."

According to the CIA: "Simonyan said on the pro-Kremlin show, "Minaev Live," that RT has enough audience and money to be able to choose its hosts, and it chooses the hosts that "think like us," "are interested in working in the anti-mainstream," and defend RT's beliefs on social media." Interestingly, the report added: "Some hosts and journalists do not present themselves as associated with RT when interviewing people, and many of them have affiliations to other media and activist organisations."

The CIA report along with Farage's response on the FBI probe raised questions as to whether he is aware of the CIA assessment that RT is a direct arm of the Kremlin and, subsequently, how this information defines (or redefines) the nature of his relationship with Russia. It also leaves more questions in respect of the former UKIP leader's adoption of a number of Russian policy positions, including on Syria, Georgia, and renewable energy, along with his apparent regurgitation of the descriptive narrative aimed at the EU, which exactly reflects that of Russian state propaganda against both the EU and the US.

I never managed to elicit a comment or response from Farage or his representatives through his EU parliamentary offices, but his denials were left in tatters in the face of the cumulative evidence.

While coming from two very different places, my investigation and the intelligence services had arrived at the same conclusions and, I found, the EU – in the meantime – had started taking more concrete measures not only to counter the Russian threat but some of the structural defects which had allowed issues like Farage and Le Pen to be left unchecked, often through the lack of effective enforcement powers in units such as OLAF.

The closer alignment of the EU and NATO was intriguing, especially in light of the risks to the transatlantic alliance posed by Russia using both US and UK as leverage and it's not beyond the realms of possibility that, at some point in the not too distant future, NATO could become something else entirely. Another clue to this was easily found in the EU developments on Ukraine.

The Dutch Senate, following the failed election attempt of far-right candidate Gert Wilders, voted through the ratification of the Association Agreement between the European Union and Ukraine in a move Russia saw as provocative. The vote came in the wake of bold statements by German Chancellor, Angela Merkel, and newly-elected French President, Emanuel Macron, both of whom had directly confronted the pervasive issues of Russian influence targeted at Western elections, and the impact of it upon collapsing international relations with the US and UK.

Responding to the Dutch vote, EU President Juncker said: "Today's vote in the Dutch Senate sends an important signal from the Netherlands and the entire European Union to our Ukrainian friends: Ukraine's place is in Europe. Ukraine's future lies with Europe. I would like to thank the Dutch government and the leadership of other parties for their efforts in bringing this process to a positive conclusion. We are nearly there. Our Association Agreement, including the Deep And Comprehensive Free Trade Area component, is now one step closer to being ratified. I would like to see the process now being finalised swiftly, in time for the EU-Ukraine Summit in July."

"The European Union is fully committed to our partnership with the Ukrainian people, which has developed into one of our closest and most valued. The Association Agreement has already increased trade between us, has brought increased prosperity for entrepreneurs, has helped to initiate and consolidate a number of reforms in Ukraine, and has brought new opportunities to European Union and Ukrainian citizens alike. Let us harness the positive momentum generated by today's vote to further strengthen our partnership," he added. In December 2016, the EU Heads of State and Government had agreed on a legally binding decision setting out their common understanding of certain aspects of the Association Agreement with Ukraine, clarifying the convention did not confer European Union membership, or offer collective security guarantees or military aid/assistance to Ukraine, or give Ukrainian nationals access to the labour markets of EU Member States. They added at the time it did not commit the Member States to financial assistance to Ukraine and underlined that the fight against corruption was an essential element of the arrangement.

To my mind, a stronger EU military force, combined with a more formal agreement with Ukraine was not only indicative of a shift in power within the EU but of increasingly bold push-back against Russia – who had effectively rolled across the UK and US without any real resistance.

The EU also recognised it needed to give its investigative departments teeth, rather than rely on referrals back to domestic governments to act or ignore the issues raised. Just after the union's defence announcement, twenty Member States reached a political agreement on the establishment of the new European Public Prosecutor's Office, under what they termed "enhanced cooperation." Once in place, the independent EU public prosecutor would be equipped with the power to investigate and prosecute criminal cases affecting the EU budget, such as corruption or fraud with EU funds, or cross-border VAT fraud. By design, it would be a strong, independent and efficient body specialised in fighting financial crime across the member states. This would target the exact type of offences I had discovered in respect of Le Pen and also cover that election misspending of Farage and UKIP, which the UK had failed to act upon. On the announcement, Commissioner Günther H. Oettinger, who is in charge of Budget and Human Resources, said:

"We have zero tolerance for fraud against the EU budget. Every cent of it needs to be spent for the benefit of EU citizens. With a strong, independent and efficient European Public Prosecutor we are strengthening our efforts in protecting taxpayers' money by ensuring a European approach to the criminal investigation and prosecution of criminal offences affecting the Union budget. This will be a substantial addition to the current means at Union level, namely the work of OLAF in the area of administrative investigations." According to the Commission, every year at least fifty billion Euro of revenues from VAT alone are lost from national budgets all over Europe through cross-border fraud. Transnational organised crime was, they said, making billions in profit every year by circumventing national rules and escaping criminal prosecution. Outside the area of VAT, in 2015 the Member States detected and reported to the Commission fraudulent irregularities for an amount of around six-hundred-and-fifty million Euro.

Identifying national prosecutors' tools to fight large-scale cross-border financial crime are limited, the new EU prosecutor would be in place to conduct swift investigations across Europe, and to provide a real-time information exchange which does not currently exist. The European Public Prosecutor's Office would operate as a single unit across all participating Member States, set up outside the existing union institutions and services. It would not seek nor take instructions from EU bodies or national authorities, making it lethal to any of the toxic groups currently abusing the system. "We have worked hard to bring as many Member States as possible on board and I am very glad that we now have 20 founding members of the European Public Prosecutor. This is a big success and it ensures that the European Public Prosecutor's Office will be efficient from day one. This is a good day for the European taxpayer. The European Public Prosecutor's Office will complement the important work of Eurojust, the EU criminal justice agency, allowing it to dedicate more resources to the fight against terrorism, human trafficking or other crimes," Commissioner Věra Jourová, EU Commissioner for Justice, Consumers and Gender Equality, said.

The European Public Prosecutor will be organised with a central office at EU level and a decentralised level consisting of European Delegated Prosecutors located in the Member States, who will also continue their function as "double hat" national prosecutors. The central level would supervise the investigations and prosecutions carried out at a national level, the Commission said: "To ensure effective coordination and a uniform approach throughout the EU." Interestingly, the plan sets out that, if the Office takes up an investigation, national authorities will not exercise their powers for the same criminal activity. This indicates a supposition domestic justice is, in specific circumstances, ineffective or, at worst, corrupted.

While the European Public Prosecutor's Office would be responsible for criminal investigations, OLAF was also set to continue its administrative investigations into irregularities and fraud affecting the Union's financial interests in all Member States of the Union. "This approach will ensure the widest possible protection of the EU's budget by increasing the conviction and recovery rates," the EC said on the announcement.

With increasing responsiveness to the changing world climate, the Commission also began making a renewed call to further accelerate the roll-out of the European Border and Coast Guard project and to fill persistent gaps in manpower and equipment as swiftly as possible. Between the lines, they had put in pace significant measures to stem the tide of people displaced by war, not only to break the back of the real problems and shut down far-right narratives but also –

from a diplomatic standpoint – to tell Russia the jig was up.

The EU-Turkey agreement had already delivered significant results, shown by a consistent reduction in irregular crossings to Greece, and in the successful resettlement of over six thousand Syrians given safe and legal pathways to Europe. Giving an update, the European Commission First Vice-President Frans Timmermans made a statement for the EC, saying: "Two years after the launch of the European Agenda on Migration, our joint efforts to manage migratory flows are starting to bear fruit. But the push factors for migration to Europe remain and the tragic loss of life in the Mediterranean continues. As the weather improves, we must redouble our cooperation – working with third countries, protecting our EU external borders, together giving refuge to those who need it and ensuring that those who have no right to remain in the EU are quickly returned. We can only effectively manage migration in Europe if we all work together in a spirit of solidarity and responsibility."

The pace of relocation programmes – taking immigrants and refugees from landing hubs in Greece and Italy and distributing them across the EU, had significantly increased in 2017 with over ten thousand people relocated since January alone — a fivefold increase compared to the same period in 2016. Of course, this isn't without issues. "Regrettably," the Commission stated, "despite these repeated calls, the Czech Republic, Hungary and Poland, in breach of their legal obligations stemming from the Council Decisions and their commitments to Greece, Italy and other Member States, have not yet taken the necessary action. Against this background, and as indicated in the previous Relocation and Resettlement Report, the Commission has decided to launch infringement procedures against these three Member States."

Despite this, progress on resettlement continued to be well on track with nearly three-quarters of twenty thousand resettlements agreed in July 2015 having already been carried out. Commissioner for Migration, Home Affairs and Citizenship Dimitris Avramopoulos said at the time: "Our Union is based on solidarity and the sharing of responsibility. These fundamental values apply to all our policies and migration is no exception. We cannot and we will not leave those Member States with an external border on their own. And when it comes to relocation, let me be crystal clear: the implementation of the Council Decisions on relocation is a legal obligation, not a choice."

The number of daily crossings from Turkey to the Greek islands had stabilised at around fifty per day and, despite some tragic incidents, the number of lives lost in the Aegean had fallen substantially. Overall, arrivals had decreased by ninety-seven percent since the EU-Turkey Statement became operational. The pace of return operations had also seen some positive developments with an additional three hundred returns carried out since the previous report in March 2017, bringing the total number of migrants returned to almost two-thousand. However, arrivals still outpaced the number of returns from the Greek islands to Turkey, leading to pressure on the reception structure on the islands. Progress in other areas of the Statement also remains ongoing, with the continuing efforts by the EU and Turkey to accelerate the delivery of the financial support under the Facility for Refugees in Turkey. Almost all of the funding for 2016-2017 had quickly been allocated (almost three billion Euro) and contracts had already been signed for a total of one-and-a-half billion Euro. In June 2017, more than six-hundred-thousand refugees in Turkey were being supported by the Emergency Social Safety Net and the number of Syrians supported through direct cash transfers was expected to increase to almost one-and-a-half million. Russian was unhappy with this blockage and it is likely this prompted a threatening announcement from their ally, Erdogan, that the six hundred thousand Syrians would be pushed to Europe. Undeterred, however, the Commission also set out the results and lessons learned under the Partnership Framework on Migration, which came a year after its launch. They stated progress was made in the fight against traffickers with "closer cooperation with key countries in Africa to tackle migration flows through the Central Mediterranean route, with a strong focus on cooperation with Libya." The EU Trust Fund, they said, had supported political priorities, mobilising around two billion Euro for projects to address the root causes of migration and supporting better management in countries of origin and transit.

Due to Brexit, the UK faces having its border controls returned from France and it will be excluded from both the European Defence project and the new Independent Prosecutor's Office. Subsequently, the country will remain vulnerable to Russia while also being ineffectively equipped to combat those working in collaboration with Putin's Federation, who will be absorbed back into national politics as the UK's parliamentary presence in the EU is closed down.

Investigating this whole mess, it struck me that the unmitigated success of the Russian hybrid conflict largely arose because of the stale organisation of Western democracy. And not just the institutions which the EU are rapidly transforming. The stagnation ended up with a certain type of person becoming the only acceptable entrant into politics or the security services – something particularly evident in Britain where the private school model has long been the norm in both. Russia, on the other hand, embraced a new style, undergoing a fluid transition from a state with criminal links to a criminal organisation with state machinery. Over the past twenty years, the role of Russian organised crime shifted considerably and Russian criminals now operate less on the street and more in the shadows, often described as "allies, facilitators and suppliers for local European gangs and continent-wide criminal networks." The Russian state has also increasingly become criminalised and the interpretation by some, of the "criminal underworld and the political upperworld," has led Putin's regime to use criminals from time to time as instruments of its rule. While there is now no doubt this incorporates hacking and disinformation, combined with political provokatsiya, Russian-based organised crime groups in Europe have been used for a variety of purposes, including as sources of dark money, human traffickers and smugglers, and even to carry out targeted assassinations on behalf of the Kremlin. According to one detailed assessment I read, Russian-based organised crime is responsible for around one-third of the heroin on Europe's streets, a significant amount of non-European people trafficking, as well as most illegal weapons imports. It is described as a "powerful and pervasive force on the European continent." However, it is also true the operations take different forms in different countries and largely works with – or behind – indigenous European networks and criminal gangs. European policing is – and I know this from experience – behind the curve when it comes to fighting Russian-based organised crime, mainly due to an understanding of these gangs which is outdated. (Police are often still chasing down the street-level gangs first identified as "colonised" in the 1990s, rather than delving behind the scenes of established organised crime to expose their Russian backing.)

Having followed the work of Luke Harding, a former Russia correspondent for some time, it was clear what makes Russian organised crime a particularly serious challenge is the direct connection between the criminal networks and the Kremlin's state security apparatus, notably the Foreign Intelligence Service (SVR), military intelligence (GRU), and the Federal Security Service (FSB) – all three of whom are also engaged in the subversion of democracy across the West. These organised crime groups have already been used by the

Kremlin and are likely to become an even greater problem as Russian's campaign to undermine Western stability and military unity continues. Even back in the 90s, Boris Yeltsin expressed his concern that Russia was becoming a "superpower of crime" and, after the fall of the Soviet Union, the old-school tattooed mobsters of the so-called *vorovskoi mir* and their *vor v zakone* leaders were succeeded by a new generation of *avtoritety* ("authorities"). These are more hybrids: gangster-businessmen who were able to enthusiastically take advantage of crash privatisation, legal anomalies, and state incapacity which characterised Yeltsin's era. One former, senior commander of the police in Moscow said at the time: "These were days when we knew the bandits had not just money and firepower on their side, but they had a better krysha [meaning "roof" and referring to political protection in Russian slang] and we just had to accept that." There was, according to academic studies, a very real fear the country could become, on the one hand, a failed state, and on the other, a very successful criminal enterprise. It became the latter. The 1990s saw organised crime spread like cancer, evolving until, by the end of the decade, a series of violent local, regional, and even national turf wars to establish territorial boundaries and hierarchies were coming to an end. The wealthiest avtoritety partnered with the vast resources of their oligarch counterparts, who had used the collapse of the old state to seize control of markets and assets. They were also joined by some small groups within the military and security structures, motivated by both perverse nationalism and their own personal interests, who acted as provocateurs aiming for a renewal of Russian state power. This is how they all came together, in the end, to put a stop to constant disorder and build something new from the ashes.

Even before Vladimir Putin was elevated to acting president in 1999, then confirmed as Yeltsin's successor in 2000, the battles were ending and, while criminals at first feared Putin was serious about his tough law-and-order rhetoric, it was soon understood his offer was a new contract with the underworld. Gangsters could go about their business without a systematic crackdown, on the condition it was accepted the state was the "biggest gang in town and they did nothing to directly challenge it." The underworld complied and, so the story goes, "indiscriminate street violence was replaced by targeted assassinations; tattoos were out, and Italian suits were in; the new generation gangster-businessmen had successfully domesticated the old-school criminals."

"This was not just a process of setting new boundaries for the criminals; it also led to a restructuring of connections between the underworld and the 'upperworld', to the benefit of the latter," wrote one academic, adding: "Connections between these groups and the state security apparatus grew, and the two became closer to each other. The result was not simply institutionalisation of corruption and further blurring of the boundaries between licit and illicit; but the emergence of a conditional understanding that Russia now had a nationalised underworld." In short, the gangsters were expected to comply with the requests of the state and, during the Second Chechen War, for example, Moscow was able to persuade Chechen gangsters not to support their rebel compatriots. The same thing, it is alleged, recurred during the 2011 State Duma elections – where criminal gangs were used to ensure a Putin vote while disrupting opposition campaigns. The genesis of managed democracy.

As a result of Putin's bold moves, and some apparent degree of growing paranoia, Russia then entered a new phase of this national step-change and the Kremlin came to consider itself at war with the West. It is no surprise, understanding this, the tactics for waging this war include using organised crime as an instrument, and this is the face Western intelligence agencies – in particular the UK, with its genetic code of private education and subsequent non-exposure to criminality – simply failed to recognise. The hybrid conflict we find ourselves in is, in part, a war of the old ways and this new hybrid. The dead languages versus the modern. If you really want to know how all of this came down so hard and fast, I believe the answer is traditional privilege met contemporary criminality and couldn't recognise it for what it was: sharper than Latin.

TWENTY:

As my own investigations came to their end, after months of speculation the former Director of the FBI, James Comey – relieved of his position by Donald Trump in May – finally took the stand before the United States Senate Intelligence Committee on the 8th of June 2017. His personal fall outs with President Trump were not my concern – these were grown men after all – but my journalistic poking around had exposed the wholesale interference in the 2016 presidential election, authorised at the highest levels of the Russian government. I wanted to hear the words said out loud and Comey's testimony did not disappoint me. He confirmed everything within the opening minutes of his testimony.

The Senate Intelligence Committee is led by North Carolina's Republican, Richard Burr, and Virginia's Democrat, Mark Warner, both of whom had been investigating the Russian operation. In opening the June hearing, Burr explained the Senate Select Committee on Intelligence exists to certify for the other eighty-five members of the United States Senate and the American people that the intelligence community is operating lawfully and has the necessary authorities and tools to accomplish its mission and keep America safe.

"Part of our mission," he continued, "beyond the oversight we continue to provide to the intelligence community and its activities, is to investigate Russian interference in the 2016 US elections" adding: "This committee is uniquely suited to investigate Russia's interference in the 2016 elections. We also have a unified, bipartisan approach to what is a highly charged partisan issue." Burr sombrely set out the absolute risks of failing to carry out the inquiry, saying: "Russian activities during 2016 election may have been aimed at one party's candidate, but as my colleague, Senator Rubio, says frequently, in 2018 and 2020, it could be aimed at anyone, at home or abroad."

"We must keep these questions above politics and partisanship. It's too important to be tainted by anyone trying to score political points," he added.

Warner's opening speech pulled no punches either. "It's not about who won or lost. And it sure as heck is not about Democrats versus Republicans," he said, before explaining the true nature of a hybrid conflict. "We're here because a foreign adversary attacked us right here at home, plain and simple, not by guns or missiles, but by foreign operatives seeking to hijack our most important democratic process — our presidential election."

"Russian spies engaged in a series of online cyber raids and a broad campaign of disinformation, all ultimately aimed at sowing chaos to us to undermine public faith in our process, in our leadership and ultimately in ourselves," Warner continued, adding "and that's not just this senator's opinion, it is the unanimous determination of the entire US intelligence community." I knew he was right as, through my Byline investigation, I had extensively documented and reported on the open source and declassified materials which confirmed it. Turning to the work yet to do, Warner continued, saying: "So we must find out the full story, what the Russians did, and, candidly, as some other colleagues have mentioned, why they were so successful. And, more importantly, we must determine the necessary steps to take to protect our democracy and ensure they can't do it again."

On the topic of Trump, Warner was scathing. "Recall, we began this entire process with the president and his staff first denying that the Russians were ever involved, and then falsely claiming that no one from his team was never in touch with any Russians," he said. "We know that's just not the truth. Numerous Trump associates had undisclosed contacts with Russians before and after the election, including the president's attorney general, his former national security adviser and his current senior adviser, Mr Kushner."

"That doesn't even begin to count the host of additional campaign associates and advisers who've also been caught up in this massive web. We saw Mr Trump's campaign manager, Mr Manafort, forced to step down over ties to Russian-backed entities. The national security adviser, General Flynn, had to resign over his lies about engagements with the Russians," he continued, concluding by saying: "And we saw the candidate him — himself, express an odd and unexplained affection for the Russian dictator while calling for the hacking of his opponent. There's a lot to investigate. Enough, in fact, that then Director Comey publicly acknowledged that he was leading an investigation into those links between Mr Trump's campaign and the Russian government."

Within opening questions, Burr and Comey explicitly confirmed the involvement of Russia in the hybrid assault on the United States. The initial exchange was swift and direct.

"Do you have any doubt that Russia attempted to interfere in the 2016 elections?" Burr asked.

"None," Comey replied.

"Do you have any doubt that the Russian government was behind the intrusions in the DNC and the DCCC systems, and the subsequent leaks of that information?" Burr asked.

"No, no doubt," Comey replied.

"Do you have any doubt that the Russian government was behind the cyber intrusion in the state voter files?" Burr asked.

"No," Comey replied.

"Do you have any doubt that officials of the Russian government were fully aware of these activities?" Burr asked.

"No doubt," Comey replied.

The Republican Senator then raised an issue of criminal behaviour beyond the confirmed espionage, saying to Comey: "Director, is it possible that, as part of this FBI investigation, the FBI could find evidence of criminality that is not tied to — to the 2016 elections — possible collusion or coordination with Russians?"

"Sure," was Comey's only response.

Burr pressed him, asking: "So there could be something that just fits a criminal aspect to this that doesn't have anything to do with the 2016 election cycle?"

"Correct," Comey replied. "In any complex investigation, when you start turning over rocks, sometimes you find things that are unrelated to the primary investigation, that are criminal in nature."

It was also clear in the subsequent exchange that Christopher Steele's infamous dossier on Trump contained a deal more than mere speculation. "At the time of your departure from the FBI, was the FBI able to confirm any criminal allegations contained in the Steele document?" Burr asked.

"Mr Chairman, I don't think that's a question I can answer in an open setting because it goes into the details of the investigation," Comey responded.

Burr then steered the questioning skilfully towards the recruitment of spies, saying to Comey: "The term we hear most often is "collusion." When people are describing possible links between Americans and Russian government entities related to the interference in our election, would you say that it's normal for foreign governments to reach out to members of an incoming administration?"

"Yes," Comey answered.

"At what point does the normal contact cross the line into an attempt to recruit agents or influence or spies?" Burr asked.

Comey responded, saying: "Difficult to say in the abstract. It depends upon the context, whether there's an effort to keep it covert, what the nature of the requests made of the American by the foreign government are. It's a — it's a judgment call based on a whole lot of facts."

Burr was surprisingly direct in response. "At what point would that recruitment become a counterintelligence threat to our country?" he asked.

"Again, difficult to answer in the abstract," Comey replied. "But when — when a foreign power is using especially coercion or some sort of pressure to try and co-opt an American, especially a government official, to act on its behalf, that's a serious concern to the FBI and at the heart of the FBI's counterintelligence mission."

The Republican swiftly reintroduced the Steele dossier, saying: "So if you've got a — a — a 36-page document of — of specific claims that are out there, the FBI would have to, for counterintelligence reasons, try to verify anything that might be claimed in there. One, and probably first and foremost, is the counterintelligence concerns that we have about blackmail. Would that be an accurate statement?"

Responding to the issue of Kompromat material, Comey didn't hesitate. "Yes. If the FBI receives a credible allegation that there is some effort to co-opt, coerce, direct, employ covertly an American on behalf of the foreign power, that's the basis on which a counterintelligence investigation is opened," he told the Committee.

Burr's questioning then delved into cyber-attacks and hacking efforts which had ultimately caused significant damage to the campaign of Democrat candidate Hilary Clinton. The exchange was brief but confirmed Russian hacking efforts had extended well beyond the DNC alone, mirroring the mass, Russian-led cyber activity in the EU which preceded the world cyber-attack that affected critical infrastructure. "Okay. When did you become aware of the cyber intrusion?" Burr asked.

"The first cyber — it was all kinds of cyber intrusions going on all the time. The first Russia-connected cyber intrusion, I became aware of in the late summer of 2015," Comey responded.

"And in that timeframe," Burr asked, "there were more than the DNC and the DCCC that were targets?"

"Correct. There was a massive effort to target government and nongovernmental — near-governmental agencies like non-profits," Comey replied.

"What would be the estimate of how many entities out there the Russians specifically targeted in that timeframe?" Burr asked.

"It's hundreds. I suppose it could be more than 1,000, but it's at least hundreds," Comey replied.

"When did you become aware that data had been exfiltrated?" Burr asked.

"I'm not sure, exactly. I think either late '15 or early '16," Comey responded.

Comey's testimony was not about whether he personally got along with Trump, or whether the President was "nasty" to him. The former FBI Director stood in front of the committee and cameras to tell the whole world Russia had attacked the US, potentially infiltrated the White House at the highest levels, and, so far, had gotten away with it. For me, having been investigating this without a safety net for months, it was the icing on a very toxic cake.

Because of the way I had arrived at the same conclusions, effectively the long way round starting with unrelated parties on the other side of the Atlantic, Comey's testimony wasn't just a confirmation of Trump's Russian ties. It was a confirmation of everything, including Brexit. One couldn't be Russia without the other, which was doubly interesting because the evidence also came on the same day as the snap general election, called by Theresa May. I contacted GCHQ on the 9th of June 2017, as the results were coming in, to ask whether Russia had been caught intervening in the election, and the spooks replied rather blandly with: "We have seen no successful cyber intervention in UK democratic processes. We have systems in place to protect against electoral fraud at all levels. The voting system in the UK uses paper ballots – both in polling stations and for postal voting, and votes cannot be cast electronically. This reduces the risk of interference." I didn't have the heart to tell them their measures were meaningless, nor that Russia didn't need to hack the vote, so to speak, because everything else they'd done had already worked so well. But I suppose that's what happens when the spies are only looking one way, which is pretty much the whole point of a hybrid war and the reason Russia found it so easy to win. The Westminster email hack followed almost immediately.

As it happened, May lost her majority in the election and ended up forced into a coalition with the Northern Irish Ulster Unionists, the DUP. This brought Leave.EU front, centre, and straight back into my line of sight – allowing me to tie up some loose ends with them which, confusingly yet unsurprisingly, unleashed a whole new round of open-ended questions. With rumours rife as to the DUP's six-figure donation during the EU Referendum campaign – over four hundred thousand pounds from shadowy Conservative linked to Saudi Arabian intelligence services, Richard Cook – and arguments over inducements from Arron Banks – which had the end of the same week as the doomed election extended to allegations Banks would use leverage' on May to push Nigel Farage into a Brexit negotiating position with the DUP's blessing – I decided to cut to the chase and ask Leave.EU's Andy

Wigmore what exactly was going on. I ended up walking away with more evidence to submit to the ICO and the Electoral Commission.

At first, Andy replied to me by saying: "You're an ex cooper you work it out dopey," but, after we concluded I had, in fact, been a police officer and never made barrels, he was more helpful. "Nothing to do with us dear boy," he told me on the DUP funding, adding: "Ask the Vote Leave lot."

I pressed him on who I should be speaking to specifically but he didn't respond so, I had a quick look around myself. It was only in March 2017 Cook was openly looking to spend his money on a unionist campaign in Scotland, with the Telegraph reporting "Cook, who chairs the pro-Union Constitutional Research Council (CRC), said "several" wealthy backers are prepared to hand over major sums to "a new and positive campaign" to keep the UK together." During the Brexit referendum, Cook's money was used by the DUP to fund a rather excruciatingly expensive cover advert in the Metro, at a cost of over a quarter of a million pounds but it's incredibly difficult to tell which campaign group this was specifically aligned to, if either. I also found that one of May's newly appointed senior advisors, Steve Baker, had openly encouraged conservative groups supporting Leave to pool their resources and create an almost unlimited number of minor campaign groups. With each having a maximum budget of seven hundred thousand pounds, like Leave.EU, Baker identified the possibility of investing an unlimited budget in the push for Brexit. Baker was also discovered on a recording, telling a think-tank his objective was not just to leave the EU but to destroy it – the clear Russian narrative used by deniable and detached assets alike.

Wigmore, however, eventually loosened up during our chat and told me: "All DUP did for Leave.eu was support us by speaking at rally's [sic] full stop." Of course, having investigated the Leave.EU and

Cambridge Analytica side of things with both the ICO and the Electoral Commission, and knowing The Guardian's Carole Cadwalladr had established potentially illegal collusion between Leave.EU and Vote Leave, relating to the use of foreign-based data companies, I was quite well versed in the rules by this time. So, when it appeared the DUP efforts may have represented yet more joint campaigning, or another donation in kind, I knew it should have been declared. As such, I referred my findings straight on to the Electoral Commission.

Still poking around I found that, according to The Times reporting on the 11th of June 2017, "Theresa May has been warned that she should hand Nigel Farage a peerage and a government job on her Brexit negotiating team or face a relaunch of UKIP that will leach votes from the Tories at the next election." Quoting from the Times article, Banks said if May turned away from any Brexit pledges he would deploy his mailing list against her, saying: "It will be ding, ding! seconds out, round two!"

On this alleged issue of Banks using leverage and Farage's insertion into Brexit, Wigmore told me it had: "Not come from me so can't answer you – I'm as intrigued as you." Of course, others had been asking if the leverage he spoke of might refer to a rumoured two million pound spend on a so-called "Tory/UKIP alliance" and, having seen the popup dark posts myself – including some attached to climate change denial content featuring Conservative politician Jacob Rees-Mogg, saying the only way to get foreigners out of the UK was to vote for the alliance – I put the question to Andy, but he did not reply. Again, such spending should have been declared by both parties.

Previously, I had stuck my nose into Banks' and Wigmore's links to the small African country of Lesotho, following the trail of company listings from the Panama Papers. Wigmore had, by the election, confirmed to me they were, as a group, supporting the

Basotho National Party in the Lesotho elections, though he also clarified the corporations listed in the Panama Papers were just "shell companies." He added their Lesotho operations include diamond mines, call centre employing 1500 people, and huge charitable donations into Lesotho. Even now, I am struggling to find relevant company records but the Lesotho National Development Corporation had issued a tender which states: "Call centre outsourcing is a big business opportunity for developing countries with a huge qualified workforce and high unemployment rates. Many organisations prefer to outsource call centre services as this is a cost saving opportunity for them while being beneficial for the hosting country as well." Of course, if a group dedicated to a brighter future for Britain outside of the EU, taking a fiercely 'patriotic' line, were also encouraging outsourcing to a foreign country, this might raise some eyebrows among their supporters. I asked Wigmore what the call centre does – if it was outsourced insurance, international or domestic services, what the company was called, that kind of thing – but he didn't reply, other than saying: "What do you think a call centre does."

I had also investigated Leave.EU's involvement in the gathering and sharing of big data and the findings of the original investigative work – which raised serious concerns over data laundering – were referred to ICO, sparking another inquiry. One of the companies I uncovered in the Leave.EU network was a relatively new outfit called "Big Data Dolphins" and no real records of its function existed. However, Wigmore told me during our conversation the company was working on "Artificial Intelligence," adding it was: "Already fully functional based out of Bristol and Mississippi for insurance/financial services." I asked him what the company focused on, if Governor Phil Bryant had been useful, and if they were using any of the databases they had established through other companies. Wigmore didn't reply. In my investigative work, and that statement sent to the FBI and others, I had uncovered those extensive links between Farage, Leave.EU, and the Mississippi governor, which connected all of them back to Trump's White House and the Russia probe. After the initial Mississippi article was published, Farage had actually hosted Governor Bryant as a guest on his LBC radio show, during which they discussed President Trump's "strong affection" for the UK's departure from the EU and talked about free-trade deals. Big Data Dolphins put not just Farage but the whole of Leave.EU squarely in the Trump-Russia arena in a way the previous connections had not so, as a result of Wigmore's comments regarding the international data company, I referred yet more of my findings to the ICO as there was a clear connection with their ongoing inquiry.

If Comey was the icing on my cake, this final chat with Leave.EU was a sprinkle of hundreds and thousands. Still, I found myself hunting around for a starting point in all this, the first step taken on the path which led to Capstone and onwards to Trump. Eventually, I discovered a book called "The Foundation of Geopolitics," which caused me to set down my coffee and whistle through my teeth the first time I saw it. My investigations were done and the original articles published by this point, the CIA and FBI, along with NATO, confirmed what I had dug up, but this was something else.

To call it by its full name, The Foundations of Geopolitics: The Geopolitical Future of Russia, is a book by Aleksandr Dugin which has had a large and prolonged influence within the Russian military, police, foreign ministries and among the elites – the oligarchs. It was published in the 1990s and, according to what is almost an urban legend, it is used as a textbook in the General Staff Academy of the Russian military – probably because it was co-authored by General Nikolai Klokotov, himself of the academy.

Another military official, Colonel General Leonid Ivashov, head of the International Department of the Russian Ministry of Defence, apparently advised on the project and Klokotov is quoted as saying the book would "serve as a mighty ideological foundation for preparing a new military command," in the future. The principal author, Dugin, has also asserted the book has become an official textbook in Russian educational institutions.

Even in synopsis, there are striking similarities in the central message of the book and the kind of things I read about the views of the Sweden Democrats at the very start of my own investigation. Dugin's Foundations declares: "The battle for the world rule of [ethnic] Russians" has not ended and claims Russia remains "the staging area of a new anti-bourgeois, anti-American revolution." The Eurasian Empire, which went on to be a centrepiece for Putin, would be constructed, Dugin said: "On the fundamental principle of the common enemy: the rejection of Atlanticism, strategic control of the USA, and the refusal to allow liberal values to dominate us." It all sounded so familiar when I first heard it, the targeting of NATO and this Moscow-centric axis of control, and military operations play only a relatively small role because the ideology of the text is centred on a "sophisticated program of subversion, destabilization, and disinformation spearheaded by the Russian special services." There was everything, the media outlets like RT and Sputnik, the additional disinformation of the alt-right, APT28 and APT29, Wikileaks, the far-right political parties. All of it. The operations, the book set out, should be "assisted by a tough, hard-headed utilisation of Russia's gas, oil, and natural resources to bully and pressure other countries." And there was Rosneft, Qatar, Gazprom, Nord-Stream. It's not a pleasant thing to realise that a roadmap to hybrid war was on the table for years and still everyone was completely blindsided and left to play catch up.

The strength of a united Europe is not underestimated by the author either, though the deeply exploitative efforts deployed by Putin's Russia seem to have had the polar opposite effect to that desired. Le Pen had clearly read Dugin's work, however. The book also envisioned Germany should be offered the "de facto political dominance over most Protestant and Catholic states located within Central and Eastern Europe," and says the "Kaliningrad oblast could be given back to Germany." The book uses the term Moscow-Berlin axis but adds France should be encouraged to form a "Franco-German bloc" with Germany, as "both countries have a firm anti-Atlanticist tradition.

Brexit itself is quite neatly shown as a successful operation in just one sentence: "The United Kingdom should be cut off from Europe."

At first, it might have been easy to dismiss this publication as another coincidence but too much of it exists in the reality of the world we now know. For example, the book says "Ukraine should be annexed by Russia because Ukraine as a state has no geopolitical meaning, no particular cultural import or universal significance, no geographic uniqueness, no ethnic exclusiveness, its certain territorial ambitions represents an enormous danger for all of Eurasia and, without resolving the Ukrainian problem, it is in general senseless to speak about continental politics." And it gets darker still, going all the way back to my concerns about Russia in the Middle East and how it interacts with the Islamic State. The book stresses the "continental Russian-Islamic alliance which lies at the foundation of anti-Atlanticist strategy," saying: "The alliance is based on the traditional character of Russian and Islamic civilization." According to the doctrine: "Georgia should be dismembered. Abkhazia and "United Ossetia" (which includes Georgia's South Ossetia) will be incorporated into Russia. Georgia's independent policies are unacceptable," while "Russia needs to create "geopolitical shocks" within Turkey. These can be achieved by employing Kurds, Armenians and other minorities." Erdogan was right there, too.

Focusing on Asia, the book emphasises how Russia must spread Anti-Americanism everywhere, saying "the main 'scapegoat' will be precisely the US," which left me with a deeply disturbing, secondary understanding of North Korea's frequent targeting by Trump, which has been spreading to the UK through ineffective intelligence analysis. China and Japan have both been horrified by the prospect of Trump's threatened nuclear holocaust against the despotic state and this has created a great deal of tension which will last long beyond Trump's stay in the White House.

As regards the US itself, Dugin outlines how "Russia should use its special services within the borders of the United States to fuel instability and separatism, for instance, provoke Afro-American racists." It adds that Russia should: "Introduce geopolitical disorder into internal American activity, encouraging all kinds of separatism and ethnic, social and racial conflicts, actively supporting all dissident movements – extremist, racist, and sectarian groups, thus destabilizing internal political processes in the US. It would also make sense simultaneously to support isolationist tendencies in American politics." Through RT they'd done this as far back as Occupy, at least, and moving forward to Bannon's Breitbart and Trump's White House, it is impossible not to agree Russia has succeeded. A number of alternative figures have also risen in the Democratic Party and the online resistance movements, too. All of this has clearly been extended to the UK, as well. For example, in the wake of the Finsbury Park terrorist attack in mid-June 2017, in which Darren Osborne – a white male from Wales – drove a van into worshippers at the mosque, it was discovered that Britain's white extremists had shifted their social media use to unregulated social networks like the Russian-based VKontakte (VK) service where they have built up a substantial spider's web of contacts through which they are radicalising each other. There was no coincidence in this, it was utterly inevitable, and in July the security services finally conceded they had seen exponential increases in white extremist terrorism since the Brexit vote. I found it desperately painful to examine the book, primarily because this adversary had already won. For now, Putin's Russia, operating from Dugin's strategy guide has been victorious – and it's not just in looking back to the dated writing you can see the reality of our situation reflected.

I was privately sent another document which lit the same, grim fireworks. In astounding written testimony, Rolandas Kriščiūnas, the Lithuanian Ambassador to the United States of America, gave blistering evidence to the US Senate of Russia's efforts to cut the transatlantic relationship between Europe and the US and undermine NATO. His statement was submitted in March 2017, two months before my own was sent pretty much everywhere.

According to the written statement on behalf of Lithuania: "Russia updated basic strategic documents, indicating NATO, and particularly the US, as threats. It is written in official documents, it is publically said by Russian politicians, and it is constantly broadcasted on TV for the public. Russia withdrew from international agreements aimed at building trust and stability and thus assuring existence of the international security system. Russia is violating basic international law norms, and is keen to change current international order." At the same time as NATO was aiming to build a strategic partnership with Russia, cutting defence structures and focusing on expeditionary forces, Russia, the ambassador wrote, had been increasing its investments into defence, modernising its armaments and military structures, reviewing its strategy, doctrine and tactics.

Turning to disinformation and fake news, the Ambassador's statement said: "Russia is extremely active in the information field, using pro-Russian media (e.g. Russia Today, Sputnik), propaganda, disinformation, fake news, trolls, leaks etc. in order to confuse public opinion and influence the decision-making. Russia also employs lobbying, PR agencies to disseminate the conspiracy theories, to discredit other states in the international arena and harasses those who criticize the Kremlin."

"Russia tends to support European extremist and anti-EU groups, strives to foment divisions and instability in the target countries, and to create divisions inside the EU and NATO. Other forms of action: cyber activity (attacks against critical infrastructure, hacked and leaked emails, and cyber espionage), initiation of population resettlement (in order to change the ethnic composition of a frozen conflict region), creation of the proxy groups (pseudo-NGOs, youth organisations, research institutes, think tanks, motorcycle clubs)." The latter made me immediately think of Sweden, its hand grenades and the motorcycle gangs I'd discussed with Manne Gerell what seemed like a lifetime before.

The statement also set out information on further Russian strategies, saying: "The compatriot policy (providing financial, health care or other kind of benefits to Russian-speakers abroad, issuing Russian passports, and justifying aggression against neighbouring countries with protection of Russian speakers' rights) is being used as an additional tool for Russia's disruptive strategies abroad."

According to Kriščiūnas, the Kremlin increasingly saw Europe's status as: "Whole, free, and at peace not as an opportunity for prosperous coexistence, but as a threat to its geopolitical agenda and regime survival."

"Moscow views the Western values – pluralism and openness – as weaknesses to be exploited. Its tactics are asymmetrical, subversive, and not easily confronted. US is presented as an abuser of a global dominant position and Russia knows a solution – diminishing US role in the world to achieve multipolar international order. Western governments have ignored this threat for too long, but finally, awareness is growing that the transatlantic community must do more to defend its values and institutions," he added.

While hybrid conflict and countermeasures were broadly covered – a topic my own investigation had delved into almost exhaustively – my central interest in the statement came back to disinformation and how it is deployed in Lithuania. The account more than echoed my long conversation with Steve Komarnyckyj and my own nosing around into RT and those other channels, which also started back in Sweden. I had been on the right trail from the very outset. Kriščiūnas wrote: "Russia pursues to influence Lithuanian and Western audiences by setting up and promoting international media channels that spread its views and disinformation on the sensitive topics – such as migration crisis, terrorism, ethnic relations, deployment of NATO troops in Central and Eastern Europe etc."

"The most active propaganda project of Russia's international media outlet Rossyia Segodnia in Lithuania is website Baltnews.lt. It realizes Russia's informational and ideological policy, disseminates articles which cover main narratives of Russian propaganda. Baltnews.lt gets funding from Rossyia Segodnia in a complex and non-transparent financial scheme through intermediary companies in foreign states," he explains. "A new Rossyia Segodnia propaganda project, Sputniknews.lt, was launched in Lithuania in December 2016. Sputniknews.lt is oriented in Lithuanian-speaking audience, but for the moment failed to gain any popularity." Citing a specific example, he detailed the most recent example of an information attack as having been an attempt by Russian media outlets and pro-Russian activists, in February 2017, to spread the fake news that German soldiers stationed in Lithuania were culpable for the rape of the teenage girl. "This particular piece of disinformation failed to attract attention of mainstream media, but the like information attacks against NATO military personnel deployed in the region are highly likely to be repeated in the future," he wrote. In Sweden, the same story had gained such traction the Defence Minister had to defend it across the nation once it crept into the mainstream media.

Further expanding on Russia's covert funding of disinformation channels, Kriščiūnas explained that Moscow's attempts to regain the influence in the post-Soviet region "materialize in Russia's efforts to weaken Lithuania's social integrity and to escalate intra-ethnic tensions. Russia employs so called compatriot policy to achieve that. Kremlin's aim is to discredit and hinder any efforts made by the authorities' to carry out a successful integration of national minorities. The main goal of Russia's compatriot policy in the Baltics is to incite ethnic tensions." He asserted the: "Fund to Support and Protect the Rights of Compatriots Living Abroad, which was established by the Russian Ministry of Foreign Affairs and the federal agency Rossotrudnichestvo, finances two Lithuanian-based organisations, which try to fuel ethnic tensions within Lithuania." The Centre for the Protection and Research of Fundamental Rights uses "various international human-rights events to blame Lithuania for violating the rights of ethnic communities. Independent Human Rights Centre, takes part in pro-Russian propaganda campaigns against the US and NATO." Both organisations, according to the evidence, receive nearly one hundred thousand Euro from the fund every year. Vladimir Pozdorovkin, the current coordinator of the Baltics in the fund, had been the chief of SVR under a diplomatic cover at the Russian Embassy in Vilnius from 1994 till 1996. Another spy directly involved, but not the only one.

KrIščiūnas also savaged Russian intelligence operations in Belarus, writing: "In 2014 Belarusian intelligence operation against Lithuanian military communications system was terminated." According to the Lithuanian diplomat, Belarusian military intelligence undercover officer Sergey Kurulenko carried out the failed operation, in which he tried to collect information about a fibre-optic cable network belonging to the national Lithuanian air navigation system. The cable was also used by the military among others for NATO communications. "Due to close military cooperation between Belarus and Russia," KrIščiūnas wrote, "it is highly likely that the Belarusian GRU shared the collected information with the Russian military intelligence GRU." He also reported that approximately one-hundred pro-Russian groups are active in Belarus – many of them paramilitary, describing some as "patriotic groups" and highlighting a portion of them are related to Belarusian Cossacks movement. These groups are most active in Belarus regions bordering Lithuania and Poland. Cossacks, his evidence says, played a significant role in the Russian hybrid warfare against Ukraine, including the Crimea takeover operation. "Belarusian Cossacks and other pro-Russian paramilitary groups operate in the same fashion as in Ukraine, using representatives of Russian Orthodox Church as liaison officers for the Russian intelligence services," the Ambassador wrote, adding: "Pro-Russian groups in Belarus can be used by Russia to pressure Belarusian president Alexander Lukashenko as well as various operations (provocations) against the NATO member countries, e.g. Lithuania and Poland." Such provocations are highly likely during the "Zapad 2017" military exercise due to take place in September, KrIščiūnas warned.

Putin, of course, continued to deny Russian involvement of any kind. Meeting German Chancellor Angela Merkel in May, he fielded a number of questions from journalists at a press conference, saying: "For years we have seen attempts to influence events in Russia via so called NGOs and directly. Realising the futility of such efforts, it has never occurred to us to interfere in other countries internal affairs," adding: "You mention the US. No one has been able to prove this, these are just rumours used for internal political struggles in the US."

Merkel, facing her fourth general election campaign in September, around the time of Zapad 2017, was having none of it, responding at the same conference by saying: "We know cyber criminality is an international challenge, and also that Russian military doctrine touches on the topic of hybrid military strategy, but I believe we will have no problems in the political campaign in Germany even if there are disagreements." It turns out she already knew at the time of the meeting that, as recently as March and April 2017, hackers had tried to infiltrate computers of NGOs associated with Germany's top political parties. Trend Microsystems attributed the attacks to APT28 and APT29, both spear-phishing with false domains under yet another of the RIS's operating names, Pawn Storm. As a result, Merkel's Christian Democratic Union (the CDU) proposed the introduction of a new defence law which would permit the country to "hack back" and shut down servers hosting hackers during attacks – in line with the NATO Article 5 approach. The Bundesamt für Sicherheit in der Informationstechnik (BSI), the German cyber security agency, was also taking on nearly two-hundred people and decided to place additional experts to work with the German election watchdog, to protect the integrity of the Autumn vote. In May, the BSI held talks with foreign counterparts, including France's online security agency, to examine best practice in countering hybrid attacks on democratic elections. Maks Czuperski, head of the digital forensic research lab at the Atlantic Council in Washington, had made sure the Germans were aware: "Since late 2016 we've been identifying attacks on Chancellor Merkel, and we are anticipating quite a strong barrage as the election approaches."

Emmanuel Macron, whose campaign was also targeted by the Russian intelligence services yet went on to win, held similarly blunt talks with Putin at the end of May, during which he openly lambasted Russia's propaganda machine, saying: "I have always had an exemplary relationship with foreign journalists, but they have to be journalists. Russia Today and Sputnik were organs of influence and propaganda that spread counterfeit truths about me." The comment was made at a joint press conference with Putin after an initial, private, meeting.

The Russian punch aimed at Merkel could well be the best-signalled and may prove to be the ultimate downfall of Putin's campaign which wiped the floor with the floor with the UK and US. Putin himself has also read the signs and started changing tack, most recently attempting to peddle a theory claiming patriotic Russians could be responsible – but without state backing. Thankfully, I know enough coming out of this to be able to dismiss this line as utter nonsense. It's a mess, all of it – of that there is no doubt – and investigating something so complex has been fraught with the dangers of any findings being dismissible as a conspiracy theory but the problem with that is: it's all true – verifiably so.

At the conclusion of the process, as an independent journalist who had once been a police officer, what I came to believe was the world needed to have all of this laid out in one place. Not just so people could go away afterwards and – most importantly – check for themselves, but because a permanent point of reference needed to be created so future generations had something they could one day look back upon and say: "Never again." I owe my children this and we all have similar debts, especially as this took place on our watch, as the saying goes. It doesn't even matter how the sorry Trump or Brexit sagas conclude because –

though I accept it is a challenging task for everyone – the reality we have to face up to, acknowledge, and fully understand is World War Three had been fought and won before we even noticed anything was wrong. It was not, in the end, the nuclear conflict feared for so many years but, rather, this only too real and wholly alien hybrid conflict being fought with the mixed methods of technology and psychology – disinformation, destabilisation, and the deployment of insidious, deniable and detached assets instead of missiles, infantry, and artillery. A war fought purely with lies – which Russia only won because it never made the official declaration.

"It was not, in the end, the nuclear
conflict feared for so many years but,
rather, this only too real and wholly alien
hybrid conflict being fought with the mixed
methods of technology and psychology –
disinformation, destabilisation, and the
deployment of insidious, deniable and
detached assets instead of missiles,
infantry, and artillery. A war fought
purely with lies – which Russia only won
because it never made the official
declaration."

J.J. Patrick

ABOUT J.J. PATRICK:

Between 2004 and 2014 I served as a police officer with the Derbyshire Constabulary and Metropolitan Police Service in the United Kingdom. I retired in 2014 after giving evidence in a parliamentary inquiry.

In 2013 I acted as a whistleblower in the course of my duties, giving evidence to the House of Commons Public Administration Select Committee on the manipulation of crime figures by the police. The final report of the committee said of me: *"We are indebted to PC Patrick for his courage in speaking out, in fulfilment of his duty to the highest standards of public service, despite intense pressures to the contrary."* I have also acted as a freelance specialist consultant on crime data analysis with an NGO in Mexico.

I am now a freelance journalist and member of the National Union of Journalists. My primary publication platform is Byline, an independent news website based in the United Kingdom. This is a non-partisan publication which holds no editorial input or sway over my work. I am also signed up to the Impress regulations. My funding comes direct from the public and is unaffiliated to advertising of any kind.

I'm still an awkward so and so.

J.J.P.

T ~~Electoral Commission + leave~~

1. Farage works for Russia BREXIT
   + all EU right populists

~~just T2 combined~~
   re Leave + Brexit

2. All Electoral Commission inquiries

3. Facebook UK story / Elections
   etc → (A → TRUMP
   what would Macon have done? —
   | Facebook is a weapon

4. EU Terror attacks
   bombs vs trucks   pattern
   + Facebook bot responses

5. NOW we know ~~about Trump~~ +
   Russia.   & EU
   THIS FILM 2 UK + Russia

6. Alt War ~ Russia attacks
   west. NATO + response
   cyber doctrine

ACTION: Bradshaw Select Committee
TO MAKE Electoral Commission
NEWS

ABOUT HOME:

Cynefin Road came to life during a period of disaster and rebirth, spawned by a heady cross-breeding of the love of both reading and writing, combined with an overwhelming desire to be happy. And what could make anyone happier than bringing beautiful books into the world? (Apart from reading them, of course).

Cynefin is the Welsh word for a place where the nature feels right — where it feels like home — and the road which leads there is paved with stories.

www.cynefinroad.com
www.cynefinroad.co.uk
@cynefinroad

Other Titles By Cynefin Road

Forever Completely
J.J. Patrick

The Rest Is Silence
J.J. Patrick

Legacy
Thomas Heasman-Hunt

The Worry Box
Lu Thomson

The Star Princess and the Kitchen Witch
Stephanie Shields

1. "Farage ~~agent of~~ works for Russia"
   + all EU right populists

2. ["Election watchdog can't protect us" (all Electoral Commiss: in quivers / Banks / DUP / micro-campaigns]

3. Facebook is a weapon. UK story. What would French have done re FB in Brexit?

4. The Bear, the Lion & the Unicorn

NN We know about ~~Trump~~ & Russia & US election. This film is Russia & Brexit

5. Alt. war. Russia attacks west. NATO response. Ukraine test bed

6 Bombs vs Trucks. Why are Russia bots on it?

ACTION) Bradshaw Sclers CCtee
Elecn
Commn

Lightning Source UK Ltd.
Milton Keynes UK
UKOW04f0558180917
309391UK00001B/1/P

9 781999 785413